FORESTRY COMMISSION BULLETIN
No. 61

# Technology Transfer in Forestry

**PROCEEDINGS OF A MEETING OF THE INTERNATIONAL UNION OF FORESTRY RESEARCH ORGANIZATIONS, SUBJECT GROUP S6.08, 'APPLYING THE RESULTS OF FORESTRY RESEARCH,' HELD AT EDINBURGH UNIVERSITY, 25 JULY—1 AUGUST, 1983**

Edited by G. H. MOELLER[1] and D. T. SEAL[2]

[1]*Principal Recreation Scientist, USDA Forest Service, 12th & Independence, SW, P.O. Box 2417, Washington, D.C., 20013, U.S.A.*

[2]*Chief Research Officer (North), Forestry Commission, Northern Research Station, Roslin, Midlothian, EH25 9SY, U.K.*

LONDON : HER MAJESTY'S STATIONERY OFFICE

*First published* 1984

ISBN 0 11 710155 9

FRONT COVER Members of a IUFRO Working Party on Norway spruce provenances visiting Hirkjolen research area, Norway. (*N2917*) *R. Lines*

# Contents

# Preface

At the 17th Congress of the International Union of Forestry Research Organizations (IUFRO) held in Kyoto, Japan, in September 1981, a Subject Group S6.08 was set up in Division 6 (General Subjects) to develop methods for the rapid worldwide dissemination and application of results of forestry research. Papers presented at this initial Subject Group meeting are contained in the Kyoto Congress proceedings.

This Bulletin contains papers presented at the second Subject Group meeting held at Edinburgh University, Edinburgh, Scotland, 25 July–1 August 1983. Papers tabled at this meeting, and some that were not contained in the Kyoto Proceedings, have been added where appropriate.

The need for efficient transfer of new forestry knowledge is critical throughout all the various IUFRO Subject Groups. Group S6.08 serves as a clearing-house for ideas related to procedures, processes and methods for application of forestry research.

There is little doubt that the need for application of advanced technologies is of universal concern, regardless of the country or area of interest. Very simply, the failure to apply the most advanced technology results in waste of valuable resource production and leads to social and economic penalties. While application of advanced technology is lagging, the rate of accumulation of new knowledge is increasing exponentially. Projections indicate that within the next 10 years, the volume of accumulated information will be four to seven times what it is today. So the void between what we know and what we apply to solving practical problems in forestry continues to widen. Although the lack of application of advanced technology will always be a problem, by focusing on it and devoting resources to its resolution, we can narrow the gap and avoid some of the penalties. The central objective of the conference was to suggest ways to foster the purposeful transfer of new forestry knowledge from research to practice.

Papers contained in this proceeding are arranged into four major sections:

Section I deals with approaches that have been used by various countries to encourage the transfer and application of new forestry information. Authors describe methods of transferring new forestry technology in Great Britain, the USA, Western Europe, Nepal and Nigeria. Regardless of the country, all authors agree that a primary determinant of successful technology transfer is the commitment of top managers, both in research organizations and research user organizations, to the need for effective technology transfer. This commitment takes many forms, from rewards to individuals for their technology transfer efforts, to providing an organizational environment that is conducive to innovation.

Section II contains 10 papers that describe both successful and unsuccessful case examples of technology transfer efforts. Through intensive description and evaluation, the authors provide valuable summarization of the key factors that contribute to successful technology transfer programs. Although each case example is different, the need for a personal and financially sustained commitment and organizational/administrative structure for technology transfer stand out as universal requirements for successful programs.

The four authors in Section III describe some general principles that experience has shown to contribute to successful technology transfer. In reading these papers, it becomes apparent that effective technology transfer in forestry will not happen without sustained effort and creative management of all resources.

On the final day of the conference, participants were divided into five working groups. Each group was asked to address two specific questions; "What can *researchers* and their organizations do to improve technology transfer in forestry?", and "What can *research users and their organizations* do to improve technology transfer in forestry?" After developing lists of specific answers to these two questions, all participants "voted" on those that they felt to be the most important solutions. These ranked solutions are summarized in Section IV of the Proceedings. These solutions are the final recommendations from this Subject Group meeting.

Among conference participants were a group of 20

students who were attending the Commonwealth Forestry Institute research course at Oxford, UK. During the conference, each student was invited to present a situation report on forestry, research, and the problems of applying results of forestry research in their respective countries. Summary situation reports are contained in the Proceedings Appendix.

The conference organizers greatly acknowledge the help of the British Forestry Commission in arranging the conference and the post-conference excursion, and in publishing these proceedings. We also greatly appreciate the help of Dr. John Blyth of the Edinburgh University Department of Forestry and Natural Resources for his help in arranging conference facilities and the excursion. The organizers are grateful too to the staff of the Institute of Terrestrial Ecology and the Forestry Commission's Northern Research Station at Bush, near Edinburgh, for arranging visits to the respective Stations. Finally, we thank Mr. A. Hall of the Younger Botanic Garden, near Dunoon, for welcoming conference participants during the excursion.

G. H. Moeller
*Leader, IUFRO Group S6.08*
D. T. Seal
*Deputy Leader, IUFRO Group S6.08*

*Note:* Where English and American spelling is at variance, the English form has been preferred. The alternative forms 'programme/program' and re-afforestation/reforestation' are used in papers of English or N. American origin respectively.

# List of authors and participants

## Authors

J. Beer, Centro Agronomico Tropical de Investigacion y Ensenanza, Turrialba, COSTA RICA
O. N. Blatchford, Forestry Commission Research Station, Alice Holt Lodge, Surrey, UK
G. A. Cooper, USDA Forest Service, Portland, Oregon, USA
G. O. B. Dada, Forestry Research Institute of Nigeria, Ibadan, NIGERIA
D. G. Embree, Canadian Forestry Service, Fredericton, New Brunswick, CANADA
J. E. Force, Department of Forest Resources, University of Idaho, Moscow, Idaho, USA
*D. M. Griffin, Department of Forestry, Australian National University, Canberra, AUSTRALIA
*S. D. Hobbs, School of Forestry, Oregon State University, Corvallis, Oregon, USA
G. D. Holmes, Forestry Commission, Edinburgh, UK
F. C. Hummel, Consultant (former Head of Forestry in the European Economic Community), Surrey, UK
*D. O. Ladipo, Forest Research Institute of Nigeria, Ibadan, NIGERIA
F. T. Last, Institute of Terrestrial Ecology, Midlothian, UK
W. H. Lawrence, Weyerhauser Company, Tacoma, Washington, USA
R. R. B. Leakey, Institute of Terrestrial Ecology, Midlothian, UK
*H. G. Marx, USDA Forest Service, Washington, D.C., USA
*V. N. P. Mathur, Canadian Forestry Service, CANADA
*T. S. McKnight, Canadian Forestry Service, CANADA
G. H. Moeller, USDA Forest Service, Washington, D.C., USA
S. A. Neustein, Forestry Commission, Edinburgh, UK
*I. Nordansjo, Logging Research Foundation, SWEDEN
D. T. Seal, Forestry Commission, Northern Research Station, Midlothian, UK
*R. Segman, USDA Forest Service, Milford, Pennsylvania, USA
W. E. Sharpe, School of Forest Resources, Pennsylvania State University, University Park, Pennsylvania, USA
K. R. Shepherd, Department of Forestry, Australian National University, Canberra, AUSTRALIA
R. W. Stark, USDA Forest Service, Portland, Oregon, USA

## Other participants

P. Adlard, Commonwealth Forestry Institute, Oxford, UK
S. Ali, Escuela Nacional de Gencias Forestales, Siguatepeque, HONDURAS
J. Blyth, Department of Forestry and Natural Resources, University of Edinburgh, Edinburgh, UK
R. W. Boyd, Department of Agriculture, Forest Service, Belfast, UK
M. Bubala, Division of Forest Research, Kitwe, ZAMBIA
D. A. Burdekin, Forestry Commission Research Station, Alice Holt Lodge, Surrey, UK
C. Cahalan, Department of Forestry and Wood Science, University College of North Wales, Bangor, Gwynedd, UK
J. Christison, School of Forestry, Inverness Technical College, Inverness, UK
R. A. Curtin, Forestry Commission of NSW, AUSTRALIA
F. K. Jetuah, Forest Products Research Institute, University of Science and Technology, Kumasi, GHANA
M. Joshi, Forest Research and Information Centre, Babar Mahal, Kathmandu, NEPAL
B. N. Kigomo, K.A.R.I., Muguga, Nairobi, KENYA
G. M. Kinyanjui, Kenya Agricultural Research Institute, Kikuyo, KENYA
B. P. Lamichhaney, Forest Survey and Research Office, Babar Mahal, Kathmandu, NEPAL
A. J. Low, Forestry Commission, Northern Research Station, Midlothian, UK

C. Meki, Division of Forest Research, Kitwe, ZAMBIA
E. Merino, Instituto Nacional Forestal, Lima, PERU
H. R. S. Mohammed, Divisional Forest Office, Ministry of Agriculture and Forestry, Kenema, SIERRA LEONE
I. Napier, Commonwealth Forestry Institute, Oxford, UK
L. M. Nelson, Forest Department, Kingston, JAMAICA
N. O'Carroll, Forest and Wildlife Service, Dublin, IRELAND
J. Ochaki, Nakawa Forest Research Centre, Kampala, UGANDA
J. A. Okojie, Department of Forest Resources Management, University of Ibadan, Ibadan, NIGERIA
F. J. Lopez Perez, Centro Agronomico Tropical de Investigacion y Ensenanza, Turrialba, COSTA RICA
M. S. Philip, Department of Forestry, University of Aberdeen, UK
J. C. L. Phillips, Department of Agriculture, Belfast, UK
S. C. Sharma, Conservator of Forest, Kanpur Zoological Park, Kanpur, INDIA
A. R. Sutton, Forestry Commission, Edinburgh, UK
H. L. Wright, Commonwealth Forestry Institute, Oxford, UK

* Did not attend conference

# I

# National approaches to organizing for technology transfer

# Applying the results of forest research in Britain

G. D. HOLMES
*Director General, British Forestry Commission*

ABSTRACT

The development and application of new techniques in forestry in Britain has been rapid and broadly successful. Reasons for this include: (1) the pressure to plant and manage forests on unfamiliar and new ground; (2) the concentration of research on defined practical problems; (3) the maintenance of close linkages between research personnel and forest managers, particularly by staff interchange; and (4) giving special attention to the form and presentation of published information, including series designed specifically for users. However, if new technology is to be rapidly introduced into future forest management, one can forsee a need for: (1) organizational changes to encourage and exploit fundamental research; (2) better methods of transferring information from researcher to manager; and (3) improved guidelines and methods for international transfer of technology.

### Introduction

There is no doubt that technology transfer is becoming a matter for concern in many member organizations of IUFRO. When opinion was sounded on this issue in 1979, organizations in 46 countries reported difficulties in the application of forestry research results and wanted IUFRO to focus attention on the problems through a special Subject Group. The willingness of the IUFRO executive board to establish such a group showed that they too shared that concern. A new Subject Group was formed at the IUFRO World Congress in Kyoto, Japan, in 1981.

The working nature of this second meeting of the Group in Edinburgh has been emphasized. Exchanging experiences on national and international technology transfer will be useful, but the objective of identifying and publishing the key requirements for effective application of research results is critically important. I suspect that this conference will be judged by its degree of success in reaching that objective.

British forestry practice and most of the forests now existing in Britain are direct extensions of research, the results of which have been applied over the last 60 years. Research, development and the application of new techniques have been a major responsibility of the Forestry Commission since 1920, and we have of necessity developed procedures and methods of interest to this conference. I propose to look at the results of this experience before considering future developments and needs.

## APPLICATION OF FOREST RESEARCH RESULTS IN BRITAIN

### Background

The Forestry Commission has been compelled by circumstances to develop and apply new techniques of afforestation, particularly during the last 40 years. Government post-war forestry policy envisaged an increase of productive forest to 2 million ha by the planting of 1.2 million ha of bare ground. Pre-war experiments indicated some promising species, site treatments and planting limits, but the technical difficulties of creating large productive new forests on bare degraded uplands were formidable, requiring intensive experimentation and prompt application of results. The extent to which the necessary techniques have been evolved and applied is shown by the fact that the area of forest had been extended from 0.9 million to 1.8 million ha by 1981, mainly by establishing exotic conifers on poor upland sites. The productivity of this area is now being reflected in rapidly rising annual sawlog production, which averaged 1.6 million $m^3$ in 1980, will reach 2.8 million $m^3$ in 1990 and approach 7 million $m^3$ by 2025. This achievement has been due in no small part to the way in which applied research has been managed and put into practice.

**Organization**

The Forestry Commission (FC) is the government body responsible for managing state forests and for encouraging and assisting private forestry. As the national Forest Authority, the FC undertakes applied research for the benefit of both the state and private sectors of the forest industry. The research function is executed by the FC's Research and Development (R&D) Division. Though distinct within the FC organization, the R&D Division is an arm of management, controlled by the Board of the Forestry Commission on which it is represented by a full-time Commissioner. The work of the Division is, therefore, directly linked with management of the state forests and the FC's role in assisting the private sector.

The R&D Division concentrates on applied research. Some basic research is also done but, in general, such research is undertaken by other organizations, notably the Universities, especially those teaching forestry, and by the Institute of Terrestrial Ecology, independently or in collaboration with the R&D Division. The Division comprises two research stations, a principal station at Alice Holt near Farnham in Surrey and a Northern Research Station at Roslin near Edinburgh. Most experimental and development work is done in the forests and locally supervised from some 40 small outstations. Project leaders are, however, located in the two research stations. The method of staffing has been a significant means of promoting the application of research results.

**Staffing**

Close linkage and a degree of interchange between personnel engaged in applied research and line management is most desirable. About half of the research project leaders in the Forestry Commission are forest officers transferred to R&D from forest management duties. The other project leaders are career scientists permanently engaged in research. The movement of forest officers into the Division, and their return after 6 years or more to field duties, has many benefits and only a few penalties. The forest officers are generally posted to those branches of R&D that are most directly concerned with general forest management, to the Silviculture, Mensuration and Work Study Branches, for example, whereas more specialized branches, Pathology, Entomology and Site Studies, are generally staffed by career scientists. This process of exchange of forest officers between forest management and research at the project leader level has greatly facilitated the flow of technical information out of, and in to, research.

Similar exchanges have been effective at the technical level. The research outstations are in the charge of foresters who have had direct experience in management of the forest enterprise. They are responsible to project leaders for the establishment and assessment of forest experiments and for local relations between R&D and state and private foresters. It is significant also that the R&D Division does not own title to its forest experiments which are established in or alongside normal plantations with the approval of the local Conservator of Forests.

The R&D Division does not operate a separate research extension service. Instead, individual research officers are responsible for keeping defined fields of interest under review and relevant enquiries are referred directly to them. This brings a heavy advisory load on matters of current interest or concern; recent occurrences of damage by Pine beauty moth and the Great spruce bark beetle put heavy loads on the Entomology Branch, for example. But by and large the arrangement works well and keeps the link between R&D and its customers simple and direct. Most research workers find this involvement with management in advice and consultation stimulating and rewarding. Also, there is no better focal point for expertise than with other people actively engaged in research on a particular topic.

**Research programming**

A close linkage with forest managers in selecting applied research projects and priorities is important. The Forestry Commission's research programmes normally cover a 5 year period and are updated annually by the heads of the research branches before examination and modification by the R&D Director, who is personally responsible for the programme. Consultation with state and private sectors is an important prerequisite of programme formulation, and customers for technical information can thereby have a strong influence on R&D programmes. They do not, however, control them. The final selection of projects remains within the R&D Division with the Director as the final judge of which portfolio of projects will be the most profitable.

There are exceptions. The R&D Division undertakes some research on contract. The Work Study

Branch works on contract for other Divisions of the Commission and other branches undertake contracts for other government departments, especially in arboriculture and industrial site reclamation. The Division also commissions research by other institutes and particularly with universities to support its applied research programme. The Division does no research on wood and wood properties. This research is contracted out to the Building Research Establishment's Princes Risborough Laboratory.

Employment of research contractors has advantages in precise definition of customer requirements and in access to skills and equipment neither available nor justified within the commissioning organization. The best balance between 'in-house' and commissioned R&D obviously depends upon circumstances and the precise nature of the work required. In developing heavy machinery for harvesting, for example, we have found it better to buy from overseas than to develop such machines ourselves. At present the great majority of our applied research is conducted by permanent staff in-house.

## Transfer of research information

The flow of information from research into practice is highly dependent upon the flow in the reverse direction. Effective applied research is also obviously dependent upon a satisfactory flow of basic scientific information from numerous sources. In our case, the basic work on tree biology and ecology undertaken by the Institute of Terrestrial Ecology is of special interest, as is research by universities, and a number of agricultural research institutes working on subjects of relevance to forestry.

We encounter difficulties further afield. Much research has, *prima facie,* no connection with forestry but may occasionally have important forestry implications. The volume of published information is now massive and comes highly diluted with irrelevant reports so that efficient and reliable monitoring presents a real problem. Centralized methods of screening and summarizing this information are helpful and the Commonwealth Agricultural Bureau abstract service is invaluable. Today, acquisition, storage and retrieval of information are critical parts of successful technology transfer, especially between research workers.

Professional forestry institutions are of importance both as sources and as channels for technical information. Research officers are encouraged to attend meetings. Similarly, periodic meetings with representatives of private growers and the timber trade can be valuable, especially when research officers are called upon to present highlights of their work. Specialist professional groups have proved very valuable markets for exchanging information. For example, in the British Isles an active group on forest soils includes members from Northern Ireland and Eire as well as from Britain. The group assembles annually and there are similar groups of forest pathologists and entomologists. These groups, recruited from a specialized stratum through different countries and research organizations, should, I think, be particularly encouraged.

## Publication of results

In the case of the Forestry Commission, results of research are normally recorded in a series of official publications and in articles in technical journals. Publications are designed mainly for forest managers and supervisors in the public and private sectors but also as records for others engaged in forestry research in Britain and other countries. In practice, we have found it best to publish short, operational guides for forest managers and to support these with separate and more detailed accounts of the research on which the guides are based. In addition, the research activities of the R&D Division and the progress of commissioned research projects are summarized in published Annual Reports.

The form of presentation of research results and practical recommendations is, of course, important, and the FC contribution is overseen by a Technical Publications Committee. This Committee has recently been scrutinizing the form and content of publications with a view to matching them more precisely to the needs of forest managers, in particular via a 'forest manager's bookshelf', that is a matched set of publications covering the full range of forest operations with a minimum of overlap and cross-referencing, with replacement to keep the bookshelf up-to-date.

## Lessons from the past

The development and application of new techniques in forestry in Britain has been rapid and broadly successful. This has been due to a variety of circumstances and causes, not the least of which in the afforestation field has been the absence of tradition and of preconceived ideas with a concurrent willingness to learn.

Research has played a very important part in influencing management, especially silvicultural practices. There are many reasons why this has been so:

a. The pressures of pioneering with the planting and management of forests on unfamiliar and new ground.

b. The concentration of research on defined practical problems.

c. The close linkage between research personnel and forest management, both in planning research and application of findings.

d. Special attention to the form and presentation of published information, including series designed specifically for users.

We look forward to hearing the experience of others and especially other countries both on the transfer of research information into practice and on the transfer of ideas from basic research into applied research; this last point being a vital topic on which I have scarcely touched.

## FUTURE TRENDS

British forestry practice and research are still changing rapidly and it might be useful to mention what I believe are important trends which will have a bearing on the central issue of technology transfer.

### 1. Organizational changes in R&D

There has been a movement towards more fundamental research in forestry during the last decade. Applied and empirical research served us extraordinarily well during the formation of the new forests and has itself stimulated more fundamental studies. There is now a need to understand the growth processes in forests more completely by encouraging more basic research and so underpin and stimulate new applied research.

This need was met by a programme of research in tree biology by the Natural Environment Research Council, undertaken by its Institute of Terrestrial Ecology. Increased interest in more basic research was also reflected in the establishment of a Tree Physiology Branch within the FC's R&D Divison.

In 1979 a House of Lords Select Commitee on Science and Technology examined scientific aspects of forestry in some detail and made recommendations to government. An increase in fundamental research and closer co-ordination, through the FC, of the research of different institutes and the universities were emphasized in the recommendations. In response, the FC formed the Forest Research Coordination Committee (FRCC) for the exchange and co-ordination of ideas on research needs and opportunities. The FRCC is representative, at senior management level, of the Universities, the Institute of Terrestrial Ecology, the Nature Conservancy Council and agricultural research Institues and Departments, and is serviced and chaired by the FC. The formulation of such a national committee is important. It is advisory, not executive, but will assist member organizations to formulate the most appropriate programmes across the 'national board'.

In summary, recent organizational changes will extend forest research into more fundamental areas. This will disperse the overall effort through more organizations but the means of co-ordination at the national level have been improved and good communication will be vital.

### 2. New technologies

It is not difficult to identify areas in forestry in any country where new techniques are urgently required.

In Britain, techniques of timber harvesting are having to change rapidly to increase output and reduce costs. The forest, now larger in area, wood volume and financial value, and under increasing threat from the greater international mobility of insect pests and diseases, justify more research into protection techniques. Endemic windthrow has become a major cause of lost revenues and we shall have to adjust forest management technique to minimize losses. Deer are as impressed by the new forests as we are, and better control techniques are urgently required. In common with many other countries, we are being pressed to adjust forestry practice to enhance the role of forests as reserves for wildlife, places of public recreation and attractive elements in the landscape.

Arising from research there is the prospect of rapid improvement of trees by breeding and new methods of screening and propagation, which raise many possibilities and questions affecting future change in forestry practice. These and other developments will bring more pressing and more complex problems of application. As usual, the forest manager will have to integrate these techniques to meet his own objectives at minimum cost. To do this, he will need more data than he has had in the past and it will have to be very clearly and succinctly presented and, preferably, accessible to him by computer.

### 3. International technology transfer

We are fortunate to have IUFRO as a network for the international exchange of technical information and experience and for generating that all important international and professional fellowship. IUFRO is well run, influential, and though not considered executive, has been instrumental in some highly creditable collaborative experiments such as the IUFRO international provenance trials. Support of

IUFRO remains a most effective means of encouraging and facilitating international technology transfer.

We have recently seen the emergence of a modest European Economic Community (EEC) scheme of financial support for research projects in the EEC and Sweden to improve the supply and use of wood as a renewable raw material. The scale of this scheme is small in relation to the financing of federal research in the USA or Canada, but it is an example of current attempts to make more international use of specialized national resources for research. Great credit is due to Dr. Frederick C. Hummel for this EEC scheme.

British contributions to international forest technology transfer are now principally made under the aegis of the Overseas Development Agency, which borrows appropriate personnel from the universities and research institutes and from the Foresty Commission for periods of detached duty overseas. The contribution of the Commonwealth Forestry Institute at Oxford has been outstanding and it is appropriate that the Oxford course for research officers should be so fully represented at this conference.

One can foresee large and difficult problems for international technology transfer in forestry, especially in developing countries. FAO has done well in some areas but much still needs to be done. The contribution on international technology transfer at this conference will therefore be of particular value and interest. There is no doubt that an exchange of experiences will be valuable but, as I mentioned at the outset, the most valuable outcome of this conference could be something quite specific; I suggest well drafted practical guidelines and priorities for efficient transfer of foresty technique into the hands and minds of those who can best use them.

# Planning for transferring research knowledge in the U.S. Forest Service

H. G. MARX and G. H. MOELLER
*U.S. Department of Agriculture, Forest Service, Washington, D.C., U.S.A.*

ABSTRACT

The void between what we know and what we can reasonably organize and apply to solving immediate problems continues to grow. Mechanisms need to be developed that ensure rapid application of new technology. The United States Department of Agriculture's Forest Service has developed a technology transfer planning process that may be of use to other institutions and organizations. The process results in development of a written technology transfer plan which is approved by all parties involved. The plan includes a commitment of time, talent and money, with administrative and technical commitment as the foundation for program development and implementation. The technology transfer plan serves as an important mechanism to ensure the rapid and efficient application of new technology and is one way to narrow the gap between accumulated knowledge and application.

**Introduction**

In his recent book on major trends in America, Naisbitt (1982) outlines why we are drowning in information. His key points:

- Between 6000 and 7000 scientific articles are written each day.
- Scientific and technical information increases 13 per cent per year, which means it doubles every 5.5 years.
- The rate of increase in scientific and technical information will soon jump to 40 per cent per year because of new, more powerful information systems and an increasing population of scientists. This means that accumulated data will double about every 2 years.
- By 1985 the volume of information will be somewhere between four and seven times what is was only a few years earlier.

But, as others have pointed out, predicted levels of information cannot be handled by present means. The void between what we know and what we can reasonably organize and apply to solving immediate problems continues to grow. We need ways to narrow this gap. We need to build mechanisms into our national and international institutions that ensure the rapid application of new technology.

## THE COMMUNICATIONS GAP

Much of the value in a sound piece of research lies in the practical application of results to solve real problems. Unfortunately, as the research endeavour has become more complicated and more specialized, the communications process has not kept pace. As a result of the communications delay a very serious information gap exists.

On one side of the research equation, we have an abundance of technical information, neatly catalogued and placed in storage. At the other end of the equation, we have a large number of potential users who do not even know that the technical information exists. So the store of unused research on library shelves grows larger each year, and the gap between available technology and applied technology widens.

Although it is a fact that publication of research results is still a vital element in the scientific process, the research process does not stop there. Publication of results is only the beginning. A 1963 report of the U.S. President's Sciences Advisory Committee on the responsibilities of the technical community and the government in the transfer of information commented:

"One of the major opportunities for enhancing the effectiveness of our national scientific and technical effort and the efficiency of Government management of research and development lies in the improvement of our ability to communicate information about current research efforts and the results of past efforts."

This Committee felt that, "the transfer of information is an inseparable part of research and development." And that all who are concerned with conducting and managing research and development must also, "accept responsibility for the transfer of information in the same degree and spirit that they accept responsibility for research and development itself."

Still the problem of communicating research results from scientists to users persists. A 1972 report of the Chairman of the U.S. Government's Federal Council for Science and Technology wrote, "Good information flow is vital not only internally within science and engineering, but also outwardly—both to practitioners who use the results of research and development, and to policy makers, managers and analysts."

The Council report states that a good flow of information means timely delivery of selected material matched to the user's need, which goes well beyond mere documentation. "Improving information flows, when well done, can be a key to better understanding societal problems, superior research and development and more effective management. It will also greatly facilitate the transfer of the technology for innovative and productive use of resource." In summary, the Science and Technology Council affirms that "technical knowledge must be regularly packaged and repackaged for use by . . . practitioners and the general public."

Many studies, that have looked at the ways in which research is transmitted to users, allude to the fact that most researchers see other researchers as their primary clients, and that they seem to be reaching these peers relatively well. However, there is an over dependence on the use of scientific journals as the best way to communicate knowledge. Little consideration is given to communicating research results through other media.

The Center for the Utilization of Scientific Knowledge at the University of Michigan, Ann Arbor, Michigan, in a 1972 study of U.S. Forest Service research management, concluded, "Journals are good at transmitting findings, but Forest Service research is a storehouse of logistical, methodological, and practical knowledge as well, and Journals don't transmit these to others very well, especially the practitioner of the knowledge." The study further concludes, "There's need for research managers to search out the best approaches for transmitting the knowledge to the appropriate audiences."

## AN EXAMPLE DELIVERY SYSTEM: THE U.S. FOREST SERVICE

The Forest Service, United States Department of Agriculture, with a long history of communicating knowledge to users, recently renewed its efforts to get results of research applied. When it had become apparent that a 'business-as-usual' approach to research application was no longer adequate, steps were taken to improve the delivery system.

The Forest Service developed a planned process for transferring technology. The genesis for the process came in 1973 at the direction of the Forest Service Deputy Chief for Research. He commissioned a small group to develop a system to hasten research application and also to serve, "as a prototype for planning technology transfer."

Working with a journeyman scientist, a pilot program was developed to transfer 20 years of accumulated research results which had been reported in over 150 technical publications. The transfer plan was designed to present this information to the general public, professional arborists, foresters, land mangers, and to the academic community.

The plan proposed that brief descriptive information illustrated with hand-drawings and presented in booklet form would be developed. And then steps would be taken to market the material to intended audiences. A series of slide/tape programs were also developed as well as posters, which highlighted a phase of research that could solve problems. An evaluation of the project indicated that the process worked well, the technology was transferred to the target audiences and evidence showed that it was being used.

Working on the premise that communications is a key to successful transfer of research from results to practice, the Forest Service's technology transfer process, which evolved from the pilot study, has the following elements:

- Identifying the technology available and ready for application.
- Identifying the target-user groups who will use the technology.
- Developing an objective and formal plan for application.
- Packaging the knowledge or technology for easy understanding.
- Selecting the media for transfer.
- Involving scientists and specialists with users and innovators.
- Troubleshooting, getting feedback, and evaluating the process and results.

The Forest Service technology transfer process is

aimed at systematically communicating the technical information developed by scientists to assure its application. The approach to technology transfer, as well as in the development of the research, involves preparation of a Technology Transfer Plan. The process usually begins with a simple proposal to transfer knowledge. It is based on user needs, availability of information, and technical and informational expertise. The Plan includes a commitment of time, talent and money, with administrative and technical commitment as the foundation for program development and implementation. This approach requires managers to consider organizational frameworks and processes for making decisions, allocating funds, delegating authority and responsibilities, measuring performance, and accounting for production and accomplishment. Thus, technology transfer planning may actually require as much management as does research and development.

The technology transfer planning process begins when a scientist or his supervisor informs top management that there are research results ready for transfer to users. A meeting is held with scientists, information specialists, appropriate people in other state and federal agencies, resource managers, technology transfer specialists, extension people, university people, and other users as appropriate.

These meetings begin with the scientist(s) sharing research results with those in attendance. The participants discuss the technology. At this point they are concerned whether or not the information is ready for transfer. With a go-ahead decision, the group prepares an itemized listing of ways to transfer the information to intended users. Due dates for completion of agreed upon actions are listed, with the assigned and responsible agencies or personnel included.

Funding needs for action items are discussed and sources for funding are explored. Usually various participants at the meeting agree to share the costs. It is not uncommon to have three sources of funds involved in one Technology Transfer Plan.

The Technology Transfer Plan is then committed to written form and sent to each participant for approval and comments. Corrections are made and the final plan is signed by appropriate managers and administrators. At this point the Technology Transfer Plan has firm commitment and becomes a real working document.

Schedules contained in the plan are closely monitored to assure actions are taking place as described. A later meeting is held with the original participants to review progress and to make adjustments as needed.

Sound management requires that a technology transfer program be well planned and executed and that it be cost effective. Planning should be handled by those who understand both the technology related to the problem and the target audiences. Therefore, researchers, practitioners, and target audiences should be involved in the planning process.

The function of a technology transfer planning team includes: outlining responsibilities, emphasizing overall program direction and co-ordination, and selecting media and the proper delivery systems. The team also develops the formal program document which contains: the message, what is being transferred; the audience, to whom the message is aimed; objectives; the expected accomplishments; the mechanisms for transferring the technology; a budget; and a system for evaluating the transfer process.

The Forest Service has published its Technology Transfer Planning process in a *Guide to help develop a technology transfer plan.* This Guide can assist others who may be interested in transferring technology to users. The elements offered in the Guide resulted from a mixture of experiences and established marketing practices. They are not absolute, but provide guidance in developing actual technology transfer plans.

The Technology Transfer Plan should serve to tie the research effort to user needs. A good plan represents sound management and helps to assure that research results reach users in a planned, systematic way. A good plan is both simple and flexible, permitting change to occur. It also ensures that an orderly transfer process takes place.

## CONCLUSION

The void between what we know and what we can reasonably organize and apply to solving immediate problems will continue to grow unless we establish institutional mechanisms to ensure rapid transfer and application of new knowledge. The formal technology transfer planning process developed by the United States Department of Agriculture's Forest Service is one approach that has proven successful over the past several years. Many other approaches are possible. The exact approach used is not as important as the degree of emphasis placed on reducing the technology transfer gap by institutions and organizations involved in generating, and utilizing research knowledge.

### Reference

NAISBITT, J. (1982). *Megatrends: ten new directions transforming our lives.* Warner Books Inc., New York. 290 pp.

# Forestry research and its application in continental Western Europe

F. C. HUMMEL
*Consultant, Surrey, U.K. (formerly Head of Forestry Division, European Economic Community)*

## ABSTRACT

The very considerable research effort in forestry and forest products research in continental Western Europe is generally of a high standard, but it is dispersed among a large number of mostly small research institutes. In some instances there has been insufficient emphasis on applied research in support of forest management and on the linking of forestry research with research in other disciplines. The identification and pursuit of priority research topics in the European Economic Community has recently been greatly assisted by Community research programmes which provide a forum for the discussion of research priorities and for financial support of particularly promising lines of research.

## GENERAL BACKGROUND

The forest area of continental Western Europe is about 120 million ha and annual production averages around 240 million m$^3$, that is about 2 m$^3$/ha. The ten member states of the European Economic Community (EEC), with which this paper is primarily concerned, have a forest area of 34 million ha and produce about 85 million m$^3$ of timber per year (i.e. about 2.5 m$^3$/ha/year). The EEC runs an annual trade deficit in the wood products sector of 17 billion U.S. dollars, which is second only to the deficit in the oil sector, and is continuing to rise. The rest of Western Europe has an export surplus of about half this amount. Most of these exports come from Sweden, Finland, and, to a more limited extent, from Austria. The first major forest policy objective throughout Western Europe is to raise wood-production. Research has to play its part in achieving this objective.

The environmental and social aspects of forestry are also very important in Western Europe. Especially in the EEC, the population density is very high and the forest area per capita correspondingly low, ranging from 0.02 ha in the Netherlands to 0.28 ha. in France. The limited forest resources are expected to serve a variety of environmental purposes, the relative importance of which vary from region to region. Thus, in the Mediterranean region, soil and water conservation are vital, in the Alps protection against erosion, in some of the western areas shelter against wind. Nearly everywhere the forests must be managed to provide habitats for wildlife, especially as the intensification of agriculture and urbanization have encroached on these habitats from outside the forest. At the same time, the general public makes more and more demands on forests for recreational purposes, especially near towns, but also further afield wherever people go for their holidays and want to enjoy nature and not just a crowded beach.

There are thus three major policy areas in which research has to play a part: production, conservation of the environment and the provision of recreational opportunities. An additional, important new field of forestry activity calling for an increasing research effort is the planting of trees outside the forest. There are two aspects to this; first there is urban forestry (i.e. the planting of trees in parks for amenity or along motorways, around airports and industrial establishments as barriers against noise and the visual impact of modern technology); secondly, there is the combination of tree growing and farming on the same piece of land. This idea is not new in Europe but disappointing results in the past led to its decline until very recently when new ideas started to revive interest and research in this field. The production and utilization of wood biomass for energy has also become a major topic of research development, not only where wood is scarce, but also in wood rich countries such as Sweden. Finally, a constant research effort is required to protect forests against the various biotic and abiotic agents that threaten them. The most alarming threat at the present time comes from a rapidly spreading die-back of forests, especially in Germany, but also in some other countries. The exact causes are unknown but are believed to be in some way associated with the cumulative effect of atmospheric pollution over a long period.

Forest products research, which is also very important, has close links with forest research, for example in the investigation of the effect of silvicultural practices on wood quality. One of the main problems of wood processing is the development of technologies which do not need very large plants to be economically viable. This problem is found also in many other parts of the world, but has received less attention than it deserves, presumably because it is of no great concern to the major wood producing countries of the world and to the major manufacturers of wood processing machinery. The question of scale is particularly significant in the pulp and paper industry.

## CURRENT STATE OF FORESTRY RESEARCH

### General

Forestry research in Western Europe is founded on a long tradition going back for centuries. Originally the emphasis was on finding the best methods to manage and regenerate particular types of semi-natural forests, many of which had been exploited in the past or degraded by uncontrolled grazing and litter collection. The basic problem was to obtain a sustained yield of timber for purposes such as ship building, or of firewood for industries such as the manufacture of salt or the smelting of metals. Some enterprises were large and required an annual input of wood of over 100 000 $m^3$. Gradually the emphasis switched from very locally oriented empirical research, much of which was conducted by forest managers, to more widely applicable research requiring greater specialization, more rigorous scientific methodology and an interdisciplinary approach.

The total forestry and forest products research effort in Western Europe is considerable. In the EEC alone, annual expenditure is of the order of 150 million US dollars and there are about 1000 research officers with university or equivalent education engaged on this research, together with about 2000 to 3000 supporting technicians and other staff. Forest products research accounts for somewhat less than half of the research manpower and for rather more than half of the expenditure. Precise figures on research expenditures are not available, partially because of the confidentiality of some of the industrial research and partially because sometimes no distinction is possible between research and teaching or even between forestry research and other research, for example, in the case of research into tree diseases or wood rotting agents by research institutes not primarily dedicated to forestry or forest products.

The way the research is organized varies considerably from country to country and depends, at least in part, on factors unconnected with forestry. Thus the federal structure of the Federal Republic of Germany (FRG) and the centralized structure of France are, as we shall see, reflected in the organization of forest research. Overall, the research effort is somewhat fragmented. Not only do even small countries have their own research institutes, but in some instances even regions within countries have established separate institutes. An exception to this is Luxembourg which depends on its neighbours to meet its research needs and also for the training of its forest officers. The differences in organization are illustrated by France and the FRG.

### France

The major forestry research activities in France are centred on the Institut National de la Recherche Agronomique (INRA) which, as its name implies, is primarily concerned with agriculture. INRA comes under the Minister of Agriculture who is also responsible for forestry. Links with forestry practice are provided by a body on which the various interests representing growers, public and private, are represented. But according to the latest forest policy review, undertaken by R. Duroure (1982) at the request of the Prime Minister, the existing mechanisms for a constructive dialogue between research and practice and for the application of research results to practice leave much to be desired and must be improved.

There are five further government research organizations in France concerned with forestry and forest products. They include the Centre Technique du Bois (CTB) and the Centre Technique Forestière Tropicale (CTFT). Some of these Government research establishments are financed in part from the Fonds Forestière National (FFN) which in turn is financed from a levy on the sale of forest products. Two research organizations controlled by forest industry are also supported in part by the FNN. These organizations are the Association pour la Rationalisation et la Mecanisation de l'Exploitation Forestière

(ARMEF) and the Association Forêt Cellulose (AFOCEL). ARMEF in particular has been responsible for some interesting practice oriented developments in logging methods and logging machinery.

Finally research of relevance to forestry is carried out at about ten universities or research establishments linked to universities.

Summing up the situation, Duroure states: "The dispersal of research effort is not bad in itself, on the contrary, but given the scarcity of financial resources, it is essential for each organization to define its objectives with precision and to co-ordinate its efforts effectively with the others in order to avoid unnecessary duplication." Much the same might be said about some other parts of Western Europe.

### Federal Republic of Germany

In contrast to France, the state forests and the forest authority functions are vested in the eleven *Länder* (states), which at one time had been virtually independent states and still retain considerable powers. Each *Land* has its own forest service, and transfers of personnel between Länder are unusual. The forest services of four Länder (Bavaria, Baden-Wurttemberg, Hessen, Niedersachsen) have their own research establishments. In the case of Bavaria, until recently, the state forest research institute was very closely linked with the forestry faculty of Munich University, professors at the faculty being at the same time in charge of sections of the research institute. A few years ago, the state forest research institute was made more independent of the university, presumably in order to give the state forest service more direct control over the direction of research programmes and thus ensure that priorities be determined by the needs of forest management. The objectives of academic research at a university obviously do not necessarily coincide with the research objectives of a government state forest service.

There are two other forestry faculties, one at the University of Freiburg and the other at Gottingen, both of which also undertake some forestry research.

At the federal level there is the large federal forest and forest products research organization (Bundesforschungsanstalt für Forst- und Holzwirtschaft) near Hamburg, which comes directly under the Federal forest service. Its links with forestry practice in the FRG are somewhat tenuous as forestry and the research to service it is almost exclusively the responsibility of the Länder, but there are obviously many research topics of interest to the country as a whole which provide ample scope for useful research. On the forest products side the Bundesforschungsanstalt is very strong in wood physics, chemistry and biology as well as in certain aspects of wood processing. It is the only major research organization in Western Europe to combine both forestry and forest products. The linkage appears to be very beneficial to both sides. The federal forests and forest products research organization is also active in support of the country's aid programmes to developing countries.

### Research at the European Community level

The question may well be asked: "With all the research going on at national and more local levels, what is the need for the European Community to get involved?" In fact, just because of the fragmentation of the research effort in the member states, the Community has a useful role to play.

In the first place, there is a need for closer contacts between the various research institutes and individual research workers in order that they may benefit from each others experience, eliminate undesirable duplication of effort (not all duplication is undesirable!) and identify gaps. The Community helps by arranging and financing meetings between research workers and visits in connection with research. Secondly, where gaps are found, the Community assists by commissioning research projects to be undertaken either at one institute or shared among several institutes. This system of commissioning research applies in particular to projects which are of interest to several member states, but exceed the human and financial resources of any one. Thirdly, research is sometimes needed in support of Community legislation, for example in connection with the enforcement of quality standards of forest reproductive material or with phytosanitary measures to prevent the importation and spread of tree diseases. Finally, the Community is well placed to view forest and forest products research in a broader perspective. This point is illustrated by the fact that Community sponsored forestry research projects occur in three separate research programmes, namely

- the agricultural research programme
- the energy from biomass programme
- the raw materials programme.

Examples of research projects in the agricultural programme are those dealing with the Dutch elm disease and with certain aspects of agroforestry. The biomass projects include the establishment, management, and harvesting of so-called 'energy plantations', these are 3 to 5 year rotations. The projects also include the more efficient harvesting and burning of wood residues (tops, branches, etc.) from normal harvesting operations. By far the largest

Community research effort in forestry is in the raw materials programme in which there is a sub-programme 'Wood as a raw material' with some 60 projects and a budget of 12 million Units of Account (about 12 million U.S. dollars) over a 4 year period. This programme will be described in more detail because it illustrates how the application of research results must be considered right from the initial planning stage of research.

**Sub-programme: Wood as a renewable raw material**

The sub-programme 'Wood as a raw material' became operational in 1982. It is divided into six research areas:

1. Wood production (selection and improvement of forest reproductive material, silviculture, prevention of losses).
2. Wood harvest, storage and transport.
3. Wood as a material (wood properties, improvement of performance, protection against deterioration, development of objective testing methodology).
4. Mechanical wood processing (manufacturing processes, adhesives and joints, constructional use of wood).
5. Processing of wood and related organic materials (e.g. straw) into fibre products.
6. Wood as a source of chemicals.

Experts from the member states advised on priority topics within each of the wide research areas. The emphasis was on research likely to yield early results for application in practice, for example the development of an economically viable sawmilling technology for logs of small diameter. The contracts for this kind of short term development work which is based more on the intelligent combination of existing machinery than on new inventions were sometimes placed with small industrial enterprises if they submitted promising proposals. At the other extreme, there were highly specialized fundamental research projects. An example is the development of cell and tissue culture techniques which will permit the rapid propagation of genetically scarce material.

About 300 projects were submitted, of which some 60 could be accepted with the available budget. This very rigorous selection means that many promising projects had to be rejected; on the other hand, a very high standard has been set, which may prove beneficial in the long run.

The Community provides up to 50 per cent of the finance for each project, the rest having to be put up by the proposing organization(s). Part of the Community contribution goes towards what is called 'co-ordination' (i.e. expenses connected with meetings, travel, etc.) and part towards the conduct of the research itself. The progress of each project is monitored by the EEC Commission which sometimes hires expert consultants for the purpose. The Commission has also appointed an advisory group of experts from the member states to advise on the selection of projects and to monitor research progress.

The research results for each project will be disseminated in two forms:

i. a detailed technical report with limited distribution to experts, which will serve as a basis for planning further research and development;
ii. a very short report for wider distribution in order to give guidance on the practical application of the results.

Participation in this programme on wood as a raw material, as in many other EEC research programmes, is not confined to member states. Other states may join in, subject to certain conditions, and a financial contribution related to their gross national product. Sweden has joined the programme. The arrangement should prove mutually beneficial because the research skills in Sweden and the member states are somewhat complementary. This example also illustrates the more fundamental principle that co-operation within the EEC is not intended as a protective barrier against the outside world but rather as a foundation upon which wider international co-operation may be built.

**EEC research priorities**

The judgement on priorities is necessarily subjective because, although there may be a broad consensus on some issues, views are somewhat divided on others; these disagreements may relate to the topic itself or to the prospects of achieving useful results on topics agreed to be important. What follows is a purely personal view of priority topics within each of the six research areas identified in the EEC programme for wood as a renewable raw-material:

1. *Wood production*

a. Selection and improvement of forest reproductive material.
b. Cultivation and management of trees outside the forest (urban forestry, agroforestry).
c. Research into the cause of and cure for the die-back of forests in parts of Western Europe which is believed to be in some way associated with atmospheric pollution.
d. (Silvicultural research, which at one time held the centre of the stage, while still of some significance is no longer pre-eminent).

2. *Wood harvest, storage and transport*

The research priorities can largely be summarized by the assertion 'small is beautiful'. The EEC's forest resources are scattered both geographically and in ownership. We must therefore intensify the search for:

a. economically viable ways of harvesting relatively small parcels of small sized material; and to do this we need:
b. efficient small machines (including for example better forestry attachments to farm tractors);
c. improvement of safety standards and working conditions (noise, vibration, etc.).

3. *Wood as a material*

Here top priority is given to the development of objective testing methodology (improvements in machine stress grading, methods for evaluating new adhesives, non-destructive and comparable test procedures for wood-based panels, criteria for acceptance of wood preservatives). The competitiveness of wood will, in the longer term, depend largely on success in the development of such testing methodology.

4. *Mechanical wood processing*

Most development work has been done by the industries themselves; what they need is a certain amount of back up research (e.g. to make wood products more decay resistent) and there are some specific problems such as safety of structures (including for example, load duration effects) and health hazards (e.g. those associated with the use of formaldehyde in glues for particle board).

5. *Processing of wood and related organic materials into fibre products*

The general research objectives in this very broad area must be the development of technology which will permit economic and environmentally acceptable working in relatively small scale plants. Specific objectives are:

- improvement of fibre yield
- reduction in raw material requirements in quantity and quality
- better use of residues
- reduction of energy consumption
- reduction in pollution
- better use of recycled waste paper and non-wood fibres.

In the pursuit of these objectives top priority should be given to new technology which has already shown evidence of commercial promise.

6. *Wood as a source of chemicals*

The possible production of a very wide range of chemicals from wood has already been demonstrated; most of these can, however, be produced more economically from coal and/or oil and this is not likely to change until there is a further substantial increase in the price of these fossil fuels relative to wood. It therefore seems advisable to give priority for the time being to the more effective chemical utilization of by products from existing processes (e.g. the utilization of lignin residues of chemical pulping).

## ASSESSMENT OF STRENGTHS AND WEAKNESSES

Any generalization on strengths and weaknesses in the existing research activities in continental Western Europe are apt to be misleading because the research is dispersed among so many institutions that there are bound to be exceptions to whatever may appear to be a general trend; for the same reason any generalizations are bound to be subjective. However, since I have been invited to give an opinion, I shall do so, fully aware of the risks; but I shall confine my remarks to the EEC. In Scandinavia, in particular, conditions are different.

Perhaps the most characteristic feature of forestry research in the EEC, apart from the general, very high standard of research scientists, is its dispersal among a large number of relatively small research establishments. This leads to a certain lack of general direction and duplication of effort, but gives the individual institutes the academic independence which they prize very highly. It seems that what is perhaps needed most is a clearer distinction between research objectives:

- applied research in support of forest management
- fundamental research aimed at a better understanding of nature and eventual major steps forward in practice (e.g. in the field of genetics and propagation)
- academic research in support of university teaching.

In this context, it is worth noting that in contrast with Britain, the research under the direct control of the forest authority is very limited; in some countries there is virtually none. This is a definite weakness which is somewhat mitigated by the fact that a large proportion of those engaged in forestry research have been trained as forest officers. Unfortunately, there is comparatively little movement of personnel between research and practice in later stages of forest officers' careers. In the case of France, the concentration of the major government forestry research activities in an agricultural research establishment (INRA) prevents forestry research from becoming too inward looking, which is a common fault of forestry research.

With regard to research areas, it would seem that forest products research in general has received far too little attention compared with forestry and that, within forestry, research relating to traditional silvicultural problems (thinnings, etc.) has dominated the scene for too long. In recent years, however, there has been a welcome change in this respect.

Forestry research in the continental EEC countries has been criticized for not being sufficiently forward looking; there may be some justification in this. On the other hand, the question arises, how far should research establishments go in pursuing topics given little priority by those who determine forest policy? For example, relatively little attention until recently has been devoted to the possible introduction of exotic species into continental Western Europe, although there are far fewer indigenous conifers than in comparable climates elsewhere in the world. But was there any point in following this line of enquiry while as a matter of policy indigenous species, subject to a few exceptions, were to be preferred?

The EEC programme 'Wood as a renewable raw material', although too recent to show results, appears to be a very promising step forward. In addition to providing an informed forum for the discussion of research priorities in forestry and forest products, it can back the conclusions of these discussions with hard cash. An incentive is thus given to the wide range of research establishments in the Community to pursue certain lines of research, but without in any way infringing their independence. It is worth noting that the expertise of IUFRO contributes to the identification of research priorities in various ways, not the least of which is through the fact that the national experts on the programme committee are members of IUFRO institutes and participate in its activities. They can thus draw on IUFRO experience in their deliberations. Also worth mentioning in this context is the fact, already referred to, that this programme, as well as the other EEC programmes with a forestry component, place forestry and forest products research into a wider perspective and thus encourage research workers to become more outward looking.

## CONCLUSION

The general conclusion thus appears to be the optimistic one that it is both possible and likely that forest and forest products research in Europe will overcome some of its weaknesses and build on its strengths.

### Reference

DUROURE, R. (1982). Propositions pour une politique globale foret-bois. *Revue Forestière Française* (numéro special). 115 pp.

# The Nepal-Australia Forestry Project: a case study of research and development

K. R. SHEPHERD and D. M. GRIFFIN

*Department of Forestry, Australian National University, Canberra, Australia*

## ABSTRACT

The Chautara Forest Division in the sub-Himalayan hills is the site of this project funded by the governments of Nepal and Australia. The project is one of, 'forestry for local community development', with major aims of providing firewood, forage and timber for the residents and surpluses for the cities of the Kathmandu Valley. Topography is extreme and subsistence agriculture on terraces cut into the hills is the main occupation. A survey indicates that per capita consumption of firewood is 291 kg/year, yielding energy of 12 MJ/day. Total energy use is 14 MJ/day, amongst the lowest recorded. Each family also needs leaves from trees for forage. Because of population pressure, popular support is essential for progress in afforestation or conservation. The project's strategy is to work with panchayats (local communities) where support through offerings of labour or land is evident. As the early benefits of afforestation activities are perceived, other panchayats seek the project's help. Nearly 40 tree seedling nurseries have been opened and others will follow as more panchayats become motivated. Tree planting occurs on land owned by the government, panchayats and individuals and protection of the existing forest has commenced. No fencing of plantations has been necessary as the local people in the motivated panchayats voluntarily restrain their stock from grazing in them. Educational activities include provision of training for panchayat forest workers and stimulating awareness of forestry in schools. Research into social and cultural attitudes as these affect the forest, into the ecology and development of regenerated forests and into questions of land-use have been fostered by the project to supply answers to questions raised by management. The project provides an example of close integration between applied research and development within an international context.

### Introduction

The Nepal-Australia Forestry Project (N-AFP) is an aid project for which the Department of Forestry, Australian National University (ANU), acts as an executing agent for the Australian Development Assistance Bureau. The present project (N-AFP/2) arose out of an earlier phase of Australian forestry assistance to Nepal, both of which are described by Shepherd (1981). N-AFP/2, centred on the Chautara Forestry Division to the north-east and east of Kathmandu, extends from October 1978 to September 1983 but is presently under review. A stage three has yet to be examined and endorsed by both the Nepalese and the Australian Government.

The Chautara project is a joint exercise in community forestry between His Majesty's Government of Nepal (HMGN) and Australian aid. The rationale for the project arose from discussions commencing in the mid-1970s, mainly between the then Divisional Forest Officer at Chautara, Mr. T. B. S. Mahat, two successive Australian Project Managers in Nepal, Mr. A. Fearnside and Dr. R. G. Campbell, and the authors. Comprehensive discussion took place with members of local communities. Signing of a Memorandum of Understanding between Nepal and Australia for this project took place at about the same time as the publication of the definitive paper on community forestry by FAO (1978).

The FAO paper provides an excellent outline of the principles of community forestry, and how to go about the process of setting up projects in any area. It does not deal specifically with the day-to-day problems of any particular place, and certainly not with the singular situation of the Middle Hills of Nepal. The concepts of community forestry had been well propounded but the developmental technology was only vaguely known in 1978 as few community forestry projects existed. In spite of this some quite large projects date from about this time, for example the joint HMGN/World Bank/UNDP/FAO Community Forestry Development and Training Project was commenced in Nepal in mid-1980.

N-AFP, like many other projects, has had to acquire the necessary expertise concerning community forestry as it went along while at the same time striving to achieve a respectable target of reforestation within the Chautara Division. This paper recounts some of that experience in research and development. It deals first of all with assembling existing information about the project areas, then with research to find out about what was not known, and finally with devising management strategies to suit the local situation.

## INFORMATION ON THE PROJECT AREA

A new reforestation project must work with what is to hand: the land, the people, the climate, the forest, and the human and financial resources of the society. Knowledge of these and of the historical roots of that society is needed before policy options can be explored with confidence.

### Historical influences

Deforestation of the Middle Hills of Nepal can easily be attributed to recent influences over the last few decades. Such thinking encourages crash programs and precipitates action. In support of this view the impact of recent population increase is cited, as is the annexation of forested land by the Crown under the Nationalisation of Forest Land Act 1956, when local communities tended to abandon responsibility for protecting local forests. Both can be rejected as primary causes for the destruction of forests in the Chautara Division although they have undoubtedly exacerbated the problem. The forests were mostly destroyed long before, probably over the last century and a half, possibly several centuries.

Some of the most destructive practices of the past have been abandoned now. Careful enquiries reveal much timber was probably removed long since to build Kathmandu. Logs were taken down the Sun Kosi River into India (Hooker, 1854). Taxes to the ruling Rana family are known to have been paid in charcoal, which was used for heating and brick making. Metal smelting was widespread, evidenced by slag which can be found in many places in the Division, probably for a small arms industry which collapsed when India agreed to supply arms to Nepal during World War I (Fr. L. Stiller, personal communication). This is confirmed by elderly residents who say widespread smelting and charcoal making ceased about 70 years ago and forest boundaries have changed little since. Research into this history is part of a Ph.D. study by T. B. S. Mahat, now a graduate student in our Department.

This is a fascinating topic and much more could be recounted here, but it is sufficient to conclude that the destruction of the hill forests has been a long process. Precipitate action is not necessary as there is time still for careful research and investigation which can result in socially acceptable, technical solutions.

### The population

The population of Nepal increased from 9.4 m in 1961 to 11.5 m in 1971, and to 15.02 m by 1981 (National Census, February 1982). In Chautara Division, the population increased from 451 000 in 1971 to 540 000 in 1981, at an annual rate of 1.8 per cent. This rate is lower than the national average, as for most hill districts, due to emigration, but it is still disturbingly high. Even if reduced to 1.4 per cent, we have calculated the population could reach 733 000 by the year 2000 and in so doing offset any gains made by increased forest productivity.

To learn about this population, the project commissioned a social survey (New ERA, 1980), which was repeated in late 1982. As expected, the population is made up of a number of caste groups which vary between communities. It is important to have information on this as castes react differently to introduced technology, for example some accept improved stoves which save fuel far more readily than others, because of cooking habits. Only 28.5 per cent of the respondents were literate. The average family was 5.8 persons, each with 6.1 farm animals but with few trees on their own land, so that most were heavily dependent on the forest for fodder.

### Land and forest resources

Lack of maps and assessment data is an intractable problem. Little land is accurately surveyed and few areas are subject to title deeds. The Divisional Forest Officer is responsible for the demarcation and survey of the boundaries of forest land and resolves any ownership disputes.

Good maps of the project area were not available when the project began. A working map was commissioned by the project, derived from old Indian Survey topographic maps which were the best available. The project eventually obtained boundary maps of panchayats (community administrative districts) only to have these changed with a redistribution due to population increase. New boundary maps have now to be acquired. A forest resource map was commissioned from private consultants in late 1982, derived from interpretation of aerial photographs taken by a Canadian team in 1977. The summary data in Table 1, and a number of additional data, have been useful in laying a foundation for management planning.

### Demands for forest products

Local people make a variety of demands on the forest, including fodder, fuelwood, timber, litter and medicinal herbs. Some demands have almost ceased (e.g. making daphne paper). Demand estimates for forest products were assembled by Ramrajya Shrestha[1] (1982) and are presented in Table 2. These data and the forest resource data in Table 1 have been employed by us to estimate fuelwood demands. Several rates of population increase and of fuelwood demand were employed. It was assumed that 1000, 1500 or 2000 ha of land were converted annually from grassland or scrub to plantation within the Division until all of the available land was planted, estimated at 59 000 ha. All of the present productive forest was assumed to remain intact.

If the rate of population increase is assumed to be 1.4 per cent per year and the use of fuelwood 0.5 $m^3$ per caput, it is estimated the demand could be met by the year 2002 if 2000 ha of plantation were to be established annually. At 1500 ha per year the demand might be met by the year 2011, but at 1000 ha per year the demand will never be met due to population increase. However, Ramrajya Shrestha's enquiries into fodder use elicited the opinion from local villagers that if forest conditions were to improve the people would keep more buffaloes and hence fodder demand would rise. Seemingly the same would apply to fuelwood use, already as low as any recorded, so that even these prognostications would be overtaken by altered demand. In any case, if the population continues to increase at the rate of 1.4 per cent per year and uses 0.5 $m^3$ of fuelwood per caput, the demand will outstrip the estimated productivity of the forest within Chautara Division in the year 2031.

These calculations were carefully considered in seeking to set planting targets for a proposed N-AFP/3. Despite the projection, a target of 1000 ha planted per year appears to be all that is possible. In the monsoon planting period of 1982 the Division achieved 700 ha, but this was in 38 panchayats with the largest single block planted being 80 ha, the smallest 0.16 ha. The operational problems in an area as steep as this with few roads are obvious.

### Politics and reforestation programs

Community forestry involves close co-operation with local leaders if the objectives of reforestation are to be achieved. Local politics are complex and obscure. Even with reasonable competence in spoken Napali the expatriate aid worker must rely heavily on the advice of local counterparts to avoid the pitfalls of local antagonisms and allegiances. Two examples serve to illustrate the problems involved.

**Table 1. Statistics on land use by districts for the Chautara Forest Division of Nepal, 1982. (hectares)**

| Land use category | District | | Division |
|---|---|---|---|
| | Sindhu Plachok | Kabhre | |
| Crop land | 74 988 | 65 647 | 140 647 |
| Forest | 115 926 | 69 989 | 185 915 |
| Grassland | 11 080 | 1 711 | 12 791 |
| Rock | 48 125 | — | 48 125 |
| Barren | 855 | 1 611 | 2 466 |
| Urban | — | 31 | 31 |
| Total | 250 974 | 138 989 | 389 975 |
| Crop land per person | 0.322 | 0.213 | 0.260 |
| Forest land per person | 0.478 | 0.227 | 0.344 |

Reforestation involves a change of land use and so inevitably must be influenced by local politics. The project seeks to begin the process of reforesting some 60 000 ha of local land over the next 30 to 50 years. Grassland and scrub now used for common grazing must be withdrawn and given over to forest if this target is to be achieved. It is important that the local people perceive the benefits of conversion, accept the new land use policies, and support them. Obtaining such agreement is a major exercise in local politics.

Aid programs bring finance and prestige into a depressed region. Assistance from local leaders is necessary but they too can see advantage in being associated with successful new initiatives in their area and so may provide assistance but for the wrong reasons. However, the project must at all times not

[1] Mrs Ramrajya Shrestha was engaged on field research for a Master of Agricultural Development Economics, Development Studies Centre, Australian National University and worked in association with the project.

**Table 2. All data on households and use of fuel and fodder in Sondu Palchok, Chautara Forest Division. Source: New ERA (1980) and Shrestha (1982)**

| | Units | New ERA | Shrestha |
|---|---|---|---|
| Family size—6 panchayats | persons | 5.8 | |
| —Chautara non-bazar | ,, | 6.1 | 6.2 |
| Fuelwood use—6 panchayats[1] | kg per caput | 291 | |
| —Chautara non-bazar | ,, | 294 | 223 |
| Fodder use—6 panchayats | kg per caput | 465 | |
| —Chautara non-bazar | ,, | 655 | 499 |
| Litter for animals—6 panchayats | kg per caput | 362 | |
| —Chautara non-bazar | ,, | 459 | |
| Manure applied—Chautara non-bazar | kg per ha per year | | 8315 |
| Large animals—6 panchayats | No. per household | 3.68 | |
| —Chautara non-bazar | ,, | 4.62 | 3.69 |

[1] In addition about 45 kg of agricultural wastes are estimated to be burnt annually.

only remain apolitical but also be seen to be apolitical. National plebescite and panchayat elections have both been held in Nepal during the past couple of years making it difficult for the N-AFP project leaders to find a middle, neutral path.

## INFORMATION TO BE ACQUIRED

The last section mainly concerned information which already exists and which merely had to be assembled for project use. Much necessary information is not available and so it must be acquired through research. In community forestry both the information needed and the method of acquisition may be a little unconventional.

### Species selection for planting

Species selection is unquestionably a difficult problem involving elements of ecology, consumer preferences and watershed protection. The original forests consisted of complex species associations which changed considerably with site. Geologically the country is naturally unstable and subject to rapid erosion and change. More recent decades have brought heavy population pressures which have vastly altered the ecological balance. Planting sites available vary considerably from the original. However, we suspect many of the more resilient of the original species are relatively tolerant of site. It is these species which constitute the volunteer forest which results from protection of degraded scrublands and possibly the first steps in reforestation might be to plant these same hardy species.

Consumer preference must undoubtedly influence the choice if the village people are to become involved in community forestry. Campbell (1983) surveyed 900 households and 180 ward leaders to identify prevailing patterns of forest resource use. His data indicate decided species preferences for five main use categories: fruit, fodder, fuel, timber and bamboo. But the species listed under these categories change by region from east to west of the country. Villagers gave greater preference to planting trees in the order given, fruit trees most, bamboo least. In another survey fruit and fodder trees were favoured for planting on private land, fuel and timber trees on panchayat land (New ERA, 1980). Thus the consumer preference system is also complex. But fortunately we find a number of the resilient species referred to above appearing on these preference lists (e.g. *Schima wallichii, Alnus nepalensis, Pinus roxburghii,* and *Shorea robusta*). Other species will, however, be difficult to establish on degraded land without protection or very careful establishment procedures (shading, fertilisers, watering, etc.). Therefore, the community may have to be content initially with a few species. More delicate species probably cannot be planted until the land is partly revegetated and some protection is available, no matter how high they stand on the preference list.

A primary aim of all community forestry activity should be to try to reforest bare land within the Middle Hills as quickly as possible to protect the watersheds. For this reason, considerable weight in the species selection process should be given to species of proven capacity to establish on highly degraded land. These are *Shorea robusta* on the valley bottoms and lower slopes (to about 1200 m), *Pinus roxburghii* on the lower to middle slopes (about 900 to 1800 m), *Pinus patula* (an exotic) on the upper slopes and ridges (1500 to 2400 m), overlapping with *Pinus wallichiana* on the higher areas above 1800 m, with *Alnus nepalensis* over the whole of this range in moist, sheltered locations. *Schima wallichii* could also be included in this list for the middle and upper slopes, even though it has not been planted in large numbers so far, as it is one of the last survivors in the process of forest degradation. Once an initial cover of hardy species is established other stages in the natural revegetation process are possible. Other species could then be introduced, as has been suggested above, in a process of phased enrichment plantings. Such enrichment planting could not be contemplated in high cost developed countries but in the community forestry situation it should not only be possible but also highly rewarding in terms of user products.

### Productivity and harvesting strategies

Most forestry projects in Nepal have barely touched the problem of how communities might harvest material from their forest yet maintain, even improve, productivity. This is not only an extraordinarily difficult technical problem, given the nature of the harvesting, but also a difficult social problem.

A 'conventional' managed forest is near fully stocked, part-harvested at infrequent intervals during a lengthy rotation which is terminated when the crop is close to biological maturity. This is the developed country textbook view on which much forest management theory and practice is based. The products harvested are derived mostly from stemwood, the leaves and branches, stump and roots are left to rot on the forest floor. In the Middle Hills of Nepal the forests which will make up most of the community forests are rarely fully stocked and 'harvesting' takes place frequently, usually daily. Leaves and twigs for fodder and animal bedding, branches and stems for firewood, straighter and sturdier members for timber, and ground litter for bedding are all taken. All species are taken, not just the favoured timber trees.

In conventional management the yield obtained is carefully spread, both in time and space, over a range of age classes, species and management subdivisions. The result is a yield carefully matched to the estimated production capacity of the forest and to be sustained over a lengthy planning period, even in perpetuity. In the Middle Hills, priorities in harvesting are determined by availability and proximity to dwellings resulting in an extremely uneven impact on the forest. Areas close to dwellings are overcut while remote areas are selectively cut for specific products. The harvesting is usually carried out in an indiscriminate and disruptive manner (e.g. lopping of crown material in oak forest). The result of this uneven cutting is that the forest closest to dwellings is overcut, retreating progressively away from inhabited areas. The land is either developed into cultivated fields or degenerates first into scrub, then to grassland, and finally to bare ground due to excessive grazing. The more remote forest areas are undercut, although the more valuable elements of it are reduced, and probably disappear even before serious overcutting begins. This set of processes has been well documented by Wiart (1983) who found his study area, a substantial tract of forest flanked on either side by villages, produced more than was harvested annually, yet was deteriorating as described.

Only now are studies beginning to place this multifaceted problem within a theoretical context, as for example in the work of Wiart (1983) noted above. The framework encompasses elements of biological productivity, forest management and sociology, and social systems dominate this type of problem more in Nepal than in most countries, even within Asia.

We have been fortunate to be able to conduct research into these problems in two ways. One is through the direct involvement of project staff in harvesting studies. The second has been through the research of a Ph.D. student from our Department, Mr. B. Mohns, who is carrying out field studies at Chautara. The two research efforts are both mutually supportive and complementary. Mr. Mohns is concerned essentially with shorter term studies over 2 years, project staff, Dr. Gilmour and Messrs. Applegate and Campbell, with longer term trials which will need to be maintained for a decade or more.

Much of this work is on areas planted to *Pinus roxburghii* about 8 years ago but which has since regenerated to natural forest due to the exclusion of grazing animals. This 'volunteer forest' has been found to contain more than 100 plant species, about 20 of these local tree species (Mohns and Banks, personal communication). Much attention is being given to *Schima wallichii* as this species is one of the most resilient in the heavily populated zone from 600 to 2200 m and is almost the last tree to be lost in the process of deforestation. Its growth rate, regeneration strategy, resistance to fire and capacity to withstand lopping are being studied. Plots harvested under various strategies are being carefully monitored.

### Regeneration strategies

Regeneration of the forest presents some unusual problems. Usually a tree is cut for only the stemwood once a minimum size has been reached, but here a tree may be replaced because it no longer produces a vigorous crown following lopping for fodder and small firewood. In the conventional forest the stem is usually grown to a considerable size and sawn into planks, but here the stem may only need to be large enough to be squared into a house timber. Thus the age and size of a tree at rotation age may differ considerably from those in forests managed on conventional lines. Will trees be cut individually as in a selection system or will group selection be used? Some species may coppice from stumps or root sprouts, others regenerate from seed, while yet others will have to be planted. Answers to these questions will require careful research and observation over a period of years.

Clearcutting systems would appear to be particularly inappropriate. The protective cover of the forest on much of the Middle Hills has been lost with disastrous consequences in these important water catchment areas. The hills are naturally unstable but the change in vegetation cover has only worsened this situation. Fleming (1978) estimated the annual erosion rate under forest canopy at 8 tons per ha, but under scrub this increased to 15, and to 30 on open grazing land. Thus the regeneration procedures recommended for both planted forests and natural forest, which have been protected and restored, must take account of the protective role of these forests.

### Social factors and the distribution of benefits

A proper understanding of the social context within which community forestry must operate is necessary. In this regard the work to date of the Motivation and Evaluation Unit within the World Bank Community Forestry Development and Training Project has been particularly valuable. Careful evaluation is needed urgently of the problems of harvesting and distributing the products of the forests as nothing will destroy community forestry more rapidly than an inflated expectation of the benefits from community forests, when combined with an inequitable distribution of those benefits.

In phase three of N-AFP it is intended to establish an Extension Unit within the Divisional Office at Chautara. This Unit will be required to advocate good community forestry practice through the schools and adult education. It will also assist in devising methods for the equitable distribution for the benefits of community forestry, especially how panchayat administration can handle the problem.

## DEVISING MANAGEMENT STRATEGIES

Forest within the Chautara Division, as in all of the Middle Hills, falls into three categories: government forest, panchayat administered forest, and trees on private land. Each requires different management strategies as the forest cover differs and the management capability available to each varies. Little documentation on this problem exists.

### Government land

The most sophisticated management capability will be available for the government forest but then too this forested land will also need to serve a variety of uses, some compatible, some not. For example, the government will need to retain responsibility for very steep lands and for the high forest above about 2500 m. These forests are essential for the protection of catchments, a fact graphically demonstrated within the Division during the 1982 monsoon when two villages at the base of the catchments were destroyed in flash floods with considerable loss of life.

Protection of these high forests is an urgent but difficult task. The project hopes to devise at least tentative proposals for management during stage three. Our preliminary enquiries suggest there are changing patterns of land-use involving summer grazing, although the impacts on the forest are still heavy (Gilmore, personal communication). Tentative proposals have been made for co-operation with the project by lamas of this area, following discussion within this group of spiritual leaders and concern being expressed amongst themselves about the deteriorating environment. This is encouraging as traditionally the ethnic groups of these higher altitudes have resented outside interference.

Government forests on less steep land and closer to habitation will be used mainly to benefit local communities, although some produce could be sold in the town and in Kathmandu. The government forests will frequently be in larger blocks than panchayat forest and may need to service several panchayats. Forest supervisors may need to reach agreement with these local communities concerning the free harvesting of minor products, while retaining control over harvesting larger timbers.

### Panchayat forest

Panchayat administrations do not have a great capacity for forest management but each could ultimately be responsible for 125 ha of planted forest and 500 ha of rehabilitated native forest. Within the Chautara Division the 176 separate panchayat administrations could ultimately be responsible for managing 110 000 ha of forest. The area will be less as some panchayats have little or no forest and little land available to reforest. Nevertheless, the problem of providing sound advice to these panchayats will be a difficult one for a forest department set up on conventional lines with little capacity for this amount of extension work.

The basis of sound prescriptions for managing these forests is not known, it falls into the 'unknown information' category as noted above. Even when sound research does provide useable results there still remains the problem of translating these into sensible prescriptions to suit the circumstances (i.e. a panchayat administration with few trained personnel and almost no technical aids). In the meantime there will be a need to provide well considered advice largely on the basis of sound observation.

One thing is certain, the panchayat will not be able to carry out this task unaided. The necessary research support will need to be provided by government sponsored systems. Technical advice will need to be available from a cadre of professional foresters and technicians who must likewise be government sponsored. Much of this problem has been discussed in FAO (1978). In the Chautara Division of Nepal these are now real problems in an ongoing community forestry project.

### Private land

Planting of trees on private land has already been noted as having the potential to increase the productivity of the land, to reduce the drain on forest land and to improve the protective cover of trees on the catchments as a whole. Fundamental investigations are needed into the 'system' which private owners might follow in integrating trees into their cropping procedures. This is the realm of agro-forestry in one or other of its various forms. Agro-forestry methods in Nepal will almost certainly differ from those developed elsewhere because of local topography, weather patterns, crops grown and livestock raised, tree species available to be grown, ethnic and social factors, etc. Nevertheless, what has already been found to be of value by ICRAF and other research organizations could be applied in Nepal, then gradually modified to suit local conditions. Some excellent examples of agro-forestry already exist in Nepal, such as cardamon underneath a canopy of *Alnus nepalensis* in the eastern hills. It is possible other, equally profitable, crops could be developed to diversify the present rather simple agriculture and at the same time introduce the many benefits of a tree canopy.

## CONCLUSIONS

In seeking to reforest the Middle Hills district of Nepal the N-AFP has found there was a need to concentrate attention on the three areas of research and development discussed in this paper. First, there was a need to sift through the existing knowledge and to annex what was useful. Second, we had to obtain new knowledge which was needed but not known. Third, we had to learn how to put this knowledge to use in the context of the Chautara region and the Chautara society to formulate policy and devise management practice for community forestry.

N-AFP is a relatively small project by most international bi-lateral standards ($US 2.5 m over 5 years) and so the research resources available were limited. Fortunately the somewhat unusual situation of a project administered by a university department brought equally unusual research advantages: people associated with the project were research oriented, the project sponsored Nepali graduate students who took up research topics relevant to community forestry, and graduate students were attracted to work in association with the project. The project sought to document and publish its experience and the project became the subject of case studies for graduate classes in development forestry in ANU. The project was thus subject to a good deal of scrutiny and examination.

Nevertheless, the research effort has been limited and some areas of knowledge have, of necessity, been neglected or given less emphasis than they should. A review of the project in late 1982 quite rightly drew attention to a number of these while, at the same time, supporting the main thrust of the work at Chautara. In a slightly expanded stage three of N-AFP, should this be approved, provision would be made for two additional Australian appointments, one for silvicultural-management investigations, the other for social motivation, survey and evaluation.

We have been conscious of the problem of strengthening local technological and research capability, as discussed by World Bank—FAO priorities towards community forestry needs, trees for fuelwood, fodder and fruit, both in the context of small panchayat forests and as agro-forestry systems on private land. But there are few forest research staff in Nepal and the very limited research capacity now existing must be strengthened in a number of ways over the next decade if it is to meet the urgent need for research support to community forestry. One way of doing this will be to co-ordinate the government research effort with the considerable research capacity of aid projects in the forestry sector. N-AFP will certainly seek to mesh its own research efforts into the wider framework of community forestry research throughout the country.

### References

CAMPBELL, J. G. (1983). *People and forest in hill Nepal: preliminary presentation of findings of community forestry household and ward leader survey*. Draft paper made available to the mid-term review team of the World Bank Community Forestry Development and Training Project. Unpublished. 7pp. + tables and graphs.

F.A.O. (1878). *Forestry for local community development.* FAO Forestry Paper 7. FAO Rome. 114pp.

FLEMING, W. M. (1978). *Phewa Tal watershed management proposals.* Phewa Tal Technical Report 5, HMG/UNDP/FAO/IWM Project NEP/74/020. Department of Soil Conservation and Watershed Management, Nepal. 90pp.

HOOKER, J. D. (1854). *Himalayan Journals.* 2 vols.

NEW ERA (1980). *A study of villagers' attitude towards forest and forestry development in Sinupalchok District of Nepal.* Consultants report commissioned by N-AFP. August, 1980. 106 pp.

SHEPHERD, K. R. (1981). The Nepal-Australia Forestry Project. *Australian Forestry* **44**, 210–221.

SHRESTHA, RAMRAJYA, L. J. (1982). *The relationship between the forest and the farming system in Chautara, Nepal, with special reference to livestock production.* Thesis for the Master of Agricultural Development Economics, Australian National University, Canberra. 106pp.

WIART, J. (1983). *Ecosytème villageois traditionel en himalaya nepalais: la production forestière suffit-elle aus besoins de la population?* Doctoral Thesis, Université Scientifique et Medicale de Grenoble. Grenoble, France. 267pp.

WORLD BANK-FAO (1981). *Forestry research needs in developing countries—time for a reappraisal.* Paper for 17th IUFRO Congress, Kyoto, Japan. 6–17 Sept. 1981. 56pp.

# The Extension and Research Liaison Unit: the new organization machinery for transfer of forestry research results in Nigeria

G. O. B. DADA
*Forestry Research Institute of Nigeria, Ibadan, Nigeria*

## ABSTRACT

The Extension and Research Liaison Unit acts as a link between the Forestry Research Institute of Nigeria and the users, the state forestry departments and the public. The Unit is expected to bring results of research to the state foresters, and forestry problems from state foresters back to the research institutes. Three issues that influence the effectiveness of the Extension and Research Liaison Unit in the transfer of research findings include: organizational framework; calibre of staff in the Unit; and status of the Unit within the research institute. Since the extension and research liaison concept is based on having an effective link between research and utilization, the Liaison Unit seems to be a promising method to encourage adoption of forestry research in Nigeria.

## THE FORESTRY SETTING

Nigeria runs a presidential system of government along the lines of the United States of America. There are two principal levels, the Federal and State goverments. Forestry activities are carried out at these two levels. The federal government is responsible for forestry research activities through the Forestry Research Institute of Nigeria (FRIN) and the Universities, while the state governments, which own the forest lands, are responsible for forest management and production. There is another federal organization, the Federal Department of Forestry (FDF) whose principal responsibility is the co-ordination of forestry activities all over the country.

These various forestry organizations (FRIN, FDF, state forestry departments and universities) have no formal links and are responsible to separate parent bodies. The only all-embracing organs are the National Forestry and Wildlife Development Committees to which the Chief Executives of these various organizations belong. The Committees meet twice a year. Their decisions are not mandatorily binding on the members.

The state forestry departments are the main users of forestry research findings. The River Basin Authorities, established recently in the country, also utilize some research results. There is no private forestry practice in Nigeria as of today for reasons perhaps well known: long waiting periods on investment, ignorance about forestry, land tenure system, etc. The research programmes of FRIN are formulated on the basis of the problems confronting the state forestry departments. Since the research programmes of the universities are not by mandate, as in the case of FRIN, which is formulated on the problems of the states, the Extension and Research Liaison (ERLS) Unit, which is being discussed, refers to the transfer of research findings from FRIN to the users.

Forestry has undergone different stages of development since about 85 years ago when forestry practice started in Nigeria. It has passed through a stage of exploitation without taking measures to replace by planting, a phase of natural regeneration, and finally that of plantation forestry. Since little quality timber remains in the forest reserves, future supplies must come from plantations. The ERLS Unit is therefore required to transfer information on suitable species, their silviculture, management, economics, etc. from research to the 19 state forestry departments. Its role is all the more important when one considers that most of the plantation species in use in Nigeria are exotic species.

## ORIGIN OF EXTENSION AND RESEARCH LIAISON CONCEPT

The concept of the Extension and Research Liaison

(ERLS) Unit started with the agricultural research organization which works on food crops. It first started in 1963 when the Ministry of Agriculture in the defunct Northern Region of Nigeria established the ERLS as part of its Field Services Division. What gave birth to this section was the realization that although the Regional Research Station at Samaru, established in the 1920s, had a lot of research results acruing from its activities, this information was not reaching the potential users (i.e. the farmers). The primary function of the section was to act as a link between research and the Ministry's extension services. This pioneer Extension and Research Liaison Service was merged with an Agricultural Research Institute in 1968, but since then it has become a full fledged independent Institute.

Most of the agricultural based research institutes, including the Forestry Research Institute of Nigeria (FRIN), came into being in 1976 as the result of a decree by the then military government. With the new status, there arose a great concern for the effective dissemination of research findings. Prior to this date some of the institutes (FRIN included) were operating as government research departments with some activities in the area of transfer of results. The departments have units variously called Information and Advisory, Publications, Communications and Information, Public Relations, etc. which perform these functions. The main method of disseminating research results was by means of publications and some participation in annual agricultural shows.

On becoming institutes in 1976, the food crop based research institute copied the idea of the Extension and Research Liaison Services from the pioneering one at Samaru by establishing ERLS Units. It was easy for them to do this without any hesitation. The pioneering ERLS Unit and these newly established ones were working on the same category of agriculture commodities while their target users were also similar. The FRIN did not adopt the ERLS idea until 1978 because of doubt as to whether the ERLS concept as applied to food crops would fit into forestry, and secondly, unlike the agricultural departments in the states, forestry departments have no existing extension units.

The ERLS Units were established essentially as a corrective instrument to accelerate the rate at which research information becomes directly opera tional and practical at the user level. It was recognized that the success and effectiveness of research institutes depends largely on a good communication system between the researchers, the extension agents and the users of the research results. The three must form a smooth working team.

## THE EXTENSION AND RESEARCH LIAISON UNIT (ERLS) OF THE FORESTRY RESEARCH INSTITUTE OF NIGERIA

The Extension and Research Liaison Unit acts as a link between the Forest Research Institute of Nigeria and the users, the state forestry departments and the public. The Unit is expected to bring results of research to the state foresters, and forestry problems from state foresters back to the research institute. Its concept has features of the 'Broadcasting' Model and Local Organized Demand Model used in transfer of research information.[1] Some of the reasons that gave rise to the Extension and Research Liaison Service as a method for the transfer of forest research results are:

a. There are no formal links between the forestry organization in the country; each organization is independent. The ERLS provides this linkage.

b. The existing methods of disseminating research results are elitist allowing for little interaction between staff of the research institute and users of the research results.

c. Lack of extension units in the state forestry departments (the main users of results).[2]

The philosophy of the ERLS is based on the concept that research institutes should not wait until users of their results come to them, but rather endeavour to inform the users about their findings for the purpose of adoption.

### Organization and structure

The ERLS Unit is a component part of the Institute. It is a division equal in status to the research division. As had been recommended by various communications and extension specialists, for example, Ward (1974), Patel (1978) and Williams (1978), the Head of the ERLS Unit is answerable to the Director of the Institute.

While the ERLS Units of food crop based research institutes in Nigeria are comprised of (a) Informa-

[1] Cornell University, Ithaca (Department of Communication Arts), Communication Planning and Strategy Course, July-August, 1980. Broadcasting Model involved the transfer of research results through the use of information resources and communication agency while Local Organized Demand Model as practised in Taiwan is similar to Broadcasting Model but the local organization (e.g. states extension Unit) demand for research findings themselves.

[2] Though there had been provisions for extension units in the state forestry department in the 1973–85 development plan of Nigeria, they have not yet been created.

tion, (b) Training, (c) Advisory, and (d) Model Demonstration sections, the Forestry Research Institute of Nigeria is organized into the following sections:

Publications Section

Audio Visual Section

Extension/Advisory Section

Media (Radio) Section and

Distribution Section

The premise for these subdivisions is as follows. The sections are based on problems which are specific to the transfer of forestry research findings in the country. As an illustration, a survey has shown that one of the impediments to full utilization of research results in forestry is that the message (in form of publications, participation in seminars, workshops and conferences, etc.) does not reach the real audience that needs to use it (Dada, 1978). It follows that a Distribution section should therefore be an essential component of the ERLS if this problem is to be solved. The Registry, which is usually responsible for dispatch of correspondence in the Institute, cannot perform this distribution function because unlike ordinary official letters which it handles, the target of the research findings is not necessarily the Head of the state forestry departments but may be somebody below him along the line, usually somebody in the field. Also, an Extension section is included because of the absence of functional extension units in all the state forestry departments.

The subdivision into the section listed above is also based on the assumption that the ERLS unit should be more of a communications unit rather than an extension unit. Any attempt to carry out extension duties may result in duplication of effort or conflict with the work of the state extension units. This may lead to total breakdown of communication with the state and this is least wanted. Figure 1 gives an ideal organigram of FRIN's ERLS Unit, the categories of staff required in each section, and the duties that they are to perform.

**The functions**

The Extension and Research Liaison Service Unit is the main link between the research organization and users. It serves as the link between FRIN and the state forestry departments, a two-way communication pipeline for transfering information from research to state forest officers and also bringing feedback and forest problems from the forest officers to the research personnel. The National Seminar on the Transfer of Research Results in Agriculture, held in 1978, recommended that the following broad functions be performed by the staff of ERLS of the Nigerian Research Institute:

a. Transfering agricultural results from the research institutions, universities and other sources to the extension arms of the state Ministries of Agriculture and Natural Resources, industry, farmers, and utilizers of farm products.
b. Provision of feedback of information from the extension personnel on the suitability of the invocations being transferred, and the problems that require research attention.
c. Fostering co-operation with the various social institutions, supply organizations and other government agencies whose contributions to the socio-economic setting will facilitate the adoption of research results.

These are the basic functions which the ERLS of FRIN performs. The links through which they are carried out are illustrated in Figure 2. In carrying out these functions, the unit adopts the following strategies:

a. Participates in project selection and organizes research reviews, seminars and farmers' festivals.
b. Organizes in-service training and workshops for state government personnel and others like those in wood-based industries.
c. In collaboration with the state forestry departments, organizes field demonstrations, forestry week and tree planting campaigns.
d. Produces extension bulletins, posters and other pamphlets in the form of practical recommendations.
e. Provides back-up support such as facilitating supply of seedlings and specialist advice from the entomologist in time of epidemic.
f. Acquaints research personnel with problems confronting state forestry personnel and those in wood based industries gathered through interaction with these groups.
g. Provides administrative assistance in the form of introducing members of the public interested in tree planting to relevant organizations, thereby facilitating the securement of inputs such as seedlings, fertilisers, loans, etc.

The ERLS Unit is also responsible for some public relations work such as conducting visitors around to show them the work of the Institute. These visitors include scientists, university and secondary school students and politicians. Being an integral part of the Institute, the staff members carry out some research work which helps them in the discharge of their duties. This research is social science oriented and is in the areas of adoption of research findings, communications and testing of innovations.

## THE EXTENSION AND RESEARCH LIAISON UNIT

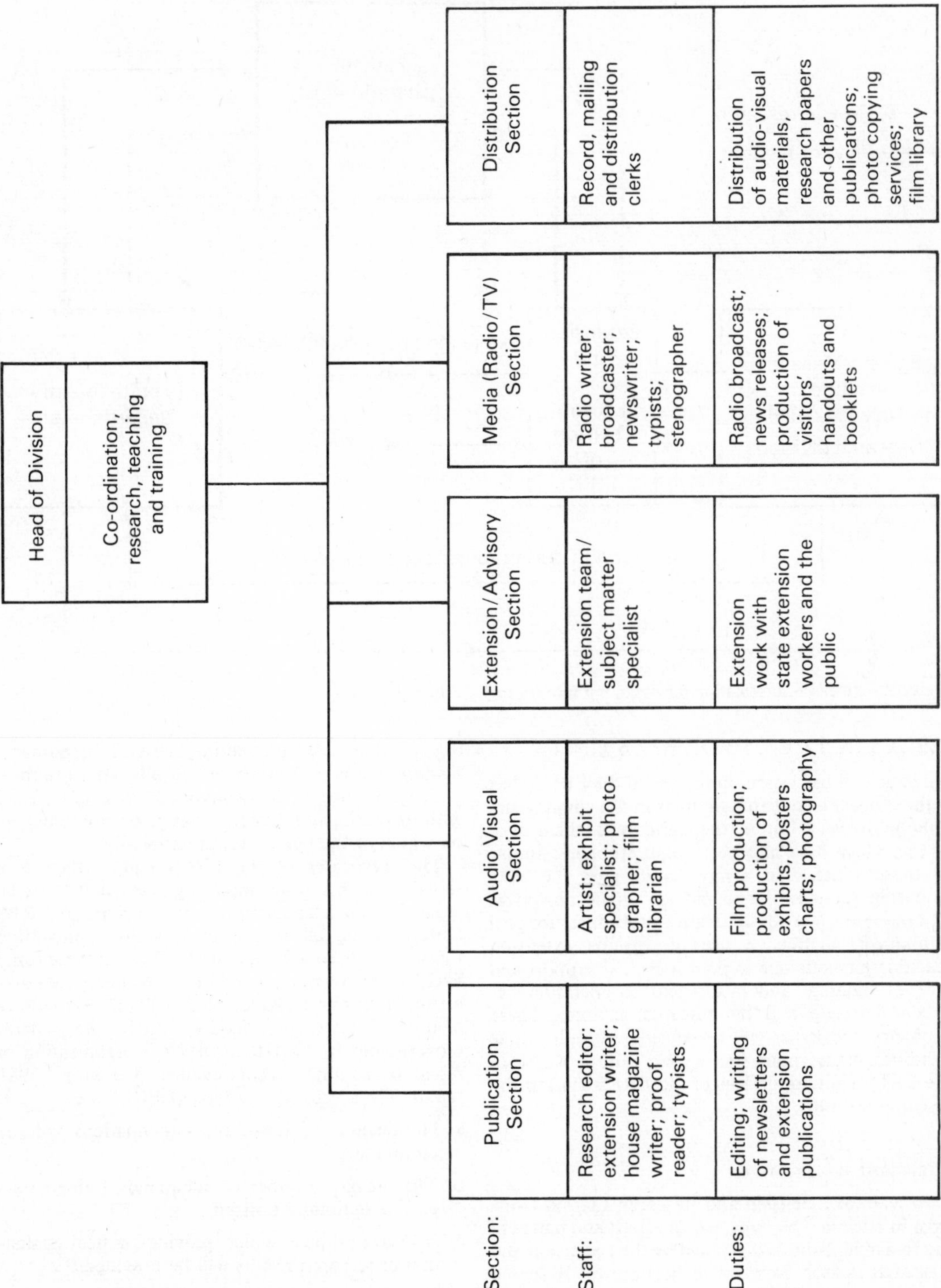


*Figure 1.* The organigram of the ERLS division.

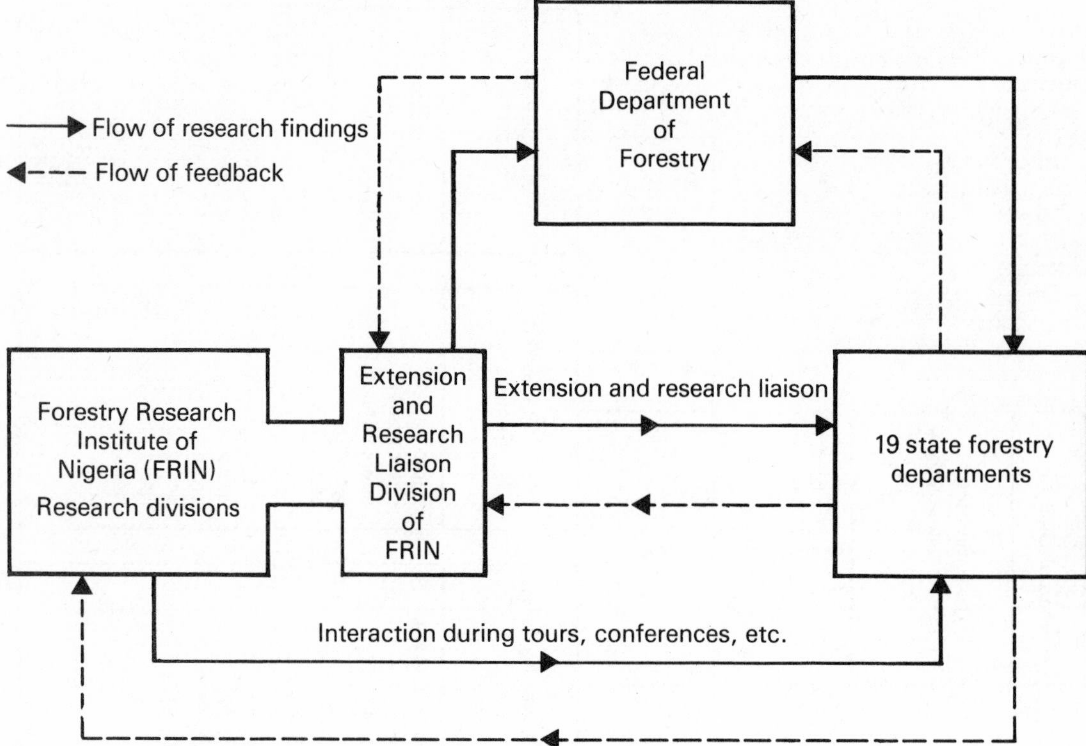


*Figure 2.* Research information flow between forestry organizations in Nigeria.

## ISSUES IN THE USE OF ERLS UNIT

An issue that has arisen on the use of the ERLS Unit is the transfer of research findings in the country, not only in forestry but in the agricultural field as a whole. There have also been some problems similar to those which had always confronted the state extension services. These include vague objectives and inappropriate administrative procedures for goal attainment, ineffective use of various extension teaching methods due to poor logistical support and lack of training, and insufficient co-operation between the state and the research institute. These problems and issues will be considered under three headings: organization framework; calibre of staff in the ERLS Unit; and status of the ERLS Unit in the research institute.

### Organization framework

Two types of Extension and Research Liaison Units exist in Nigeria. One type, which is part and parcel of the research institute, is typified by the Extension and Research Liaison Services of the Forestry Research Institute and most other agricultural research institutes. The other type operates entirely as a separate organization. The pioneering AERLS in Samaru, Kaduna State, is the only one in this latter group.

The existence of the two types in the country each with its merits and demerits, has given rise to debate on which of the two to adopt nationally.

The advocates of the ERLS Unit, which is a separate organization, have suggested that these be organized on a zonal basis with each zonal ERLS Unit covering all aspects of agriculture, including forestry, in its zone of operation. Three of these zonal ERLSs were recommended by the National Seminar on the Transfer of Research Results in Agriculture held in 1978. A committee set up by the Federal Government in 1981 to review the organization of research institutes recommended five in its 1981 report. The merits of this type of ERLS are:

a. Duplication of result recommendations will be eliminated.

b. The meagre number of adequately trained staff can be optimally utilized.

c. A clearing-house which provides critical evaluation of research results will be provided.

One disadvantage of this type of ERLS Unit, however, is that it will lack easy access to the findings of the research institutes and will be deprived of full opportunity to participate in all stages of research programme development and execution which an ERLS Unit, which is part of the Research Institute, has.

Other problems of a zonal ERLS Unit may be the huge initial amount of funds which will be required to set them up, since they will require a core of administrative staff such as Directors, Assistant Directors, Chief Accountants, etc. Another fear with regard to the idea of separate ERLS is that government departments do not generally co-operate with themselves. They always try to tackle segmentally common problems which are better solved together. These departments regard themselves as rivals. When representatives of departments sit on committees, they often feel and act as custodians of the opinion they represent, loosing sight of the singleness of purpose. One may therefore ask, "If we have separate ERLS Units, will there be co-operation between these units and the research institutes?" My guess is that there will not be.

Those who support the idea of each research institute having its own ERLS Unit argue that access to research results will be easier and participation in programme development by the staff will be more direct. The staff of the ERLS Unit can also easily acquire expertise in the commodities in which the particular institute works instead of being 'jack of all trades', which a zonal ERLS would encourage. As discussed earlier, a zonal ERLS will tend to approach the transfer of research results of all commodities in a standard way. As an illustration, the transfer of forestry research results whose users are State department officials will require a different approach from that of cereal products whose users are rural farmers. A zonal ERLS Unit may be too all-embracing to recognize this.

**Calibre of staff for ERLS Unit**

Right from their inception, the type of training required for the Head or principal officers of the ERLS Unit had occupied the minds of the Research administrators and the ERLS staff themselves. As illustration, Ekpere (1978) asks:

> "The idea (of an ERLS) sounds fine, but who operates the system? ... The extension-research liaison specialist is a rare commodity in Nigeria, consequently a good idea badly implemented could be counter productive in the future."

The qualifications of personnel presently in the ERLS units of various research institutes in Nigeria vary greatly. Some have degrees and postgraduate degrees in agricultural extension, some have first degrees in general agriculture or forestry, while others specialize in aspects of agriculture with post-graduate degrees in agricultural journalism or related fields.

Some suggestions as to the calibre of staff essential for the smooth operation of the ERLS system have been put forward. Patel (1978) recommends:

> "The staff of this department before their appointment should have been well recognized by their research contributions in their own fields of specialization."

While it cannot be generalized that being good in research means that one will be good in extension-research duties, Patel adds that the staff of the ERLS Unit will need special training in extension education and communication processes, programme planning and administration. Williams (1978) approached the issue by comparing the subject matter specialist with the generalist in agriculture. He stated that a broadly trained generalist with more training at the master's degree level with courses in social and behavioural sciences, extension philosophy, principles and methods, will be more suitable for the ERLS work. It has also been suggested that the Head of the ERLS Unit should have a first degree in the subject concerned and a master's degree in communications (or agricultural journalism) and some post-graduate training in the subject concerned (Dada, 1978).

All these suggestions are useful since they seem to point to one crucial and important factor; that of the credibility of the ERLS staff. An adequate knowledge of the subject whose results are being transferred and the skill to carry this out as well as the knowledge of all the groups of people involved in the process are the essential prerequisites for ERLS duties.

**Status of the ERLS Unit**

As with other developing countries, the major bulk of the programmes of research institutes in Nigeria are financed by the government. There are still only isolated cases of organizations, such as industries, financing research projects. The research programme of institutes are therefore oriented towards specific targets in our economic and social progress. The measure of the success of research institutes is (or should be) by the ultimate acceptance and adoption of their results by the users. It follows therefore that three main aspects should be identified in the work of a research institute. These are: research administration, research execution, and research results communication.

While research administration and research execution have been well recognized by most Directors of research institutes, the research results communications symbolized by the ERLS Unit is still to be given the prominence it is entitled to in the work of a research institute. Part of the reason for this is the newness of the ERLS Units themselves but this is just a minute part. The major reason is that a research institute is still not judged by how much of its results have been utilized (or are utilizable) when its contributions are being assessed. Indeed, the 'publish or perish' mania of the universities is invading the Nigerian research institutes. One of the criteria for promotion is now the number of papers produced in a year, not how many 'useful' papers were produced. One would have expected that in a public supported research institute reward or sanction ought to be based on 'on-the-ground' application of research findings!

The ERLS Units, as they exist in research institutes, are of varying status. While in some institutes, such as the Forestry Research Institute of Nigeria, it is a division equal to the research divisions, in some other institutes, it is part of other divisions or sections of lower status. Even in research institutes, where they are full-fledged divisions, they are sometimes not involved in programme planning and their staff not called to meetings from where they could provide feedback from users or gather information for the performance of their duties. The place of the ERLS Unit in the research organization has been studied by various scholars (Ward, 1974; Williams, 1978; Patel, 1978).

Some of their recommendations are as follows:

a. The status of the ERLS Unit should not in any way be inferior to any of the research units of an institute.
b. The Head of the ERLS Unit should be responsible to the Director of the Institute.
c. The staff of the ERLS Unit should be involved in planning and execution of research programmes.

These and some other recommendations are ideals without which the ERLS Unit cannot effectively perform its functions.

Most of the ERLS Units are presently understaffed and poorly equipped partly as a result of the low status still conferred on them. As time goes on, this condition will definitely improve, more so now that politicians and other policy makers are becoming more concerned about accountability in government institutions.

## CONCLUSIONS

Since the Extension and Research Liaison concept is based on having an effective link between research and utilization, this seems to be a promising method to encourage adoption of research results in forestry in Nigeria. Like any continuously evolving process, the structure and functions may change from time to time. If the idea of private forestry becomes accepted, for example, and individuals or groups of individuals become interested in investing in forestry, a method of reaching them will have to be developed by the ERLS Unit.

The development of the ERLS concept, especially the ideal training for the staff, will develop with the activities. How fast or well this concept develops will, however, depend on the operators of the concept (i.e. the existing staff of the ERLS). As a relatively new concept, the staff themselves will need to continue to 'spread its gospel' especially to the Directors of research institutes, until it is given its due recognition. Unfortunately, without this recognition the ERLS can never function effectively.

### References

AHMADU BELLO UNIVERSITY (1976). *Agricultural Extension and Research Liaison Service.* ABU, Zaria, Nigeria.

DADA, G. O. B. (1978). *Communication strategies for bringing forestry research results and information to the general public in Nigeria.* An unpublished M.P.S. Thesis. Cornell Univesity, Ithaca, New York.

EKPERE, J. A. (1978). Agricultural extension and research liaison services: problems, issues and suggestions. In. *Proceedings of national workshop on the role of agricultural extension and research liaison service in improved technology transfer in agriculture.* University of Ife (I.A.R.T.), Ibadan, Nigeria. 6–10 February, 1978.

NATIONAL SCIENCE AND TECHNOLOGY DEVELOPMENT AGENCY (1978). *Recommendation of the national seminar of the transfer of research results in agriculture.* Ibadan, Nigeria (NSTDA). 21–24 November, 1978.

PATEL, A. U. (1978). Whither agricultural extension and research liaison services of the national institutes of agriculture research? In, *Proceedings of national workshop on role of AERLS in improved technology transfer in agriculture.* University of Ife (I.A.R.T.), Ibadan, Nigeria. 6–10 February, 1978.

WARD, W. B. (1974). *Creating agricultural communication centre for training, research and information services.* Papers in communication, Department of Communication Arts, Cornell University, Ithaca, New York.

WILLIAMS, S. K. T. (1978). Subject matter specialists or generalists in the extension research liaison division of the agricultural research institutes. In, *Proceedings of 1st national workshop on the role of AERLS in improved technology transfer in agriculture.* University of Ife (I.A.R.T.), Ibadan, Nigeria, 6–10 February, 1978.

# II

# Case examples of technology transfer

# Applying research results from 'fringe disciplines': lessons learned from integrated pest management RD & A programs

R. W. STARK

*Program Manager, International Spruce Budworms Program (West), USDA Forest Service, Pacific Northwest Forest and Range Experiment Station, Portland, Oregon, U.S.A.*

## ABSTRACT

Integrated pest management (IPM) is an ecological approach to regulating damage from forest pests. It involves forest planning and management and is based on silvicultural practices and intensive knowledge of the ecology of the pest/host system. Developing IPM programs in the United States uses simulation modeling and depends heavily on computer capability. From experience in three IPM programs, 10 'lessons' on effective technology transfer were: (1) technology transfer should be included in research planning; (2) it should be continuous during and after the program; (3) maximum effort should be devoted to users, not researchers; (4) fringe disciplines should write in a language familiar to the user; (5) the plan should be flexible, allowing for degrees of complexity; (6) emphasis should be to agencies or units whose prime responsibility is technology transfer; (7) premature release of information should be avoided; (8) personal contacts are more effective than mass media; (9) outputs should be designed to meet user needs and practices; and (10) awards for technology transfer in research organizations should be roughly equivalent to those for research productivity.

### Introduction

Destiny and circumstances have precipitated my involvement in managing two Research, Development, and Application Programs over the past decade. The first was a 5-year National Science Foundation/Environmental Protection Agency sponsored program to develop principles and practices of integrated pest management for bark beetles attacking pine forests in the United States. The second was 'The Combined Forest Pest Research and Development Program' administered by the Secretary, U.S. Department of Agriculture, specifically the Douglas-fir Tussock Moth Program centred at the Pacific Northwest Forest and Range Experiment Station (PNW), Portland, Oregon (Wright, 1977). The third is the Canada/United States Spruce Budworms Program (CANUSA)-western component, also located at the PNW (Anon., 1978).

Although a research scientist for 30 years and a professor for over 20, my perception of technology transfer was rather shallow when I began my managerial tasks. As a scientist, I dutifully reported my work, published in journals (preferably respectable, refereed, scientific ones), and assumed that my works would be promptly absorbed by those who could use them. As a professor, I passed on current technology to a stream of students and assumed they would go forth and practice what I preached. As my forest managerial experience increased, my complacent world was shattered by reality. From these three programs, I learned lessons about my discipline and transfer of information to the practice of forestry that I hope will improve our future efforts. I am pleased with this opportunity to share them with this IUFRO group. I present the lessons in two parts: the first is directed to what I call 'fringe' disciplines; the second to planning and conducting a research program. Although learned from accelerated RD&A programs, I believe they apply to research management generally. Lastly, as charged, I have tried to make a constructive suggestion on transfer of technology from my 'fringe' discipline to less developed countries (LDCs).

## LESSONS FROM A FRINGE DISCIPLINE

A problem, perhaps peculiar to North America, is that forest entomology is considered a 'fringe' discipline of forestry (pathology too, I suspect). The fault, if it is one, lies in both camps. For example, entomology is a required subject in less than half of forestry schools in the United States. In the U.S. Civil Service jobs classification system, entomologists are defined as entomologist, not as forest entomologist or foresters. In the Forest Service, entomology and pathology are in a discrete unit, Forest Insect and Disease Research (FIDR). Most, if not all, are graduate foresters, usually at the baccalaureate level. Their advanced research degrees are in entomology or pathology, and they consider themselves to be specialists in these disciplines. To illustrate, a Forest Service colleague recently passed on the latest entomology joke:

> "Dear Abby,
> I am a forester, my brother is an entomologist. Our mother died insane when I was three. My father has been in prison for 20 years for selling drugs. My two older sisters are prostitutes. I recently fell in love with a woman just released from prison for grand theft. My problem is: should I tell her my brother is an entomologist?
> Sincerely, Ashamed Forester."

Entomological research has largely concentrated on the insect, somewhat less on insect/tree interactions, considerably less on insect/stand relationships and rarely on the insect/forest ecosystem. Relegation to fringe status was somewhat deserved and relatively tolerable until recently. The emergence of integrated pest management (IPM) or integrated forest protection (IFP) clarified the role of forest entomologists (Stark, 1980). IFP is now recognized as a component of forest management policy, planning, and implementation. The output from insect and disease research provides information and analyses that support decision-making in forest management. Its goals are those of forest management-optimization of forest resources. With this recognition, the traditional mode of technology transfer (i.e. publications only in discipline-oriented journals) is no longer adequate (Lundgren, 1981).

The problems described are diminishing, largely because of structured R&D programs. More and more research entomologists and pathologists are recognizing their role in forestry. That is, they are becoming more concerned that their results be used and recognize that, for this to happen, they must take part in the technology transfer process. Further, they are learning that they must work with users to present the technology in an acceptable format. Both university and research agencies are also more attentive to the importance of a linkage between research results and use.

The award system for research scientists, however, is based largely on publication of results in primary sources, reviewed by peers of their discipline. Recognition of technology transfer activities by a researcher range from none to little. One major university has a point system based on the prestige and type of journals. Extension papers by researchers rank at the bottom. This is less of a problem in federal research establishments, but I have been told by participants on promotion panels that such 'prejudices' do exist (Leary and Nishizawa, 1981).

## LESSONS LEARNED FROM ACCELERATED R&D PROGRAMS

The lessons learned from program management are cast within the framework of effective technology transfer so ably summarized by Muth and Hendee (1980) and by Rogers and Shoemaker (1971). The major factors influencing speed of adoption of new research (innovations) are: (1) characteristics of the innovation; (2) the media used for communication; (3) the processes required for adoption; and, (4) the characteristics of the social system in which they are to be used.

### Characteristics of the innovation

● *Relative advantage*
For example, can we measure impacts of insect outbreaks more precisely, thus aiding in decisions on the need for treatment? Can we suppress outbreaks at lower cost?

● *Compatibility*
Does the innovation run counter to the beliefs and prevailing attitudes of potential adopters? For example, a highly sophisticated sampling scheme that requires whole-tree sampling over large areas is not compatible with the needs of most forest insect surveys.

● *Complexity*
Can the innovation be easily understood and used? For example, much of the output of current R&D projects consists of simulation models for projecting insect population events and forest stand growth. Even with detailed users' guides these models demand some familiarity with computer language and use. This has delayed use of such models because not enough people have these capabilities, even in North America. Computer use may also restrict adoption or application of such innovations in many LDCs.

● *'Trialability'*
Can a trial of the innovation be implemented? Few managers are willing to change current practices, however imprecise, on an all or nothing basis.

Fortunately, most outputs from pest-management research can be tested on a small scale first.

● *Observability*
Can the effect of an innovation be readily observed? This is a problem in pest management. The effects of tactics to suppress populations, for example, chemicals, bacteria, and viruses, are readily observable from reductions in defoliation or tree mortality, or actual kill of the insect. Long-term prevention strategies, such as alteration of silvicultural practices, must be observed over long periods.

The perception by users of new research presented as a *fait accompli* varies in direct proportion to their familiarity with it. Without any prior knowledge of the research or its development, the first reaction may well be negative, and a long dialogue addressing the five characteristics might ensue. Users were generally not considered, or, at least, not involved in the planning of the research. As a result, much of the research produced is still debated by many potential users, although adopted by others. In the tussock moth and CANUSA programs, users helped plan and monitor research from the beginning, and thus the products were (are) generally designed with these five characteristics in mind.

In the CANUSA program, potential users formed the majority of a Technology Transfer Working Group. Their advice was sought in designing outputs for users (as opposed to those for researchers). Wherever possible, users, particularly those specializing in technology transfer such as Forest Pest Management personnel, were asked to be authors or to co-author with scientists, the users' manuals and 'how-to's'. The crucial output, a comprehensive set of procedures and simulation models describing budworm processes and impact on various resources, was examined in depth at a workshop to develop a decision support system for forest managers. Users from private industry and state and federal agencies were asked to review the proposed system in the context of their decision-making process (Twardus and Brookes, 1982). As a result of this workshop, alterations in the system were made to hasten its eventual adoption. The final product will be reviewed in a similar workshop.

## Communication methods

Personal contact and mass media are considered to be the most efficient communication methods for effective TT: mass media to get their attention; personal contact to persuade them to try it. The NSF/EPA program, as a research funding enterprise, suffered on both counts because it was seen only as a research program. Because of the size of the award (over $6 million) and scope (six major crop systems), it received considerable publicity in the newspapers and journals at the outset. In the forestry segment, continued communications were largely with scientists until the end of the program. Publication was largely in research journals. The importance of suitable language and publication outlets soon became apparent. We learned that outputs must be written in the language of the user, with emphasis on 'must-know' material and a minimum of 'nice-to-know' information and technical jargon, for example, how-to's designed for use by field foresters, managers, or both? Another category of general publications can be of value: accomplishments reports, designed to provide summaries for research managers and politicians involved in policy, planning and budget decision-making.

The two other R&D programs benefited from being Federal, enjoying the logistical support of information outlets of the Department of Agriculture and the Forest Service. Some differences in the programs are worthy of note. Although both acknowledged the importance of technology transfer from the beginning, the tussock moth program had neither budget nor manpower devoted to technology transfer that was included in CANUSA planning. The CANUSA program published a regular international newsletter for all who conceivably might be interested. Although both programs have an 'applications co-ordinator', whose responsibilities included technology transfer, the tussock moth co-ordinator had no support staff. In the CANUSA program, four regional representatives were appointed from Forest Pest Management and one from Timber Management to work with the applications co-ordinator. They are key to the success of acceptance of new research because their normal duties include implementing current research in the field and maintaining regular contact with forest managers, both public and private.

Increasing roles for information specialists have also been a part of improving technology transfer efforts. Two information specialists were hired late in the tussock moth program to help produce specific publications already planned by program management. From its earliest meeting, the CANUSA-West Technology Transfer Working Group has had the help of information specialists, including the editor from the tussock moth program. Now on fulltime assignment to CANUSA as information co-ordinator, this editor draws on established working relations with both users and researchers to serve as an important link in the technology transfer system.

The kinds of outputs did not differ significantly, but in the CANUSA program, additional time and effort were devoted to tailoring publications defined by users. Further, an entire year after the termination of research, projects will be devoted solely to activities related to technology transfer.

**Processes required for adoption**

The five stages for reaching a decision are: awareness, interest, evaluation, trial, and adoption. Some people decide more quickly than others; how people behave is influenced by their position in the social system.

Awareness is most effectively accomplished by mass media presentations, for example, posters, brochures, audio-visual displays. At this stage, only the advantages are usually presented. Interest depends largely on the impression the innovation makes, particularly its relative advantages.

Once interest is gained, more information can be transmitted to persuade the user that it may be worth evaluating. The media are still important for giving more detail, but personal contact is usually necessary at this stage and is essential during evaluation and trial.

The progress from awareness to trial takes time if the innovation is presented without the user's having had any prior knowledge of it. In the United States, we became aware some time ago that we were not in step with the world on the use of the metric system (hardly an innovation, but!) and passed a 'law of intent' in 1975 to proceed with metrification. (Did you know that the U.S., Brunei, Burma, and North and South Yemen are the only countries that have not officially adopted the metric system?) Awareness includes recognizing that it was hurting our international trade and that exchange of basic military hardware with our military allies could be a problem. We are still largely in the evaluation stage. Only 37 states require that the metric system be taught in schools and then as a backup system; the traditional English system is still emphasized.

In both the tussock moth and CANUSA programs, potential users were made aware of program goals from the beginning. In fact, many users participated in their creation. Interest was implicit because the goals of the programs included developing ecologically sound, economical, and efficient methods of pest management. As results of research were obtained, users themselves help evaluate them. Mutual efforts ranged from the simple (for example, a sampling method for monitoring pest populations) to the complex (determining whether a simulation model of stand growth that was developed under one set of forest conditions or management situations was applicable to others). Similarly, researchers and users participated in field trials. For example, the use of pheromone traps for early detection of increasing populations of the tussock moth was tested by a mix of federal, provincial/state, and private foresters. It worked. Researchers, working with private and public landowners, have run simulation models in specific locations, which has led to their use in several national forests and by private companies.

We believe that adoption of most of the useful technology developed in these two research and development programs has and will be accelerated by the majority of users and researchers. The CANUSA program has a distinct advantage over the tussock moth program because more attention was paid to technology transfer activities, and considerable attention was given to post program continuity of unfunded or promising research leads and responsibility for the continued training and transfer of esoteric technology, such as simulation models of pest damage within the context of forest growth (Allen *et al.*, 1982).

**Individual traits**

Within any large aggregation of individuals, social research has determined that they can be classified into categories relevant to reception of technology transfer: (1) innovators (2 per cent), who generally will try anything (they are suspected by both sides); (2) early adopters (13 per cent), who are constantly on the lookout for innovations and improvements and reach the evaluation-trial-adoption stages quickly; (3) the early majority (34 per cent), who reach the final stages relatively quickly after deliberate evaluation and trial; (4) the late majority (34 per cent), largely sceptics, who view all innovations with extreme caution (their favourite expression is "If it ain't broke don't fix it"); and (5) the laggards (16 per cent) who cling to the past and are openly suspicious and resistant to innovations (their common expression is, "But we've *always* done it this way!"). Consider the implications for transfer if the last two categories become decision-makers! Fortunately, social scientists assure us that people in categories 2 and 3 are the ones that usually rise to the top.

Programs, such as the last two described, have provided safeguards and a 'screening' mechanism to ensure that their planning groups and task-forces were not overloaded with the last two categories. First, the innovators, early adopters, and early majority were among the first to volunteer. Second, in selecting members for such panels as the Technology Transfer Working Group, some discretion of choice was possible. This is not to say we deliberately avoided sceptics and laggards; healthy scepticism can be a valuable asset (to avoid being carried away by reckless innovators) and laggards with responsibilities must be educated. In the environment in which these programs were conducted, however, such individuals were rare.

### Social structure

A social system is defined as a collection of individuals oriented to common goals. Structured research programs such as CANUSA, the Forest Insect and Disease Units of the USDA Forest Service, and Forest Pest Management, are all subsystems within a larger social system, the Forest Service. The FS is a system within the Department of Agriculture, which is one within the Civil Service, and so on.

The hierarchy of a social system determines whether adoption of an innovation is encouraged or discouraged. Individuals with various influence, depending on their own traits, may further affect technology transfer. In the Forest Service example, individuals may be responsible to the processes of several social systems. For example, they may be members of an R&D program of specific duration. Within that program they may be, or become, innovators who espouse early adoption. At the end of the program, however, they may return to a system where the administrators are late adopters or even (perish the thought) laggards. Further, a subsystem such as CANUSA or FIDR must interact at various levels within the larger system; that is, outputs from the program may be of value to many branches of the Forest Service. Formal mechanisms of communication within such a complex system may impede the flow of technology.

Again, the tussock moth and CANUSA programs had fewer constraints imposed by the social structure than the NSF/EPA program because they were mandated from the larger social systems, that is, the Department of Agriculture and the Forest Service, whereas the pine bark beetle program was an aggregation of University subsystems representing primarily fringe disciplines. No matter what the individual traits of potential users within the federal system were, they were obligated to co-operate and be receptive. The criteria for acceptance, therefore, were based primarily on the merits of the innovation proposed. Again, involvement from the beginning of all levels of management and users, strengthened potential acceptance. Where recalcitrants were identified, social pressures could be brought to bear. A social system can work for you as well as creating problems.

## SUMMARY

The lessons learned from my managerial experiences in research and development programs are:

1. Technology transfer does not just happen, whether the research is from isolated projects or large structured programs. It must be planned from the beginning.
2. Technology transfer should be continuous during the conduct of the research and after the project or program is over.
3. Maximum effort in transfer of technology should be devoted to users, not the research community. Researchers are adequately provided for through normal publication processes.
4. Fringe disciplines such as entomology and pathology must learn to present applications of their results in outlets appropriate to users and in an understandable form. Co-authorship with potential users is recommended.
5. Success in early transfer depends heavily on the characteristics of the innovation; some are more complex than others. Hence, a technology transfer plan must be flexible, capable of devoting more effort in training users, if necessary, in the use of complex material.
6. Research units must devote particular attention to interaction with units whose primary responsibility is transfer of technology, for example, Forest Pest Management, USDA Forest Service, extension agents in land-grant universities and so on. Staff from such units should participate in planning and application of research from the outset.
7. Once adopted by opinion moulders and decision-makers, the transfer process cannot be easily controlled. The technology to be transferred MUST be ready for trial, adoption, or both, before it is espoused too enthusiastically. A failure because of premature release can cause the demise of or lengthy delay to adoption of valuable innovations.
8. Although mass media are important in the early stages of technology transfer, the importance of personal contact throughout cannot be over-emphasized. Further, in selection of personal contacts, their individual traits and spheres of influence should be considered.
9. Particular attention must be paid to the form and content of published material for users. A weighty book containing all information known is of little value to a forester who only needs guidance in sampling.
10. Award systems in research establishments should give appropriate weight to effective transfer of research results to users. (It is ironic that, in most universities, if research produces profitable patents, the rewards to faculty are great. Efforts to implement use of research in the public domain, even if widely adopted, are given little recognition.)

## TRANSFER OF IPM TECHNOLOGY IN LESS DEVELOPED COUNTRIES

Integrated pest management (IPM) is based on a thorough understanding of the ecosystem in which the pest operates. Ecological studies to gain this understanding may be extremely complex and data rich. The simulation of ecological processes, for example, the projection of population fluctuations, is well-nigh impossible without computers. The decision-support systems derived for several North American pests are heavily dependent on computers. The value of these decision support systems has been demonstrated in both agricultural and forest ecosystems. Many lesser developed countries, however, have neither the computers nor enough personnel trained to develop models and to use computers in pest-management systems. McCracken and Braden (1980) discuss other problems in transfer of integrated pest management technology to such countries.

The recent creation of the position of a special co-ordinator for research in tropical regions and developing countries (IUFRO NEWS No. 39 (1/1983)) may provide an opportunity to address this problem. Specifically, the co-ordinator could work with lesser developed countries and donor organizations to upgrade computer capabilities and provide training for protection specialists in using generic simulation models, and researchers in creating models peculiar to their pest problems.

### References

ALLEN, D. C., CLELAND, D. I. and KOCAOGLU, D. F. (1982). Accelerated forest pest research and development program—a new approach. *Bulletin of the Entomological Society of America* **28**(1), 21–25.

ANON. (1978). Joint spruce budworms program formalized. *CANUSA Newsletter* **1**(1), 1–2, Ottawa, Ontario, Canada.

LEARY, R. A. and NISHIZAWA, M. (1981). Adopting high technology to onsite forest management decisions. *Proceedings XVII IUFRO World Congress,* Kyoto, Japan, Division 6, 457–463.

LUNDGREN, A. L. (1981). Research needed to improve management decisions for tomorrow's forests. *Proceedings XVII IUFRO World Congress,* Kyoto, Japan, Divison 4, 399–408.

McCRACKEN, R. and BRADER, L. (1980). Transfer of IPM to LDCs. In: *Proceedings of the U.S. strategy conference on pesticide management.* U.S. Department of State and U.S. National Committee for Man and the Biosphere, June 7–8, 1979, Washington, D.C. Government Printing Office, Washington, D.C. (629–322/1302), 54–62.

MUTH, R. M. and HENDEE, J. C. (1980). Technology transfer and human behavior. *Journal of Forestry* **78**(3), 141–144.

ROGERS, M. and SHOEMAKER, F. F. (1971). *Communication of innovations—a cross-cultural approach.* 2nd Ed. Free Press, New York, 476pp.

TWARDUS, D. B. and BROOKES, M. H. (1983). *A decision-support system for managing western spruce budworm: Report from a workshop.* USDA Forest Service, Pacific Northwest Forest and Range Experiment Station, Portland, Oregon. Administrative Report. 18pp.

WRIGHT, K. H. (1977). The Douglas-fir tussock moth research and development program. *Bulletin of the Entomological Society of America* **23**(3), 167–180.

# Two contrasting examples of technology transfer in the Maritime Provinces of Canada

D. G. EMBREE
*Canadian Forestry Service, Fredericton, New Brunswick, Canada*

ABSTRACT

Successful application of scientific discoveries comes about when the scientist or, more likely, some innovator recognizes the practical potential of a particular discovery. But this is only half the battle. The new technique or idea, once developed, first has to be accepted by the potential user and acceptance usually comes about only through salesmanship. The fact is, new ideas are often regarded with suspicion. Some mechanisms of achieving dialogue between the scientist and the potential user are discussed in relation to two technology transfer efforts; the Spruce Budworm and the Christmas Tree Industry. The part of the world where this account took place is the Maritime Provinces ('the Maritimes'), a region of eastern Canada that relies heavily on its forests for economic survival.

## SCOPE OF FORESTRY IN THE MARITIME PROVINCES

The Maritime Provinces of Canada are New Brunswick, Nova Scotia, and Prince Edward Island. Together they encompass 52 000 square miles (134 000 km$^2$) and support 25.6 million acres (10 376 000 ha) of forest. Of a population of slightly over 1.5 million, 21 000 Maritimers rely directly on the forest industry for their livelihood, and another 40 000 are employed in associated industries. Small woodlots and Christmas tree farms provide part-time employment for an additional 70 000 individuals. There are 14 pulp or paper mills, 482 sawmills, 3 composite-board mills and 2 veneer and plywood mills constituting an industry that produces a value added of almost $600 million a year.

The forest research community consists of the Faculty of Forestry at the University of New Brunswick and the staff of the Maritimes Forest Research Centre, one of six regional centres of the Canadian Forestry Service. Two research institutes, the Nova Scotia Research Foundation and the New Brunswick Research and Productivity Council, along with the faculties of the eight universities (including the University of New Brunswick) provide additional scientific input.

The management of the Maritimes forest is a provincial responsibility and each province has its own forest service. In co-operation with the forest industries in the region, the three provinces also support a Maritimes Forest Ranger School and a Maritime Lumber Bureau but, otherwise, the provinces operate independent of one another.

Information flow from the forestry sector to research organizations is through research committees established separately in each of the three provinces. The committees are composed of provincial forestry officials, university representatives and industrial foresters, and are designed primarily to aid and influence the research and technical services program of the Maritimes Forest Research Centre. The committees meet at least twice yearly to decide on research priorities and review research plans and results. Their existence is partly the result of past failures in communication. Research establishments had previously worked diligently at what they perceived to be the forestry problems of the region or what excited their curiosities, but had little or no dialogue with people responsible for actually managing the forests. Then they wondered why they were ignored! Until 10–15 years ago, the forest industry put very little effort into silviculture or any form of forest management other than the regulation of harvesting schedules.

## THE SPRUCE BUDWORM

The presence of a single insect, the spruce budworm

(*Choristoneura fumiferana* Clem.), has influenced the nature of the forests in the Maritimes. Almost every action related to forestry, voluntary or otherwise, since the mid nineteenth century has been a reaction to this insect. Five successive outbreaks of the pest have occurred during the past 180 years and are responsible for the species composition and age structure of the spruce/fir forests which cover most of the Maritimes. Outbreaks are widespread. For example in 1975, a particularly bad year, 150 million acres of eastern Canada were infested.

One of the Maritime Provinces, New Brunswick, has protected its forests through an on-going aerial spray program over the past 32 years, spraying up to 4 million acres annually.

Nova Scotia which had until 1979 elected not to protect its vulnerable forests, lost 9 million cords of timber over a 4 year period.

One obvious result has been that this one insect, was and is, the dominant object of research in the Maritime region of Canada and, in fact, most of eastern Canada.

At last count, some 2800 scientific journal publications, theses, and dissertations have been written on the spruce budworm and related subjects. Presently, some 350 scientists in Canada and the United States, and a few in Europe, are engaged in some form of research on this obnoxious pest.

This wealth of information, or at least preponderance of scientific fact, was to many as enigmatic as the budworm itself. The information existed in many forms and was available through many sources. There was simply no way that forest managers alone, or even in groups, could assemble it in a comprehensible form to be used sensibly in decision making or policy formation. As a result, budworm forest management abounded with misconceptions, myths and false theories. There was certainly no forward-looking planning.

Up to 11 years ago, the only strategy for spruce budworm control was to spray the forests threatened by the insect and to support research efforts which hopefully would lead to some 'cure' for this insect. The upper limit of effort in each case was controlled by available funds. What this meant to the spray operation was that frequently all of the threatened forests were not protected. And what this meant to research was that budworm research, in spite of its critical need, was inadequate, somewhat disjointed and often without specific objectives.

The strategy satisfied no one and while discussion and arguments abounded around scientific fact and philosophy, forest managers were uncertain about what to do. And to make matters worse, traditional harvesting patterns which could have been adjusted to at least partially alleviate the problem, were maintained.

The following account of an action that was initiated in 1972, and that led to sensible planning in budworm forest management research and operations, is not a new one. It has been reported by Baskerville (1979), Cuff and Baskerville (1982) and Fisher (1982). However it has had such an impact on the forest policy in the Maritimes area that it bears repeating.

A team of builders of mathematical models from the University of British Columbia, researchers from the Maritimes Forest Research Centre, and foresters from the New Brunswick Department of Natural Resources, combined their talents to construct a mathematical model of the spruce budworm and the spruce/fir forests of New Brunswick. The model became known as the MFRC-UBC model. All conceivable information available was incorporated into the model but there were many gaps. Unsupportable, although logical, assumptions had to be made. As a result the model was soundly criticized. Some scientists even refused to take part in the model building exercise and devoted their time to destructive criticism. However, most of the team involved were convinced that the model represented the best evaluation of the budworm situation in New Brunswick. It clearly demonstrated that the Province faced a much more serious wood shortage than had been previously realized, if the existing forest was allowed to go unprotected from continuing depredations.

The model confirmed that there was little likelihood that a 'key factor' existed that, even if found and manipulated, would bring this pest under some form of miraculous control.

The model and the outcome it predicted was presented to senior forest managers in the region through a series of carefully prepared seminars in which the managers were taught to use the model themselves. The reaction was slow initially, but the ultimate impact was profound.

The forest industry accepted the predictions of the model, which were elaborated on by a subsequent task force (Baskerville, 1976) and invested large sums of money in a corrective program. Fortunately, at about this time, forestry agreements were negotiated between the Provincial Government and the Federal Government of Canada making available large sums of money that helped the Province put the plan into action. The prime mover of the model was hired as assistant deputy minister in the Provincial Government with the major tasks of designing a program that would allow the Province to live with the budworm. The program was so comprehensive that it involved the complete disruption of historic harvesting patterns and the reassignment of forest lands. Most important, the Province emerged as the ultimate controlling agency for the management of the crown-lands forests, a role which it had traditionally allocated to the forest industries. A program of forest renewal, coupled with a protection strategy, was designed to maintain the present day maturing forest until the year 2020, at which time the new forests will be ready for harvesting. This new forest is expected to be of an age and species structure which will lend itself more easily to proven protection methods against the budworm.

The point of this example is that virtually every known fact and observation of budworm research was used to construct a model that served two functions: it permitted logical predictions to be made on the future of the existing New Brunswick forest and it provided a vehicle through which the complicated and wide variety of information on the budworm could be assimilated by forest managers. Once the situation was made clear, they were able to make proper decisions. The second consideration is that the model was understood by all to be incomplete and was considered to be a 'best estimate'. But most important it was accepted and used, whereas the individual opinions and pronouncements of numerous learned scientists over the years were not.

I consider this to be a successful example of technology transfer of erudite scientific data which led to a comprehensive forest management plan involving extremely large acreages of forests. The true test, of course, will be the evaluation of the correctness of the plan, for which time will be the judge.

## THE CHRISTMAS TREE INDUSTRY

It is one thing to extol a successful application of research when its purpose is to combat a major threat, such as the spruce budworm, to the total economies of at least two provinces. At times in their search for a solution, forest managers seemed willing to try anything. It is quite another matter to promote technology to improve an already successful enterprise. Successful enterprises, because they do not appear to have the need, do not readily search out new, and perhaps, radical ideas. This is the situation with the Christmas tree industry in the Maritimes. Small in comparison to the pulp and paper and saw mill industry, the Christmas tree industry nevertheless employs upwards of 6000 persons and brings an estimated 6 to 10 million dollars of revenue into the region.

The industry in the Maritimes accounts for over one-half of the trees exported from Canada. A large number of individuals must harvest, sell, grade, package and ship over 2 million Christmas trees to areas throughout eastern North America, all in the space of 6 weeks. These trees are produced on year-round farms which vary from less than 1 acre to 500 acres. (One large company controls 20000 acres, although not all this acreage is devoted to Christmas trees). Silvicultural techniques are highly sophisticated. It is also a very private industry. Everyone likes to grow trees, and they do. Doctors, lawyers, teachers, join with a phalanx of farmers and woodsmen to form a Christmas tree producers fraternity.

Intense pressure from the Christmas tree growers was instrumental in coercing the Maritimes Forest Research Centre into undertaking a research program on Christmas tree production. Scientists at the research centre were usually involved with large forest companies or provincial forest agencies and, as a result, usually dealt with woods superintendents, district foresters, plant managers, etc. While individuals fill such positions, dealings were, in reality, with the institutional position, rather than with the individual person. In dealing with the Christmas tree industry, scientists were confronted with actual growers. In such dealings, personality and trust were paramount. Relations frequently became modified even further when the scientist, as a government employee, was dealing on a one-to-one basis with the Christmas tree producer. The producer frequently assumed the role of a direct employer with the scientist realizing, sometimes for the first time, the full implication of being a public servant.

Scientists have been accused, not always unfairly, of being impractical, unable to converse in any meaningful fashion with 'lay' people. So to win the confidence of the Christmas tree producers, an approach was adopted by the MFRC which was designed to instill in the grower a degree of confidence in the scientist. The approach was for the scientist to literally go into the Christmas tree business with the grower. This was done by establishing three average size experimental Christmas tree farms in major Christmas tree areas in co-operation with local producers' associations and provincial forest extension services. The areas supported variable stands of natural regenerating balsam fir (*Abies balsamea*) (L.) Mill., the major Christmas tree species in the area. Each farm was divided into ten 200 ft (60 m) square blocks, and each block was divided in half. One half was managed by the Christmas tree producers, using current cultivation techniques, the other, controlled by the scientists, was the primary experimental and testing area for new techniques.

Each tree beyond knee height was tagged with a coded number indicating its exact location to the nearest square foot according to a precisely surveyed grid lay-out for each farm. All records were tied to grid numbers through a computer program.

All research plots were provided with signs which explained the experiments underway. The farms were symmetrically laid out, with straight roads, and were located at accessible, highly visible sites along main paved roads. The growers sold all trees on the research side of the blocks as well as their own, and thus were able to compare the quality of the research trees with theirs, as well as the appearance of the research side with the producers side of each block.

The grid numbers provided a means to keep complete and accurate records of responses of trees to a variety of treatments, responses which varied from a simple record of profits to detailed measurements of needle colour, number and length. These records were made available to the growers. One measurement was based on a Christmas tree classification system which served also as a basis for the commercial grading system. Christmas trees are essentially objects of art and general acceptance of a grade, which is equated with agricultural crops, has been slow. The classification system divided 72 recognizable types of balsam fir Christmas trees into six grades.

The general research program was begun in 1970 and is now almost complete. Growers immediately accepted new fertilizer prescriptions, and pesticide recommendations, even before the research was completed. Interest in any new silvicultural technique was keen and research related to shearing, nursery, and planting techniques was followed closely. However, most producers tended to ignore studies designed to improve management techniques such as the orderly development of harvesting schedules, the economic necessity of maintaining full stocking, and lessons to be learned from marketing research on tree quality. The industry has completely ignored predictions of saturated markets by 1985.

Nevertheless, Christmas tree producers have great expectations that research some day will solve their problems which they see as twofold. They foresee the geneticists developing the perfect tree that will require only planting. From soil and foliage samples, they expect precise fertilizer recommendations containing many trace elements, which will be custom designed for their particular farms.

Initially, the scientist believed that producers would be most receptive to practical and simple recommendations. However, events have proven otherwise. For example, a practical recommendation that two, 50 lb bags of ammonium nitrate per acre (112 kg/ha) is the optimum fertilizer prescription for a dry site is regarded with suspicion because it appears too imprecise. On the other hand, a recommendation of 60 lb a.i. of N per acre (67 kg/ha), which is the same recommendation, based on foliar analysis showing a normal range of N, is generally accepted because it is couched in more technical language.

In theory, fully stocked acreages of even-aged Christmas trees harvested in blocks, not piecemeal, is the most efficient means of Christmas tree production. If the scientist learned one thing from the close association with producers, and from the practical experience of operating farms, it is that this ideal is far from obtainable. The difficulties involved with developing similar sized trees in large blocks have, so far, proved insurmountable, a fact any Christmas tree producer would attest to, well before any research was undertaken.

A major lesson has been the reinforcement of the idea that successful application of research results generally depends as much on salesmanship as good science. The user is not instantly impressed, if at all, by the brilliance of scientific discovery; he has to be convinced. How the user is convinced will vary with the urgency of the problem involved, and the nature of the user.

## AN EVALUATION

### The spruce budworm

Why was the MFRC-UBC model a successful tool in the transfer of spruce budworm technology? A primary reason was the manner in which the workshops were conducted. The forest managers were able to manipulate and refine the model together with the scientists so that in effect the managers determined for themselves that a serious wood-supply problem existed. Had the model been developed in isolation and simply been demonstrated by the scientists to the managers, it is unlikely that this would have had the same effect. An underlying reason is, of course, the message the model gave. It provided 'the-moment-of-truth' for the forest industry in New Brunswick by forecasting a bleak future. It was the same sort of message as that given to Scrooge by Marley's ghost. Because of the momentousness of the problem and with the large number of financial resources available to the industry and the province, they, like Scrooge, responded positively.

### Christmas trees

Why was technology transfer in the Christmas tree industry successful in some instances and not in others? As with the spruce budworm project, the successes were due to the co-operative nature of the experimental farms. By providing a medium in which the grower could work side-by-side with the scientist, the grower was able to judge the usefulness of the research.

The process was made easier by the rapport between scientist and grower. Because the scientist had developed a full understanding of the deceivingly complex Christmas tree industry through his venture into the practical world of commerce; dialogue was as grower-to-grower.

The failures that occurred were related to techniques involving management strategies, and were due to the ambivalence of the grower to the desirability of obtaining optimum profits. This ambivalence is caused by the nature of the Christmas tree industry.

In spite of its size and complexity, the industry is largely made up of individuals who work their farms themselves, have limited financial backing, and who have other occupations that provide additional income. Their approach toward the making of profits varies according to personal outlook (some growers simply enjoy growing trees) and financial circumstances. But virtually all take great pride in the quality of their trees.

Consequently, the ideas and techniques that catch the imagination of growers, as a group, are those that are designed to improve tree quality or to reduce work load. Ideas and techniques that require financial input, increased work load, or cause inconvenience without some immediate gain, are the least attractive and last to be accepted. Moreover, these are the very techniques that maximize profit from improved management strategies.

In fairness to the growers, however, the study is only partially completed and they have not had the opportunity to judge the final results. Present plans are to develop a simulation model for Christmas tree farms, similar in nature to the budworm model, that can be used as an educational tool. A simplified version along the lines of the game 'Monopoly' is planned for family entertainment and education. With such a model the growers and their families will be able to look into a hopefully realistic future and will be better able to judge the value of the longer term techniques.

The above evaluation of the two projects is presented from the researchers point of view, and is unavoidably subjective. It is easy in such an exercise to delude oneself that failures to promote new technology result from the short-sightedness of the intended users. One must be cognisant that failures in any form of technology transfer may occur because the technology itself is impractical, inadequate, or just plain useless, a fact that may be obvious to the potential user but not to the scientist.

## References

BASKERVILLE, G. (1976). *Report of the task force for evaluation of budworm control alternatives.* Department of Natural Resources, Province of New Brunswick. Fredericton, Canada. 210 pp.

BASKERVILLE, G. (1979). *Implementation of adaptive approaches in provincial and federal forestry agencies.* A paper presented at the Environmental Policy Seminar, International Institute for Applied Systems Analysis, Laxenburg, Austria. June 18–20, 1979.

CUFF, W. and BASKERVILLE, G. (1982). *Ecological modelling and management of spruce budworm infested fir-spruce forests in New Brunswick.* Paper presented at the Third International Conference on State of the Art in Ecological Modelling, Colorado State University. May 24–28, 1982.

FISHER, R. A. (1982). *Two decades of budworm simulation: a retrospective view of comprehensive simulation models.* Paper presented at the Third International Conference on State of the Art in Ecological Modelling, Colorado State University. May 24–28, 1982.

# Research and development work by Costa Rican farmers: lessons for agro-foresters

J. BEER

*Investigator, Tropical Agricultural Centre for Research and Training, Turrialba, Costa Rica*[1]

## ABSTRACT

It is important to start new agricultural research and development projects with studies of the existing farming systems. This paper suggests that it is also worthwhile to study the empirical research and extension techniques that farmers have used to develop their traditional systems, in order to provide guidelines on how to convince farmers that new results are worth adopting. The stages in the empirical development of some agro-forestry techniques in Costa Rica (silvo-pastoral, living fence posts, shade trees over perennial crops, improved fallow slash and burn) are discussed in order to demonstrate the importance of seven research and development techniques used by farmers. These are: demonstration plots; adaptation of existing techniques; preference for multiple-use species; identification of desirable tree characteristics; directed succession; and observation of crop phenology as a silvicultural indicator.

## INTRODUCTION

The usual goal of agricultural and agro-forestry projects is the adoption, by farmers, of new or improved technology. Unfortunately this process is an unknown field for most foresters. Since the majority of the existing knowledge on agro-forestry is empirical (traditional) many agro-forestry research projects have been initiated with studies of the systems which the farmers have developed. However, this approach could be taken one step further; i.e. in order to increase the probability that agro-forestry research results will be accepted by farmers, study and adopt the ways in which the results of their own empirical research have spread from the instigators.

Four examples of the progressive development of an agro-forestry technique in Costa Rica are given below. The ways in which these developments occurred are used as a basis for specifying topics which should be considered when an intensified use of agro-forestry is being promoted.

[1] The financial support of the United Nations University (UNU) and the Deutsche Gesellschaft fur Technische Zusammenarbeit (GTZ) are gratefully acknowledged.

## EMPIRICAL DEVELOPMENT OF AGRO-FORESTRY TECHNIQUES IN COSTA RICA

### Silvo-pastoral

The grazing of domesticated animals on natural pasture, in unmanaged dry tropical forests, is still a common practice throughout the world. The technique has been transferred to more humid areas but partial clearance of the forest is then necessary in order to permit pasture establishment. Some residual high forest trees are usually left, partially because they will provide shade for the animals.

Increasing wood prices have prompted many Costa Rican farmers to establish such silvo-pastoral combinations, by selectively clearing secondary forest leaving valuable pioneer species (50–400 trees/ha) to develop to maturity over the planted pasture, e.g. the cabinet timber species *Cordia alliodora* and *Cedrela odorata.* However, these species do not germinate in a complete grass sward. In some farms the existence of a combination is a consequence of past management. For example, germination of

*Cordia alliodora* on the bare soil in a coffee plantation, may result in a silvo-pastoral combination if the coffee is later replaced by grass. Under continuous grazing it is doubtful whether these combinations can be maintained after one rotation of the trees, unless the farmer adopts the next development: tree planting in pastures.

In the high altitude dairy zone (above 1400 m) many farmers have planted *Alnus acuminata* 'wildings' at regular wide spacings ($12 \times 12 \pm 4$–5 m) over *Pennisetum clandestinum, P. purpureum* and *Axonopus scoparius* (Combe, 1979). The planted seedlings (1–2 m) are usually naturally regenerated stock collected from roadsides or riversides. They must be protected from browsing animals by encompassing individual barbed wire fences. Further evidence that these farmers practice silviculture is given by the crude pruning of older trees. The fact that they frequently leave 1–2 m branch stubs indicates that their purpose is improvement of the underlying conditions, in order to increase pasture productivity, rather than any attempt to increase wood quality. This species provides low quality construction timber and fuelwood. The final developments by Costa Rican farmers include: the planting of nursery stock (their own or commercial); vegetative propagation of trees in pastures; grazing in young plantations. Examples are rare and the tree species involved are: *Alnus acuminata* and in seasonally dry areas *Citrus* spp., *Mangifera indica* and *Tamarindus indica; Erythrina poeppigiana* (legume for soil improvement and forage); and *Pinus caribaea,* respectively. A related development, the planting of valuable species in fence-lines, is described in the following section.

**Living fence posts**

The origin of this practice is thought to be in the use of toxic, caustic or spined species to form impenetrable hedges around the homes of Central American Indians (Saver, 1979). With the advent of cattle ranching the repellent properties of such species became less important than the rooting ability of large stakes, in order to rapidly provide support (typically at 1–2 m intervals), for a barbed wire fence. Farmers have selected several multiple use species which provide fruit, e.g. *Spondias* spp. Another living fence post species, *Yucca elephantipes* provides an edible flower and can be used to control erosion on steep roadside banks. The latest development has been the establishment of valuable timber species (e.g. *Tectona grandis*) in fence lines.

**Shade trees over perennial crops**

The management of *Theobroma cacao* under shade trees (e.g. *Gliricidia sepium*) also pre-dates the Conquistadors (Cook, 1901). The crudest way to cultivate perennial crops under shade is to plant them in a partially cleared forest. This situation is non-sustainable since the original forest trees will eventually be harvested or die. In order to maintain the shade, the farmer must either promote natural tree regeneration or plant shade species. The next development in Costa Rican coffee management was the planting of *Musa* spp. for the provision of a second product as well as shade. The establishment of approximately 150–400 leguminous shade trees per ha, by rooting 5–20 cm thick stakes (e.g. *Erythrina* and *Inga* spp.), was a parallel development (Fonseca, 1968). This latter technique has been designed to maintain a low (3–7 m) light shade canopy. The latest development involves the care of naturally regenerated timber species (e.g. 200–400 *Cordia alliodora*/ha), which form a third canopy over the leguminous shade trees and the coffee (Beer *et al.,* 1981). In rare cases farmers have planted both exotic (e.g. *Eucalyptus deglupta*) and native (e.g. *Alnus acuminata*) timber species.

**Improved fallow slash and burn**

'Slash and burn' is the most common agricultural technique in the humid tropics. In the simplest version of this technique no attempt is made to influence the species composition during the fallow period. One restricted example where farmers are favouring one useful fallow species can be observed in Pacayitas, Canton de Turrialba, Costa Rica. Their rotation involves the fuelwood tree *Lippia torresii,* maize *(Zea mays)* and sometimes grazing. The three farms where this system has been observed are situated between 1000–1200 m above sea level in a 'Premontane Wet Forest' area (Holdridge, 1976). According to the farmers, the system begins when pure stands of the pioneer species 'Caragra' *(L. torresii)* regenerate naturally in maize fields established on recently cleared forest areas. Cattle may be permitted to graze on the area after the maize has been harvested, but if pasture cleaning is carried out the *L. torresii* are not cut in order that they may develop into a monospecific tree overstory. Eventually these trees can be felled for fuelwood, and maize planted again into the resulting slash (branches/foliage). It is debatable whether the farmers really influence the course of natural succession during this first rotation but by preferential cleaning they certainly halt further succession to the typical mixed secondary forest of the area. On clearing the *L. torresii* for a second planting of maize they leave 0.5–1 m stumps which coppice vigorously. The continued existence of a pure stand of *L. torresii* depends in part on how they manage these coppices. If continually slashed back it is probable that pure pasture or a more heterogeneous secondary forest will result.

## RESEARCH AND DEVELOPMENT TECHNIQUES USED BY FARMERS

### Demonstration plots

Farmers are more impressed by visual evidence, such as a demonstration plot, than by written or verbal information. This is even more important in the tropics where many live at a subsistence level and are illiterate. They learn from each other by copying what appear to be successful practices and hence if a development worker wants to influence them a demonstration plot is probably his most effective option. In order to draw attention to a demonstration plot a large signpost is invaluable since the extension effect is then somewhat independent of the project. The target group for agro-forestry projects is much larger (millions of farmers), than is the case for traditional silvilculture (often only a few public organizations and private firms). Establishment of a large number of demonstration plots is one of the few ways of extending results to such an enormous group, but it is important not to over-reach project resources. A few well managed demonstration plots are better than many neglected sites. Their value can be greatly increased by using them for student training exercises as well as for field days for farmers.

### Adaption of techniques familiar

Subsistence farmers do not have large margins for error. They are wary of radical innovations and are more likely to adopt systems, techniques or species which seem familiar. Thus the empirical development of their four main agro-forestry techniques, which are described above, has occurred gradually or in a step-by-step process. In order to sell the farmers an innovation it is advisable to imitate this process. For example: the promotion of windbreaks in an area where they are unknown could be achieved by initially persuading some farmers to replace their fence-posts with a suitable timber species. Alternatively, or subsequently, they could be persuaded to include living fence posts, which produce fodder, within the line of the timber species. Finally the idea of planting not one but several parallel lines of trees could be proposed. Assuming that suitable species are chosen, the farmers will gradually be convinced that the advantages far outweigh the loss of land, since some of the advantages will be demonstrated *before* they are required to accept a reduction in cropping areas.

Management techniques which are adaptations or imitations of methods used by farmers stand a higher chance of being accepted than those which are completely new. For example, in Costa Rican coffee growing areas it is common practice to plant annual crops (chiefly maize and beans) between coffee rows during the first one or two seasons after establishment. It should not therefore be difficult to promote the 'Taungya' technique (intercropping of forestry plantations during the establishment phase) in these areas. In this particular case there is however an example of a negative drawback associated with prior experience. These farmers tend to make tree planting holes far too large, and to take such excessive care in planting each tree seedling, that establishment costs can be unnecessarily increased!

### Multiple-use species

The subsistence farmer with a limited land area has obvious reason for choosing multiple-use species, such as the *Spondias* spp., which can provide fruits, medicine and even forage as well as fuelwood when no alternatives exist. Although there is often no ecological justification for opposing the promotion of exotic species, there may be social justifications for preferring native species with which the farmers are already familiar.

### Identify the most important component

Farmers will frequently favour one component of a 'crop' association at the expense of the others (Mead and Willey, 1980); for example, the *A. acuminata* pruning described above favours pasture production but not wood production. Another example is that many farmers will not accept a coffee shade tree that provokes large reductions in coffee bean yields, even if the value of the combined tree and coffee products exceeds that from a pure coffee plantation.

### Desirable characteristics of agro-forestry

Farmers choose tree species which favour, or at least are not strongly detrimental, to the associated crop. A study of the characteristics of the species of their choice is advisable before attempting to suggest alternatives (Beer, 1981). For example, it is arguable whether *Enterlobium cyclocarpum* (wide crown) is an alternative *T. cacao* shade tree to *C. alliodora* (narrow crown), because much more extensive damage of the *T. cacao* is caused by the felling of the former. Judged by growth characteristics in Costa Rica, a much better alternative is the African species *Terminalia ivorensis,* which like *C. alliodora* has a narrow crown, is self-pruning, forms a straight unbranched stem and has rapid apical growth. However, it is noteworthy that many of the agroforestry tree species, selected by Costa Rican farmers, also coppice strongly.

### Directed succession

The development of the improved fallow for the slash and burn technique is an example of directed succession. The high weeding costs associated with the planting of *Pinus* spp. in continuously humid tropical areas, is an example of the consequences of opposing succession. When profitability is marginal (e.g. fuelwood) it may pay to put more emphasis on the management of naturally regenerated stands, which have little or no establishment costs, and less on plantations.

### Tree-crop interactions

It may be necessary for foresters to study the physiological needs and/or phenology of associated crops, when developing agro-forestry systems or techniques. For example: the traditional pruning schedule of *Erythrina* and *Inga* shade trees is determined by coffee phenology; specifically flowering and fruiting. In fact this reasoning has a sound physiological basis when the resulting moisture regime and nutrient uptake of the coffee bushes are considered.

## CONCLUSION

If agro-foresters would study not only existing agroforestry practices but also the way in which these practices have developed, they would obtain valuable guidelines for the orientation of their research and extension work.

### References


BEER, J. W. (1981). *Advantages, disadvantages and desirable characteristics of shade trees for coffee, cacao and tea.* Turrialba, Costa Rica, CATIE. 14 pp. (Mimeograph).

BEER, J. W., CLARKIN, K., DE LAS SALAS, G. and GLOVER, N. (1981). A case study of traditional agroforestry practices, in a wet tropical zone: The "La Suiza" project". In *Simposio Internaccional sobre Ciencias Forestales y su Contribucion al Desarrollo de la America Latina.* Edited by M. Chavaria, San Jose, Costa Rica, Conicit—INTERCIENCIA—SCITEC, 199–209.

COMBE, J. (1979). *Alnus acuminata* with grazing and mowing pasture: Las Nubes de Coronado, Costa Rica. In *Proceedings of the Workshop on Agro-Forestry Systems in Latin America,* edited by G. De las Salas, Turrialba, Costa Rica, CATIE, 199–201.

COOK, O. F. (1901). *Shade in coffee culture.* Washington, D.C., US Department of Agriculture, Division of Botany. 79 pp.

FONSECA, M. T. (1968). El poro. *Revista de Agricultura (Costa Rica)* **40** (6–7), 102–112.

HOLDRIDGE, L. R. (1967). *Life zone ecology.* San Jose, Costa Rica. Tropical Science Center. 207 pp.

MEAD, R. and WILLEY, R. W. (1980). The concept of a 'Land equivalent ratio' and advantages in yields from intercropping. *Experimental Agriculture* **16,** 217–228.

SAUER, J. D. (1979). Living fences in Costa Rican agriculture. *Turrialba* **29**(4), 255–261.

# Eruptions and applications

G. A. COOPER
*USDA Forest Service, Pacific Northwest Forest and Range Experiment Station, Portland, Oregon, U.S.A.*

## ABSTRACT

In the week following the May 18, 1980, eruption of Mount St. Helens in Washington State, the USDA Forest Service, Pacific Northwest Forest and Range Experiment Station, planned the research needed to develop forest resource management guidelines for the damaged acres and obtained funds to conduct the research. A workshop involving major land managers near Mount St. Helens and researchers identified the questions having highest priorities. The workshop was also the start of the communication and co-ordination processes between managers and researchers needed for subsequent development of research information. Application of the findings was rapid because of this close working relationship and the strong motivation on both sides to work out the answers. Technology transfer was tailored to the audience and, at the same time, took into account the problems of time, weather, and public safety. The eruptions created intense public interest as well as pressure from the news media. Working in the middle of a media event was a mixed blessing: there was the pressure from all sides to produce results; but there was also tremendous scientific opportunity, funds quickly made available to do the necessary work, and co-operation from all involved.

## INTRODUCTION

Mount St. Helens, the Mount Fuji of the American Northwest, was a beautiful, quiet volcano in south-west Washington State for 123 years. There was major volcanic eruption in 1842 followed by intermittent volcanic activity until 1857. Nothing unusual occurred from then until March 1980. For several weeks that spring small eruptions of steam, gases, and ash and numerous concentrated earthquakes signaled bigger events. A bulge of rock appeared on the north face of the mountain. It grew at the rate of 1.5 m per day. As quakes increased in frequency, a 'Red Zone', or danger keep out area, was established in early April.

At 8.32 a.m., Sunday May 18, 1980, a sharp earthquake triggered the bulge into an enormous avalanche, and the pressure released from the avalanche spewed billions of tons of rock, ash, and ice over the land. A prioclastic flow of mud and superheated gases shot down the volcano's northern flanks, filling rivers and lakes and burying old-growth forest over 150 m beneath it. Continuous eruptions formed a crater 1 mile wide and 2 miles long. The elevation of the summit was reduced by 387 m. Thirty-six people were killed and 23 others are still missing and presumed dead. The area directly affected by the blast was 61 000 ha, and tephra blanketed the earth for 800 km downwind. Within a week a cloud of ash had encircled the earth. Federal resources damaged or destroyed included 4 million $m^3$ of timber, 160 km of streams, 2300 big game animals, 27 recreation sites, 100 km of road, 13 bridges, 318 km of trails and 15 Forest Service buildings. The estimated value of the private and public losses in timber, agriculture, fisheries, rivers, roads and bridges, and ash clean-up, was $1.2 billion. Over 200 homes were destroyed, and many people suffered grievously in other ways as well.

State, federal, and private industry resource managers faced huge responsibilities: to keep fires in the fallen timber and dead trees along the fringe of the blast areas from burning into surrounding green timber; to cope with the effects of 250 cm of winter precipitation on highly erodable, ash-laden slopes; to protect population centres downstream from flooding; and to deal on a daily basis with many members of the public and to help eager reporters through a bureaucratic maze. How to cope? What would work and what would not? What should be avoided that might eliminate future options for meeting resource responsibilities? What could we expect nature to do? Would the volcano ever stop so we could go to work? These are the questions that managers asked and for which there were few immediate answers.

How biological research needs were defined, met, and applied to assist those resource managers is the scope of this paper.

## DETERMINING WHAT WAS NEEDED

Forest land managers asked researchers to provide quick help to cope with the eruption impacts.

On May 19, 1980, six of the leading scientists from the Pacific Northwest Forest and Range Experiment Station were assembled into a think tank. Their task was to brainstorm potential research efforts that would be responsive to anticipated needs of the forest resource managers near Mount St. Helens. We had only 5 days in which to write a proposed research program for our Forest Service headquarters in Washington, D.C. It had to include study objectives, expected duration, necessary funding, and projected impacts of the research on restoration of the resources. On May 22 we sent a proposal that outlined problems with forest productivity, watershed restoration, anadromous fish habitat, fire, salvage operations, and reforestation. This initial program proposal worked out well, and it was the basis of a successful budget request to fund our work through 1982. As we learned more we were able to sharpen the focus of research within the original prospectus.

With planning completed and funding assured, we, and everyone else, were anxious to get into the blast zone for a close look at the damage. Rescue operations were substantially completed by June 1 and the volcano, under intense observation by the U.S. Geological Survey (USGS), was deemed calm enough to permit our first helicopter reconnaissance on June 12. That trip caught six normally loquacious scientists and resource managers totally unprepared: they were silent for over an hour as they viewed the devastation. From that view, though, they were able to delineate zones of damage, and begin to formulate a plan for assessing the damage, establishing research plots, and meeting the future needs of the managers.

Since so many people were involved, co-ordination and communication were the first organizational needs. What had initially been a quagmire, by July was transformed into a reasonably cohesive communications network involving eight agencies responsible for public protection. Another overlapping network within the resource management agencies quickly coalesced due to the similarity of the problems. The Gifford Pinchot National Forest (a federal agency), the Washington State Department of Natural Resources (DNR), and Weyerhaeuser Company (a private wood products corporation) collectively managed 90 per cent of the land in the blast and damage zone and each had a research facility available to respond to their needs. These three organizations formed the St. Helens Forest Land Research Co-operative. I represented the Pacific Northwest Forest and Range Experiment Station (PNW) and had six leading scientists helping me; DNR and Weyerhaeuser had similar teams. We met regularly, attended planning sessions of the resource managers, and co-operated in entering the Red Zone to assess the damage. We were not involved in the earth sciences or research on volcanism, that work was done by USGS, but we did embrace and provide co-ordination for all federal, state, and private research in the biological sciences. There were numerous helicopter entries, plenty of photographs taken, accurate maps made, and total resource losses calculated.

By late August we had enough data to co-ordinate a complete initial assessment of research needs to support the development of management plans. The stage was thus set for the single most important event in the subsequent success of the application of research results: The Technical Needs Workshop. On September 4–5, 1980, 50 of the leading federal, state, and private resource managers and their counterpart scientists met at a Technical Needs Workshop. Each person represented a specific viewpoint or discipline that related to the impacts of the volcano and the associated recovery on the lands around it. The resource managers stressed the need for technical assistance from scientists on problems demanding immediate attention and indicated which items could wait for results from longer-range research. Together, the scientists and managers identified 40 separate elements needing further study (St. Helens Forest Lands Research Co-operative, 1980a).

They also documented the work already underway. Because there was such a significant increase in scientific pursuits around Mount St. Helens, a comprehensive listing of current research was needed by everyone involved: scientists for co-ordinating research planning; state officials, who were responsible for overall planning and management, to complete their understanding of research activities; and journalists to serve their audiences who wanted to know what was happening. Thus the first 'technology transfer' (in this case, a comprehensive listing of research projects) occurred on September 5 (St. Helens Forest Lands Research Co-operative, 1980b).

That listing was subsequently updated and published four more times (Winjum, *et al.*, 1981a, 1981b, 1982a, 1982b).

The Technical Needs Workshop accomplished four important things:

1. It identified the immediate as well as long-range needs that research has to meet, and it established priorities.
2. It brought together the people who had the needs and those who would answer these needs.
3. It established and solidified a climate of co-operation and co-ordination: teams of scientists and managers with common interests combined their goals to avoid redundancies and to make efficient use of the limited opportunities for access by helicopter into remote areas.
4. It broke down barriers, both real and perceived, between researchers and managers: researchers agreed to drop the 'publish first' posture and all the attendant peer reviews, so the managers could put the research results into use as quickly as possible; and managers and researchers, together, accepted the risks involved.

Right after the Technical Needs Workshop a major research effort called the '1980 Pulse' was begun to accomplish as much as possible in a 2-week time period before weather or an unco-operative volcano stopped all work. Sponsored by PNW, 117 researchers from 21 organizations put in 663 research-days and installed more than 150 sample plots. They identified critical areas that had to be reserved for scientific or educational purposes and prepared maps of major terrestrial and aquatic features for use by the managers and planners of the National Volcanic Area. They identified and recorded potential problems from erosion and sediment transport; they recorded early stages of ecosystem recovery; they established baseline transects and plots to monitor changes; they collected samples of ash, vegetation, water, insects and soils to assess impacts of the blast; and they made on-site recommendations to resource managers.

By October 1, 1980, the needs had been well identified and a strong, co-ordinated research effort was underway to meet these needs.

Looking back at this particular phase of the research-to-applications sequence, we can see why it worked. First, circumstances forced researchers and managers to work together from the very beginning. Second, specific audiences defined specific needs directly to the research specialists who could meet those needs: there was almost no lost time or effort in determining the audience and reaching it. Third, effective communication and co-ordination was achieved but only after considerable bureaucratic manoeuvering and some battles over 'turf'. Fourth, we by-passed many of the formal buffers and failsafe procedures normal to research. The biggest reason for this was a universal recognition that time would not permit any other course of action. Danger helped too, limited and uncertain access to the mountain dictated either efficient operations or failure. More than any other reason, though, this phase worked because the research scientists and resource managers developed mutual respect and dependence.

## DEVELOPING THE INFORMATION

We estimate that $3.3 million was budgeted by all participating organizations for research in the area around Mount St. Helens during the first year following the major eruption (Winjum, *et al.,* 1983). By February, 1981, there were 195 separate studies that we know of; 42 supporting organizations; scientists came from Great Britain, Germany, the Netherlands, Japan, Canada, Mexico, Costa Rica, as well as 20 states in the United States. These scientists shared four things: (1) a burning desire to examine the rapidly changing ecosystems; (2) hassles over helicopter entry; (3) danger of eruptions; and (4) constant watch by the media and public.

There were several reasons for what were perceived as hassles, but which were all really systems designed to mitigate potential danger. One area of concern was air safety. Geologists from USGS had first priority for air space and available helicopter service because they monitored the volcano's tremors, gas emissions, bulges, lava domes, landslides, and flood hazards. Biological scientists had to wait for the geologists to say the mountain was safe, and then had to wait for their agencies to determine the safety to helicopter operations. Researchers had no accidents, but others did: freak air currents rather than unsafe procedures were the cause. But there were frequent delays due to ensuring safe entry into the area of devastation, and extraordinary efforts were taken to provide enough helicopter service at the right time and to have the aircraft and operators certified as safe by various agencies.

A second, but less disruptive, problem was the health risk from exposure to ash and highly polluted waters. The ash threat was quickly over; rain settled it for the most part, and face masks provided very effective, albeit uncomfortable, protection. Water pollution was another matter. Our scientists, particularly those working on aquatic systems, were exposed to numerous pathogens; most worrisome was an unidentified pneumonia virus which can sometimes be fatal; the illness caused by this virus is known as 'Legionnaires' Disease'. A few researchers had flu-like symptoms after splashing about collecting samples from the lakes and streams in the blast area. Public health officials were alert and provided constant monitoring, and no widespread problems occurred. Aquatic biologists quickly developed sampling procedures that eliminated any unsafe exposure to pathogens, and following that development no one became ill. Legionnaires' Disease was never diagnosed, but all polluted water was continuously monitored, and plans for draining impoundments were carefully reviewed to preclude unwanted effects downstream. Places accessible to the general public were posted with warning signs.

The constant attention from the various news media was a partial impediment, even though the journalists and photographers rightfully sought to tell their audiences what the Forest Service was accomplishing. The general public quickly became aware that researchers existed and wanted to know what they were doing. News about available technology and research findings reached the media audiences daily. Sometimes that was unsettling to the researchers and the resource managers, however, because the situation was changing so quickly, ideas and recommendations reported one day might be changed just a few days later. Then the public would want an explanation of why we said one thing and later did another. Information officers were kept busy, and researchers and managers quickly learned if they found out anything that could have an influence on an upcoming management decision they should alert each other as early as possible. Thus the focus of the media created added impetus for fast technology transfer and even closer co-ordination between researchers and managers.

Our combined research efforts, co-ordinated by the principal Forest Service scientists, used the talents and support of university, state and private organizations. In the 2 years following our start, we estimate that this combined effort cost almost $12 million; $1.1 million of which were Forest Service funds.

There were six major interrelated categories of studies for developing the information needed, and supported by the resource managers:

1. *Aquatic ecosystem recovery*
   To develop management guidelines on: how to treat streamsides and stabilize pools during salvage operations; how to enhance fish habitat and the return of anadromous fish; and how to deal with lakes of bacterial soup.
2. *Erosion and channel change*
   To monitor rill and surface erosion, predict sediment transfer, determine role of plant recovery, and the effects of fallen timber.
3. *Terrestrial ecosystem recovery and revegetation*
   To monitor plant recovery on various sites, and develop recommendations for reforestation.
4. *Utilization of fallen timber*
   To estimate timber breakage and residues so managers could conduct salvage sales, estimate fuelwood availability, and evaluate forest fire fuels.
5. *Physical and chemical characteristics of ash*
   To determine the effect of ash and tephra on the biology of the forest floor and conifer regeneration.
6. *Wildlife recovery*
   To enhance recovery of ecosystems, and develop guidelines for game management in the environs around Mount St. Helens.

This overall effort was successful in providing research results, but it also was a big contributor to the success of subsequent application of the results. We believe the development of close relationships with resource managers and the logistical support provided by management kept researchers right on target. Also, scientists and managers both learned how to exercise personal diplomacy with journalists, and that contributed to the quick transfer of information to other scientists and managers. Finally, researchers played an active role in developing management prescriptions, environmental impact statements, and in making on-the-spot management decisions. They saw their recommendations accepted because of the respect and understanding they had generated amongst managers.

## PACKAGING AND TRANSFERRING THE INFORMATION

Packaging and delivery of research results were tailored to the audiences we were trying to reach. Our primary audience was forest managers in the Pacific Northwest, but we also reached other scientists, other countries, and the public in a variety of ways.

Our most effective transfer of new information came through on-the-ground workshops with multidisciplinary teams of scientists and managers addressing complex problems incorporating many trade-offs. Representatives from Weyerhaeuser Company, Burlington Northern Railroad, and Washington State Department of Natural Resources met frequently with Forest Service administrators and scientists because they shared the same problems on their lands located in the blast zone. There were almost monthly sessions and, in the first 2 critical years, there were 17 full-day field sessions with agenda and briefing papers. We also huddled over maps and photographs at hundreds of conferences: these meetings, trips, and joint work sessions became almost daily fare.

The working conferences were followed by summary statements, written recommendations, or a brief analysis of alternatives to consider. The record of the research at the session was often little more than data tables and initial conclusions. No one waited for publication, peer review, or editing: if they were confident they had it right, it was passed to management; if they were unsure, it was qualified and risks were sometimes taken. Surprisingly, this backfired infrequently and the time saved was an immense advantage. No scientist felt compromised by the lapse of scientific discipline.

Dealing with other scientists at seminars, symposia or professional society meetings was another matter. These forums for digging out errors and shedding more light on new subjects operated in the traditional manner. By the end of 1982 there had been over 20 seminars in which scientists from our Mount St. Helens effort were involved. Papers were presented and eventually published in journals following review by peers. There are no bibliographies which include all the manuscripts published by scientists working on Mount St. Helens. Findings from research conducted by the Forest Service has resulted in 45 publications in 1981 and 1982, and we know of dozens more in preparation. The university contribution has also been large, but figures are incomplete.

International exchanges between scientists were successful in transferring technology both ways. One such technical exchange was with Costa Rica: the visit by our scientists to Volcano Irazu provided us with direct knowledge of watershed rehabilitation in areas affected by volcanos. In return we were able to assist them with their analyses of volcano and earthquake hazards in Costa Rica. We had similar exchanges with scientists from Mexico and Japan, and we learned as much from them as they did from us.

Our most demanding clientele was the populace in the areas surrounding the volcano. Regardless of the positions about the management of the area advocated by individuals and groups, they all sought our research to support their varied viewpoints. The greatest controversy was preservation *v.* salvage. As researchers, we too had viewpoints on the matter, but our emphasis was on providing facts rather than offering opinions. And we had plenty of facts for both sides. By the time long-term management decisions were being discussed, research had helped to document all the issues of concern, and we collaborated with the resource managers to describe the pros and cons of alternative management strategies. These were published in several documents (U.S. Department of Agriculture, 1981a, 1981b) and circulated to the public for their comments and information.

In retrospect, technology transfer worked quite well. We employed many methods: the selection of a method was based on the audience and what would be most timely and appropriate. It was also a case where technology transfer could not have been curtailed even if we had tried to do so. If we had any problem, it was that not enough information was available, early enough, to keep all the transfer pipelines full.

## APPLICATIONS

The Mount St. Helens National Volcanic Monument was created by Congress in August 1982 with the USDA Forest Service as the managing agency. Our Land Management Plan outlined in the Final Land Management Plan (U.S. Department of Agriculture, 1981b) was the one Congress chose for us to follow. Under its guidelines, a 45 000 ha area has been dedicated for protection of geologic, ecologic, and cultural resources with full use for scientific study and research. This area is not managed for production of timber or other resources.

The remaining blast area (about 16 000 ha), and all the affected surrounding general forest area, is being managed for renewable resource production. It is here that the results of research are being intensively applied. And we are not making hasty decisions or operating with less than firm research data. Researchers and managers together solve problems and arrive at management prescriptions. Research is represented on the interdisciplinary team charged with developing the detailed comprehensive management plan for the National Forest areas both within and surrounding the National Volcanic Monument. Researchers are frequently asked to assist in resolving plan implementation problems: where should a bridge be placed to minimize stream habitat impacts? How can erosion on hillslopes best be managed? What planting techniques are most likely to succeed? How close to waterways should salvage operations be conducted? What should be done to hasten restoration of fish habitat? Our recommendations are translated into on-the-ground actions, and that is the greatest satisfaction a researcher can have.

## CONCLUSIONS

The application of the results of research conducted around Mount St. Helens was, and continues to be, very successful. It happened fast, it produced the desired effects, and it gave scientists much satisfaction. This occurred primarily because:

Resource managers and scientists worked together from the start.

Together we established communications, defined priority needs, and obtained funding.

Scientists were strongly motivated by the unique research opportunities.

We used the whole community of available research talent involving many agencies and organizations.

Researchers were pushed by weather, danger, rapid ecological changes, public interest, and managerial needs.

And we accepted risks that we might be wrong.

### References

ST. HELENS FOREST LANDS RESEARCH CO-OPERATIVE (1980a). *Minutes of the Technical Needs Workshop.* Olympia, Washington. 36 pp.

ST. HELENS FOREST LANDS RESEARCH CO-OPERATIVE (1980b). *Mount St. Helens: available information on research planned or underway.* (Unpublished report). 33 pp.

U.S. DEPARTMENT OF AGRICULTURE, FOREST SERVICE (1981a). *Mount St. Helens land management plan, draft environmental impact statement.* U.S. Forest Service, Pacific Northwest Region. 162 pp.

U.S. DEPARTMENT OF AGRICULTURE, FOREST SERVICE (1981b). *Mount St. Helens land management plan, final environmental impact statement.* U.S. Forest Service, Pacific Northwest Region (update). 288 pp.

WINJUM, J. K., ANDERSON, H. W. and COOPER, G. A. (1982a). *Research associated with Mt. St. Helens and the volcanic eruptions of 1980.* St. Helens Forest Land Research Co-operative, c/o Weyerhaeuser Co., Centralia, Washington 98531. 128 pp.

WINJUM, J. K., ANDERSON, H. W. and COOPER, G. A. (1982b). *Research associated with Mt. St. Helens and the volcanic eruptions of 1980 (update).* St. Helens Forest Land Research Co-operative, c/o Weyerhaeuser Co., Centralia, Washington 98531. 129 pp.

WINJUM, J. K., COOPER, G. A. and JAMISON, D. W. (1981a). *Active research associated with Mt. St. Helens and the volcanic eruptions of 1980.* St. Helens Forest Land Research Co-operative, c/o Weyerhaeuser Co., Centralia, Washington 98531. 67 pp.

WINJUM, J. K., COOPER, G. A. and JAMISON, D. W. (1981b). *Active research associated with Mt. St. Helens and the volcanic eruptions of 1980 (update).* St. Helens Forest Land Research Co-operative, c/o Weyerhaeuser Co., Centralia, Washington 98531. 114 pp.

WINJUM, J. K., COOPER, G. A. and ANDERSON, H. W. (1983). *The scope of research resulting from the 1980 eruptions of Mt. St. Helens.* St. Helens Forest Land Research Co-operative, c/o Weyerhaeuser Co., Centralia, Washington 98531. 5 pp.

# Transfer of forest products technology

T. S. McKNIGHT AND V. N. P. MATHUR
*Canadian Forestry Service*

ABSTRACT

Events leading to development of two recent research innovations, a lumber slicer and a new method of finger-jointing, are analyzed to determine the factors that contributed most to application. The general conditions which should be met include: (1) a highly-motivated research group; (2) open research time for curiosity-minded trials; (3) responsible research management that recognizes 'winners'; (4) early and continuing involvement of potential clients; (5) availability of funds; and (6) competent, technologically-aware managers or research users.

**Introduction**

The forest products research program of the Canadian government was for over 50 years carried out in two laboratories, the Eastern Forest Products Laboratory (EFPL) in Ottawa and the Western Forest Products Laboratory (WFPL) in Vancouver. Latterly, the forest products program was combined with the Canadian Forestry Service of the Department of Environment because the industrial utilization of the forest resource was recognized as an important aspect of the broad range of subjects encompassed by forest-related research and development.

With the growing connection of the forest products laboratories with the industrial users of the technologies being developed, as well as the provincial governments which are directly responsible for the management and utilization of the forest resource, the government decided in 1979 to 'privatize' the forest products program. By this is was meant that the responsibility for the management and financing of the program would be taken over by a private, non-profit corporation. The name of the new corporation, in which there is broad industry, provincial government, and university involvement, is the Forintek Canada Corp. There also remains a substantial federal government involvement in the 'privatized' forest products program because of the important national benefits to be derived from improvements in the utilization of a major resource, i.e. the forest resource.

There were two earlier precedents for this form of spin-off of a government program in the forest resource field which are provided by the formation of the Pulp and Paper Research Institute of Canada and the Forest Engineering Research Institute of Canada. The pulp and paper research program had its start within the government forest products research program and was later split off to form the present Institute. The forest engineering programs of the Pulp and Paper Research Institute of Canada and the Canadian Forestry Service were combined and placed under the management of a new non-profit corporation which was named the Forest Engineering Research Institute of Canada.

These events illustrate one approach to achieving the transfer of technology and improving the commercialization of the most viable of new developments. In these cases it was desired to obtain the close involvement of the potential clients in the management of the program, in the choice of projects to be included in the program, and in the application of the findings which the program generated in response to the stated needs of the clients.

These conditions can be met by other forms of organization and by other forms of research/client relationships. In this paper two examples, taken from many, will be discussed which arose from the forest products research program while it was under the management of the Canadian Forestry Service. In a recent review of research and development in solid wood products, Mathur (1978) commented on technology transfer from both laboratories. Some recent achievements of these laboratories in forest products research include non-leachable fire retardants, waterborne preservative formulations, a steam press for manufacturing thick composite boards, a variety of methods to improve the process of wood and basic information for the engineered uses of wood in structures and housing. The two examples selected for this paper are the lumber slicer developed at EFPL and the WFPL method of finger-jointing. The first of these developments is now entering the commercialization stage, while the second is already in use in a number of industrial operations.

The general conditions which should be met in the invention, development and commercialization of a new technology seem to be:

1. The existence of a highly-motivated research group in touch with the research and industrial communities.
2. Some open research time for curiosity-motivated trials.
3. Responsive research management for the recognition of winners among the research ideas.
4. Early and continuing involvement of potential clients.
5. The availability of developmental and commercialization funds for promising inventions.
6. The existence of a technologically-aware and competent management group among the clients who must accept and utilize the new technology.

In forest products research there is another special condition which must be taken into account: familiarity with the changing nature of the resource and the problems associated with those changes. In the two examples being discussed, the relationship with resource problems is very clear. The balance of the forest resource is swinging with increased harvesting, from trees suited for production of long solid products of large cross-section to those more suited to fibre production. To counter this trend, the building-up of large-dimensioned solid products from smaller elements becomes very important. Finger-jointing is one of the more important techniques available to do this, and improvements in the technology such as that accomplished through the WFPL method become very important. The lumber slicing technology addresses another resource problem which is the increasing need for efficiency in utilizing a diminishing resource. The elimination of sawdust generation by the use of a slicing technology would release additional solid wood for other products to the extent of tens of millions of tons per year in Canada.

Of the above six conditions the first four can be established by the management of the research organization. To some extent the research organization can influence condition 6 as well by the transfer of appropriate information and advice to groups of clients. However, the need for greater numbers of highly trained scientific and management personnel is now being recognized as a priority and greater support of university programs to provide the requisite training is being suggested with increasing frequency.

Condition 5, dealing with developmental and commercialization requirements, is met to some degree within government by special funding associated with many R&D programs. One of the successful special funding programs conceived and originally managed entirely by the National Research Council of Canada is the Pilot Industry/Laboratory Program (PILP). The purpose of PILP is to support the development by industry of inventions by government researchers which have been developed and demonstrated at the laboratory level. PILP funds are playing an important role in the development of the lumber slicer to the commercially viable stage.

Condition 5, is also supported in Canadian government departments by the activities of Canadian Patents and Development Limited (CPDL), a Crown agency which is responsible for patenting inventions made through government programs as well as licensing their use so as to achieve maximum exploitation.

More details on each of the inventions follow:

## WFPL METHOD OF FINGER-JOINTING

The development of the finger-jointing of lumber at any given moisture content resulted from a spin-off from the basic research on the phenol-resorcinol resin systems at WFPL during 1975–77. Need for such a technology was apparent from the market trends. A reduction in clear grades and premium length of lumber was expected due to gradual disappearance of old growth forest stands and emergence of second growth stands with smaller average log size. At that point in time, the available technology required lumber to be at a moisture content of about 12 per cent. Use of radio frequency (RF) heating to obtain rapid cure of the glue lines, in order to obtain reasonable productivity from the jointing and assembly equipment, was prevalent.

Research at WFPL under Dr. Suzone Chow suggested that the best approach to the problem was to avoid the use of radio frequency entirely, either to set the glue lines or to pre-dry the wood.

For the conventional glues to function properly, the moisture content of the wood must be below about 20 per cent. Fundamental studies on the curing reaction for a phenol-resorcinol and phenol-formaldehyde resin explained the low temperature curing property of the former and this property was used to develop the WFPL finger-joint method.

In the WFPL method a simple technique was utilized that not only predries the surface of wood in the area to be glued, but also preheats the wood so that the desired rapid cure of the glue line can be obtained from the stored heat. The simplest means of accomplishing this is exposure of the piece to hot air, at a temperature that will not produce damage to the wood surface. The technique developed by the WFPL was granted a patent (Chow, 1976) in the U.S.A. and Canada.

The WFPL technique was demonstrated to produce joints on green lumber of as acceptable quality as those in kiln dried lumber. The green finger-jointed lumber met all the requirements of the Canadian Standard Qualification Code for manufacturers of glued end jointed structural lumber. An economic analysis from WFPL concluded that the new technique is economically viable and would provide substantial returns on the investment from finger-jointing green lumber for structural end uses. These activities convinced industry of the value of the new technique and at present six industrial plants in British Columbia are successfully utilizing the WFPL technique for finger-jointing green lumber for structural lumber end uses.

Acceptance of the WFPL method by industry has been aided by expeditious licensing arrangements made by CPDL and the willingness of WFPL staff to advise industrial users on the application of the new technology. An additional factor was that finger-jointing in other forms was already widely known and accepted for non-structural uses.

## LUMBER SLICER

Compression slicing of wood to produce lumber is a new technique that does not produce sawdust. It is also almost noiseless and introduces little wood dust or wood flour into the work environment. Such a slicer should also require much less maintenance than conventional saws.

J. S. Johnston and A. St-Laurent of EFPL were granted patents on the method of kerfless cutting of wood both in Canada and the U.S.A. (Johnston and St-Laurent, 1975, 1976). The lumber slicing technique involves applying a lateral pressure to the cant while a slicing knife penetrates it and cuts it into lumber. The pressure needed is of the order of two-thirds of the stress at the proportional limit of the wood. The wood can be sliced from the side or from the end. The most practical way is to do it from the end and to apply the lateral pressure by means of a non-friction device such as tyres or a caterpillar track. This lateral pressure device can also drive the cant past the knife to obtain slicing through the whole length of the cant.

A prototype slicer capable of operating at speeds of up to 100 m/min was built under PILP sponsorship by Black Clawson-Kennedy Ltd. who also assessed the prototype in mill trials. Because the original developmental contractor was not interested in further commercialization activities the license was granted by CPDL to Gar-hagon Ltd. PILP support is being extended to Gar-hagon for the development of a cheaper commercial model of the lumber slicer which will be expected to excite enough interest for substantial market penetration. It is thought that there is a market for about 500 such lumber slicers in Canada and the U.S.A.

The involvement of the private sector in the development and potential commercialization of the lumber slicer has been made possible by PILP support, CPDL co-operation, and the continuing involvement of the original EFPL inventors at each stage of the process.

## CONCLUSIONS

The inventions considered in this paper illustrate the importance of the six conditions covering the process of deriving an invention and the commercialization of it. These conditions were met while the forest products program under which most of the work was done was within the government departmental structure. However, there is no reason to suppose that a program under industrial or institutional forms of management need be any less productive.

The initial conception of the lumber slicer and the new method of finger-jointing was made by inventive and knowledgeable research scientists who had extensive outside working contacts and some spare time for curiosity-oriented trials. The management of the program made time available for extensive relevant applied research and called in a number of potential clients for information transfer and planning sessions. Guidelines for some of the applied research were provided by safety and product quality/performance standards such as those of the Canadian Standards Association.

At the appropriate point in development the services of Canadian Patents and Development Ltd. were called upon with regard to securing patents and also to plan subsequent exploitation. Mill trials were also arranged, as appropriate, with interested clients.

In the case of the new WFPL method for finger-jointing, conditions were right for an immediate application by industry, and this was done. However, there is usually a bridging period, with substantial financial requirements, for further development and engineering work related to commercialization. This is the stage to which the lumber slicer has progressed under PILP sponsorship.

Of the chain of events leading to the commercialization of the inventions, probably the most critical under current conditions are the existence of: (1) technically competent and action-oriented 'receptors' among management personnel in the private sector, and (2) funds from government or private sources that are specifically intended for the commercialization of new products or processes which have reached the end of the possibilities available under laboratory conditions.

**References**

MATHUR, V. N. P. (1978). *R&D in solid wood products.* Canadian Forestry Service, Information Report DPC-X-7.

CHOW, S. (1976). *Method of joining bodies of green lumber by finger joints.* U.S. Patent No. 3985169.

JOHNSTON, J. S. and ST-LAURENT, A. (1975). *Method for kerfless cutting wood.* U.S. Patent No. 3916966.

JOHNSTON, J. S. and ST-LAURENT, A. (1976). *Method for kerfless cutting wood.* Canadian Patent No. 932032 and 1044576.

# Planning and implementation of an acid precipitation technology transfer program

W. E. SHARPE

*School of Forest Resources and The Institute for Research on Land and Water Resources, Pennsylvania State University, University Park, Pennsylvania, U.S.A.*

## ABSTRACT

The philosophy of technology transfer is discussed within the framework of a research organization sponsored program. An example of technology transfer program planning for the restoration of waters acidified by acid precipitation and increasing public awareness about acid rain is given. Key planning elements are enumerated and a brief discussion of both the research and technology transfer resulting from planned implementation is presented. It is recommended that international technology transfer programs be adequately funded and that such activities should be part of the mission of international research organizations. It is further concluded that technology transfer planning will better utilize scarce available funds.

The terms 'information dissemination' and 'technology transfer' are often used to describe transfer activities. These terms are used interchangeably by many, while others insist that they describe two distinctly different activities. I would like to start by defining and explaining these terms. 'Information dissemination' can be defined as the act of informing or providing information about technological changes and advances through visual, audio, and written media. The end result of information dissemination is to create awareness and stimulate interest in new technological developments. Examples would be news releases, newsletter stories, brochures, and pamphlets designed to make audiences aware of new developments.

'Technology transfer' is the sum of those activities leading to the adaptation, adoption, or demonstration of new technology where the audio, visual, and written media provide a partial vehicle for accomplishing the transfer. As such, it includes, but is not limited to, information dissemination. An example would be an in-depth technical manual showing how new technology can be incorporated into existing procedures and techniques. Technology transfer is, by definition, a longer, more involved, active process and has the ultimate goal of seeing the technology transferred and incorporated into the accepted way of performing everyday functions or solving everyday problems. The process includes those products and situations that are directed toward a specific user's needs.

The technology transfer process most often requires extensive personal contact between the user of the technology and the individual responsible for transferring the technology. Although computerized literature retrieval systems, workshops and conferences, publications, technology demonstrations and mass media information techniques are important technology transfer methods, there is no substitute for one-on-one technology transfer. No matter how well technology is presented, it cannot suffice in easing the user through the clouds of doubt that are almost sure to appear at one stage or another in the implementation process. The most essential ingredient in any technology transfer program is personal contact. Personal contact is the mortar that binds all the techniques just discussed into the solid structure of a viable technology transfer program. When new technology is ready for demonstration, the more innovative users agree to try it. The success or failure of the demonstration will depend on many factors, but the probability of its failure will certainly be greatly increased if personal contact is not well established.

Information dissemination often precedes and follows technology transfer. That is, information dissemination, by creating an awareness of new technology, stimulates receptivity to the transfer and subsequent adoption of that technology. Once this has occurred, information dissemination is then used to tell that audience or other audiences of the experience. For discussions in this paper, technology transfer includes information dissemination.

An organization's basic philosophy of setting research priorities and determining areas of critical research needs will influence what technology transfer can take place. If immediate or future societal needs are not fulfilled by a research endeavour, transfer of the technology involved is likely to be difficult. Technology transfer must be recognized as a vital part of the organization's research mission; it is the economic payoff for the money spent for research. This payoff has often been measured in economic and social terms. Technological breakthroughs such as miniaturized circuitry and antibiotics are readily identifiable as having economic and social value. Unfortunately, the vast majority of new technological developments do not have such immediate and readily demonstrable payoffs. This is often the case with developments in forestry and water resources.

Once the technology transfer organization is in place there are many things to consider in planning specific technology transfer programs. A listing of key plan elements that we used in the planning of a lake restoration program for the now defunct Office of Water Research and Technology (OWRT), within the US Department of Interior, may serve as a useful example.

1. *Background*
   A brief description of the problem which led to past/present research and development efforts. Discuss how the results of the work can help in solving the problem. Discuss your organization's past involvement in increasing knowledge in this problem area.
2. *Identification and characterization of primary and secondary users*
   Identify all users who will at some time be on the critical path for the implementation of the results. Characterize these users by number, geographic distribution, required contribution to implementation, and the point in the implementation strategy where they must have the required information.
3. *Description of needs of primary users*
   Describe the type of information needed by each user group and the use to which the user group will apply the information. Discuss and identify the level of detail and limits of the required information.
4. *Identification and format of desired technology transfer products*
   Identify the technology transfer products required for each primary user group. Provide a suggested outline for the topics which should be covered in the technology transfer product. Review available technology transfer products.
5. *Analysis of cost to benefit for required products*
   Demonstrate that the results from preparing and distributing the technology transfer products will produce sufficient benefits to justify their preparation. Compare likely sequences of events for cases where the products are, and are not, produced.
6. *Recommendations for dissemination*
   Identify the most cost-effective method for disseminating each of the technology transfer products. Discuss major alternatives with the rationale behind the selection of the recommended mechanism.
7. *Recommendations for dissemination to secondary users*
   Outline the benefits and costs of including secondary users in the dissemination plan.
8. *Estimate of cost for total recommended program*
   Provide an estimate of the resources required to carry out the recommended strategy.

The scope of effort applied to plan preparation will of necessity be limited by the resources available to the planner. If the proposed effort is large, a detailed plan requiring a considerable amount of work may be necessary. The lake restoration plan was prepared for OWRT following this format at an approximate cost of $15 000 U.S. dollars. A less detailed plan would have cost less, a more detailed plan, more.

Adequate funding of technology transfer is essential to the success of a research program. Natural resources technology transfer programs have traditionally been underfunded in comparison to their companion research programs. In my view a minimum of 50 cents of every research dollar must be spent on technology transfer if the research-technology transfer program is to be of maximum benefit to society. The lake restoration technology transfer plan will not be implemented because OWRT was eliminated by budget reductions. The OWRT water resources research program would probably be alive and well today if it had made a stronger commitment to technology transfer.

In the development of the lake restoration plan considerable emphasis was placed on the judgements of professionals working in technology transfer or allied research in the subject matter area. Their input was solicited in detail during interviews that in some cases were a full day in length. The plan largely reflects those points of view upon which there was consensus among the interviewees.

Interviews of those individuals working on acid precipitation effects mitigation in the U.S. agreed that a large scale technology transfer program would be premature. Most of these individuals felt that additional research and demonstration of mitigation techniques was still required; consequently, the recommendation to OWRT was that they should not at that time proceed with plans to begin a technology transfer program on acid precipitation effects mitigation. However, it was suggested that OWRT prepare a popularized pamphlet informing users of the research that was underway on acid precipitation, including currently available results. The suggested vehicle was a research capsule report in the OWRT capsule report series. If such a pamphlet had been produced, it would most surely be enjoying much current popularity as the debate over acid rain control strategy rages in the U.S.

A major weakness of this plan was its failure to adequately evaluate the significant work conducted outside the U.S. on acid precipitation mitigation, particularly in Sweden. Acid lake rehabilitation in Sweden has moved beyond the demonstration phase to adoption and implementation; consequently, the recommendations in this plan may have been modified by more international input. The existence of a strong international technology transfer organization providing English translations of Swedish research on acid rain mitigation would have no doubt resulted in a better plan.

Our acid rain research program has been strongly influenced by the completed lake restoration technology transfer plan. We have begun a large research and demonstration project on the restoration of fisheries to acid rain impacted streams. Techniques such as instream refuge construction and groundwater development which have not been attempted elsewhere will be researched and demonstrated. As has been indicated earlier in the paper, research and technology transfer cannot be divided into two distinct parts, one totally separate from the other. They are companion activities with many interrelationships. The lake restoration plan could not have been completed without talking to both researchers and technology transfer specialists. In so doing some assessment of research needs is inevitable. Our current research and development effort in fisheries restoration was an obvious beneficiary of the lake restoration technology transfer assessment. In the future it may be feasible to obtain support for technology transfer planning if it is more closely aligned with research planning.

The lake restoration technology transfer plan called for an effort to increase public awareness about the acid precipitation problem through wider dissemination of research results. Our organization has begun to implement this recommendation in a variety of ways. Summaries of research findings have been prepared and numerous discussions have been held with news media representatives. These discussions have resulted in a number of printed stories in Pennsylvania newspapers. A concerted educational program mounted by a coalition of labour and environmental organizations has relied heavily upon these research result summaries in the preparation of a popularized pamphlet describing Pennsylvania's acid rain problem. A summary of acid rain research at The Pennsylvania State University has been prepared and published as a feature in the Institute for Research on Land and Water Resources Newsletter. Lastly, a colour slide program emphasizing currently available research results has been prepared and is being presented to interested civic groups.

This activity and similar ones by many other organizations have contributed to a much greater awareness and understanding of acid precipitation problems in the U.S. As a result of these awareness programs, the acid rain problem is currently receiving a great deal of attention at the federal government policy level. The culmination of this awareness program will be legislation that adequately reflects the current state of knowledge on acid rain, and effectively deals with the problem. Such legislation is likely to be enacted in the near future.

The lake restoration technology transfer assessment is an example of how to plan and implement a technology transfer program. I hope that its iteration here is helpful to the development of the IUFRO technology transfer program.

It seems to me that the problems of establishing an effective international technology transfer program are the same as those confronting national programs, only perhaps considerably more difficult and requiring greater resources. If at all possible, such a program should be tied very closely to a strong well funded international research organization. Careful planning must be done to maximize the benefits gained from the inevitable scarcity of funding. Such planning is essential to co-ordinate the many diverse activities being carried on around the world under a wide variety of sponsors. Emphasis should be placed on long term program continuity. The technology transfer organization should maintain a high degree of professional visibility so that it is well recognized by professionals around the world.

The United Nations Educational Scientific and Cultural Organization (UNESCO) has been a leader in co-ordinating world-wide water resources technology transfer programs. The recently released International Hydrologic Program (IHP) Phase III (1984–1989) plan details water resources technology transfer needs. According to this document, 70 per cent of the world's population has 5 per cent of the world's research and development capability. A monumental technology transfer task is indicated. In a letter asking for University support of the IHP program, the U.S. National Committee on Scientific Hydrology stated that UNESCO could not provide financial support. The IHP report states "Transfer of knowledge and technology as a means to increase the endogenous capacity of developing countries was one of the basic motivations of past IHP activities. However, the results achieved were not always at the level of expectations." It seems clear that adequate funding is not being provided for the UNESCO program. Technology transfer, like research, does not occur without funding. Adequate funding and good planning will spell success for international programs just as it has for national ones.

## References

DASCHBACH, M. H., ROE, E. M. and SHARPE, W. E. (1982). *Lake restoration technology transfer assessment.* Project completion report, Office of Water Research and Technology. Institute for Research on Land and Water Resources, The Pennsylvania State University, University Park, Pennsylvania, USA. 56 pp.

ROE, E. M. and SHARPE, W. E. (1983). *Water resources technology transfer handbook.* School of Forest Resources. The Pennsylvania State University, University Park, Pennsylvania, USA.

SHARPE, W. E. *et al.* (1977). *Water resources technology transfer: A guide.* Miscellaneous report of the Institute for Research on Land and Water Resources. The Pennsylvania State University, University Park, Pennsylvania, USA. 24 pp.

SHARPE, W. E. and DeWALLE, D. R. (1982). *Restoration of trout fisheries to headwater streams of the Laurel Hill area impacted by acid rain.* Research proposal submitted to Richard King Mellon Charitable Trusts, Pittsburgh, Pennsylvania, USA.

UNITED NATIONS EDUCATIONAL SCIENTIFIC AND CULTURAL ORGANIZATION. *International Hydrologic Program, Phase III (1984–1989).* Unpublished report.

# Safeguarding the resources of indigenous West African trees: an international venture exploiting physiological principles

F. T. LAST[1], R. R. B. LEAKEY[1] and D. O. LADIPO[2]
[1] *Institute of Terrestrial Ecology, Midlothian, U.K.*
[2] *Forest Research Institute of Nigeria, Ibadan, Nigeria*

## ABSTRACT

There is a predictably continuing and increasing demand (internal and external) for indigenous tropical hardwoods. In recent years the widespread planting of exotic pines, eucalypts and *Gmelina*, has begun to safeguard the supplies of fuelwood and pulp in tropical countries; but how should the resources of hardwoods be managed to ensure the commerical advantage accruing to the producer-countries and at the same time minimize pressures on surviving areas of intact natural forest ecosystems?

A collaborative study between the Forestry Research Institute of Nigeria, Ibadan, and the Institute of Terrestrial Ecology, U.K., has shown, since it was started in the early 1970s, how fundamental studies of branching patterns, including apical dominance, can be used with advantage to guide applied developments. From these studies it has been possible to (a) devise a predictive test that facilitates the early identification, within a few months, of genotypes that grow into trees of good form and appreciably better than average annual increment, and (b) develop methods of stockplant management to ensure a constant supply of uniform cuttings for vegetative propagation (from predictably desireable genotypes).

These advances were made with *Triplochiton scleroxylon* (Obeche). Because this major economic species produces relatively few germinable seeds and because this deficiency cannot yet be offset by artificial flower induction, it was essential to resort to vegetative propagation to ensure a predictable supply of planting stock. Bearing in mind that there are indications that clonal plantations of *T. scleroxylon* may yield marketable timber within 40 years, compared with 150–200 years in natural stands, isn't there a case for applying the same principles, but with different details (*vide* the predictive test for 'form'), to the conservation of hardwoods that produce seed prolifically, such as species of *Nauclea, Terminalia, Lophira* and *Lovoa* and, if pest problems can be resolved, *Chlorophora, Entandrophragma* and *Khaya?* It is argued that the management of selected clones is preferable to that of trees from unselected seed, at least in the short-term.

'Applying the results of forest research': by having this conference it is assumed that we have something to learn from each other and *ipso facto* this implies that there have been, and/or are, problems.

Our brief refers to the resources of indigenous West African trees. In this instance the problem can be characterized by a consideration of the rates of (i) deforestation and (ii) re-afforestation in relation to the sizes of the surviving natural resources. Whereas the annual rate of deforestation in seven contiguous coastal West and Central African countries is 772 000 ha, the area of plantations in these countries including species of *Pinus,* and broadleaved trees (species of *Eucalyptus, Gmelina,* and *Naclea diderrichii*), only totals 331 000 ha. That is, the annual loss is greater than the area of plantations ever established (in the seven countries); further, the annual loss is on average 1.4 per cent of the surviving resource. But this figure masks the conspicuous differences between the different countries. In the Ivory Coast the annual loss is 7.0 per cent; in Nigeria it is 4.8 per cent (Table 1).

Within each of these countries, many species contribute to the exports of roundwood, a major source of revenue (Table 2). In Nigeria species of *Afzelia, Antiaris, Guarea, Khaya, Terminalia, Ceiba pentandra, Chlorophora excelsa, Entandrophragma*

**Table 1. Forest statistics for some West and Central African countries in 1980 (areas in thousands of ha) (see Leakey and Last, 1983).**

| | Total area of moist forest | Annual losses by deforestation | Total area of plantations |
|---|---|---|---|
| Sierra Leone | 740 | 6 | 5.8 |
| Liberia | 2000 | 41 | 6.3 |
| Ivory Coast | 4458 | 310 | 44.9 |
| Ghana | 1718 | 27 | 75.3 |
| Nigeria | 5950 | 285 | 163.3 |
| Cameroon | 17920 | 80 | 18.5 |
| Congo | 21340 | 23 | 16.8 |
| Total | 54126 | 772 | 331.0 |

*cylindricum* and *E. utile, Gossweilorodendron balsamiferum, Lovoa trichilioides, Mansona altissima* and *Pycnanthus angolensis* have all contributed significantly, $>10^3 m^3 yr^{-1}$, but *Triplochiton scleroxylon* was predominant, as it has also been in Ghana and Ivory Coast. At different times *Entandrophragma cylindricum, E. utile, Lophira alata, Tarrietia utilis* and *Terminalia superba* have been pre-eminent in the other countries.

In Nigeria, *T. scleroxylon,* Obeche, reached a peak of 500–550 $10^3 m^3/yr$ in the late 1950s and early 1960s thereafter declining with a total export prohibition in 1975 (Figure 1). This drastic but understandable decision has not yet been taken in Ivory Coast, where *T. scleroxylon* is being seriously depleted. But shouldn't steps be taken now to ensure that the commercial advantage accruing to West, and Central, African countries from this, and other species, is not lost? However, time is short. In transfer of apposite techniques developed in other fields of applied biology it is essential to increase the awareness and understanding of politicians, and other decision makers, to the need to lessen the

**Table 2. Total volumes (1000 m³) of roundwood of the 14 most important broadleaved trees exported from Ivory Coast, Ghana, Nigeria, Cameroon and Congo during 1964 (Trade names in brackets).**

| | |
|---|---|
| A. Exported from all five countries | |
| *Entandrophragma utile* (Utile) | 680 |
| *Terminalia superba* (Afara/Limba) | 290 |
| *Khaya* spp. (African mahogany) | 230 |
| *Entandrophragma cylindricum* (Sapele) | 180 |
| *Lovoa trichilioides* (African walnut) | 45 |
| *Entandrophragma candollei* (Omu) | 24 |
| B. Exported from only four of the five countries | |
| *Triplochiton scleroxylon* (Obeche) | 1200 |
| *Entandrophragma angolense* (Gedu nohor) | 130 |
| *Chlorophora excelsa* and *C. regia* (Iroko) | 93 |
| *Mansonia altissima* (Mansonia) | 60 |
| *Afzelia* spp. (Afzelia) | 57 |
| *Ceiba pentandra* (Ceiba) | 32 |
| *Guarea* spp. (Guarea) | 31 |
| *Terminalia ivorensis* (Idigbo) | 29 |

Data taken from *Bois et forêts des tropiques* (1965).

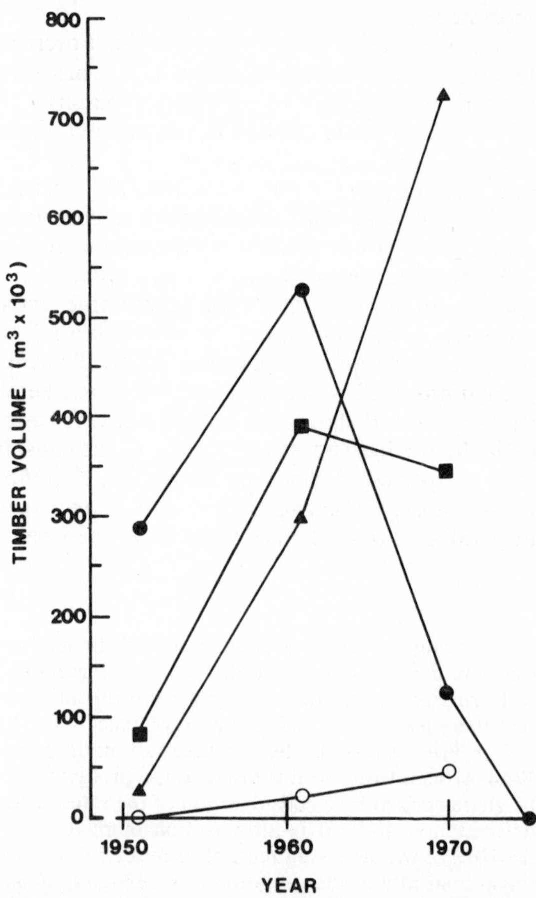


*Figure 1.* Annual round- and sawn- wood exports of *Triplochiton scleroxylon* from Cameroon (○), Ghana (■), Ivory Coast (▲) and Nigeria (●).

addition to the rapid pressures on surviving areas of natural forest, so conserving their soils and living gene-banks of differing assemblages of plants, animals and microbes. Conservation and the maintenance of economic advantage would both be served by the greater domestication of indigenous hardwoods (Leakey *et al.*, 1982b).

At this stage we would like to turn to *T. scleroxylon* and a case study. For a time it was tacitly assumed that the resource of this species, like others worldwide, would be sustained by natural recruitment and regeneration, but as we all know, the need for larger areas of agricultural land and the apportionment of land to towns and infrastructure and domestic animals, consequent upon effects of a burgeoning population, have, as in so many parts of the world, conspired to prevent this. But with *T. scleroxylon* there was another problem, namely the supply of seed.

In the early 1970s, members of a collaborative Nigerian/U.K. team, receiving funds from the U.K. Overseas Development Administration, investigated methods of maintaining seed viability. Howland and Bowen (1977) were able to show that the viability of seeds from green undried fruits was appreciably extended when stored at 0°C, instead of 30°C, an approximation to room temperature. Bowen *et al.* (1977) indicated that the ability to germinate was retained for 18 months, and probably longer, if the fruits of *T. scleroxylon* were slowly dried (1 per cent weight loss per hr) to 14 per cent moisture before being stored at −18°C. While these results are of continuing importance for the maintenance of gene-banks, they have had relatively little impact on man-made plantings because foresters have not been able to rely on dependable supplies of seeds. *T. scleroxylon* flowers erratically (Jones, 1974) and the development of fruits and seeds can be seriously impaired by pests and pathogens (Ashiru, 1975; Odeyinde, 1975). But this is not to imply that interesting plantings have not been made in mast years, e.g. the Kennedy plots at Sapoba.

Without plentiful supplies of viable seeds, how can we conceive of mounting a regular programme of *T. scleroxylon* re-afforestation? What of the potential of vegetative propagation? Iyamabo (1975) indicated that attempts were made in Nigeria between 1962 and 1966 to root cuttings from juvenile tissues of *T. scleroxylon* but they met with severely limited suc-

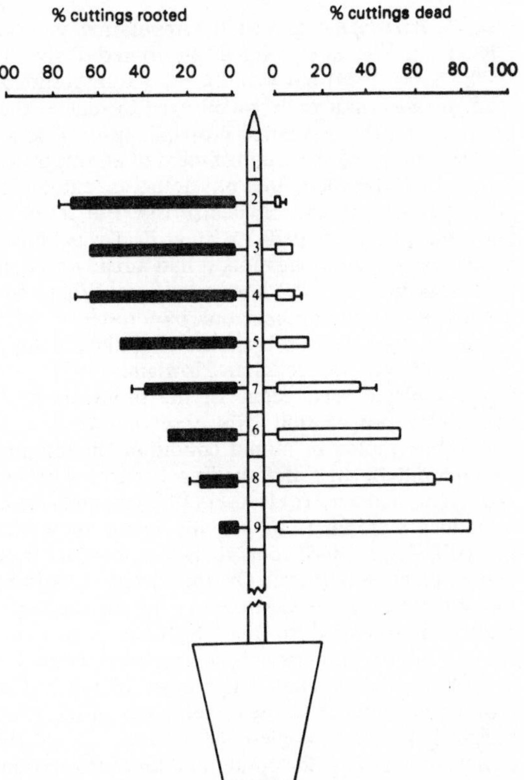


*Figure 3.* Mean effects, after 10 weeks, of node positions on rooting and death of single-node leafy mainstem cuttings from undecapitated stockplants of three clones of *Triplochiton scleroxylon* (Leakey, 1983).

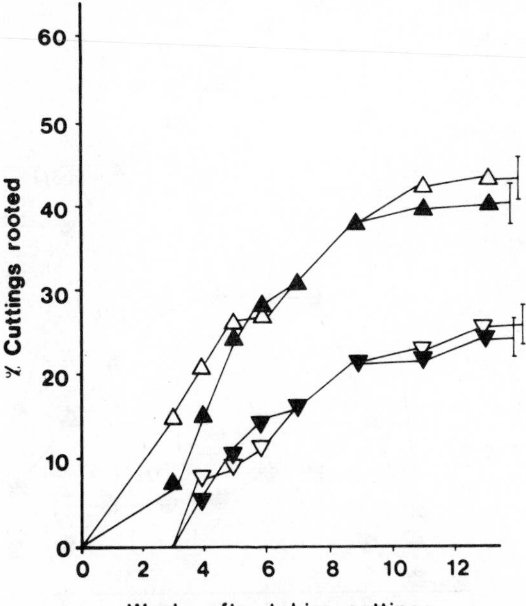


*Figure 2.* Effects of pretreating stockplants for 16 weeks with liquid fertilisers on subsequent rooting of leafy single-node cuttings of *Triplochiton scleroxylon* (Leakey, 1983) (▽, ▼, 0.4 per cent fertilisers; △, ▲, 4.0 per cent fertiliser).

cess. *T. scleroxylon* gained the reputation in both Ghana and Nigeria of being a 'shy-rooter' (Britwum, 1970; Okoro, 1974) but was this reputation justified? Iyamabo was sufficiently encouraged to suggest that the problem, the vegetative propagation of *T. scleroxylon,* warranted the establishment of an integrated team of tree breeders, tree physiologists, entomologists, mycologists and silvilculturists. But, even at that time (the early 1970s) a great deal was known about vegetative propagation, it had already become the stock-in-trade of horticulturists. What was needed was greater appreciation by foresters of what was being done in other branches of applied biology. With such an appreciation Howland (1975) was rapidly able to solve many of the problems of *T. scleroxylon* propagation. His observations that *T. scleroxylon* rooted in humid conditions maintained by intermittent mist and shading confirmed earlier deductions made by: (a) Heuser (1976) that it is easier to induce material from juvenile plants of woody perennials to produce roots than it is material from mature plants; and (b) van Overbeek *et al.* (1946) who found that leaf tissue was necessary for the successful rooting of softwood cuttings. Subsequently, many facets of propagation have been amplified (Leakey *et al.,* 1982a): the optimal temperature of the bed of rooting substrate, 28°C; the optimal area of leaf to be attached to each single-node cutting should be decreased to 50 cm$^2$, the optimum taking into account rooting and economy of space in propagating beds; the optimal application of auxins to the freshly cut basal ends of *T. scleroxylon* cuttings 10 $\mu$l MeOH droplets with 8–40 $\mu$g of a 50 : 50 mixture of $\alpha$-naphthalene acetic acid (NAA) and indole-3-butyric acid (IBA), according to clone.

The application of horticultural techniques to problems associated with root development in *T. scleroxylon* has obviously been richly rewarded. However, further progress has relied heavily on the physiological concepts of apical dominance or correlative inhibition, terms used to explain the control of branching in which terminal apices regulate the development of lateral shoots (*vide* Leopold, 1964; Wareing and Phillips, 1970).

In practice, apical dominance is broken when terminal buds are removed from stockplants when harvesting material (shoots/branches) for cuttings. As a result the remaining axillary buds develop into lateral shoots to produce the next crop of cuttings. But detailed investigations have unravelled an unexpectedly complex pattern of differences in rooting abilities (Leakey, 1983). It is one thing to get cuttings to root but another to obtain a consistent supply of uniform, easily-rooted cuttings: stockplant management is of fundamental importance. Applying a 4 per cent, instead of 0.4 per cent, complete fertiliser solution to stockplants for 16 weeks before harvesting cuttings significantly increased the rooting ability of that batch of cuttings (Figure 2). In contrast, rooting ability was decreased when cuttings were taken from stockplants that had been exposed to full, instead of 10 per cent sunshine, although the proportion of axillary buds which started to elongate after mainstem decapitation was greater (72 per cent) in full, than in partial (10 per cent), sunshine (Leakey and Ladipo, 1983). In addition to these external influences, rooting ability is strongly related to internal factors. When Leakey (1983), instead of decapitating stockplants to leave residual stems with a constant number of nodes, examined the effects of manipulating numbers of nodes in the range 10–30, he found that rooting ability of cuttings taken from the many lateral branches of 30 node-stockplants was less, 20 per cent compared with 85 per cent, than that of cuttings from the few lateral branches that developed on 10 node-stockplants, there being a strong inverse correlation between numbers of lateral shoots developing after mainstem decapitation and the ability of cuttings to root.

For the stockplant manager it is necessary to strike the right balance between numbers of nodes retained after decapitation (pruning) and the rooting ability of the cutting material that develops, he must optimize

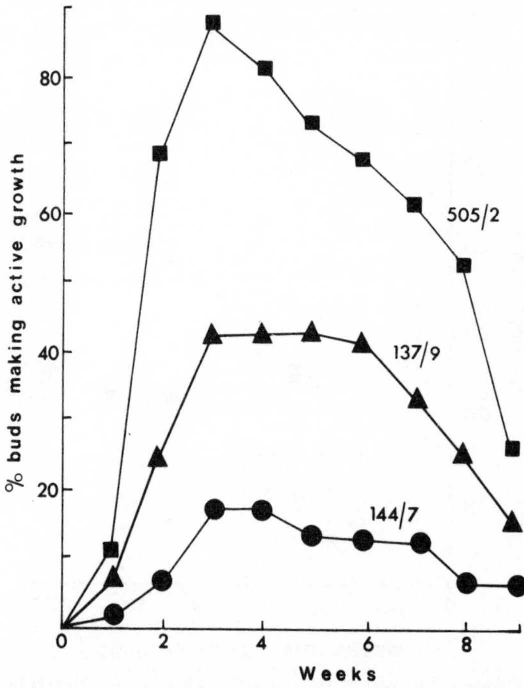


*Figure 4.* Proportion of axillary buds making active extension growth, >2 mm wk$^{-1}$, after decapitating small single-stem plants of three clones (137/9, 144/7 and 505/2) of *Triplochiton scleroxylon* (Leakey and Ladipo, 1983).

his yield. But there is another factor of importance, the stockplant manager's calculations must be made separately for each clone because the response of different clones to pruning differs greatly. Whereas every axillary bud developed a lateral shoot when stockplants of clone 505/2 were decapitated, only 20 per cent developed on clone 144/7 (Figure 4). This observation, however, is of more than immediate significance; it could, as will be seen later, be the key to the selection of clones for re-afforestation with *T. scleroxylon.*

While techniques of stockplant management and root induction have been evolved in glasshouses and nurseries in Edinburgh, U.K., and Ibadan, Nigeria, series of field trials have been planted in most years at Onigambari, a field station of the Forest Research Institute of Nigeria. With Dr. Ladipo, who became a fully integrated member of the team in the late 1970s, spending about half of each year at home in Ibadan and Onigambari and the remainder in Edinburgh, Dr. Leakey and Dr. Grace found that there was a strong direct relation (r=0.93) between: (a) total numbers of branches per tree, counted 4 years after establishing field plantings of rooted cuttings, and (b) the percentages of axillary buds developing after decapitating stockplants (Figure 5). Thus, what may appear to be a productive stockplant, that is a plant that responds to pruning (decapitation) by the prolific development of laterals, is the antithesis of the silviculturist's requirement. However for reasons attributable to the effects, already discussed, of internal and external factors, the propagator's ideal stockplant would only produce two lateral shoots after decapitation.

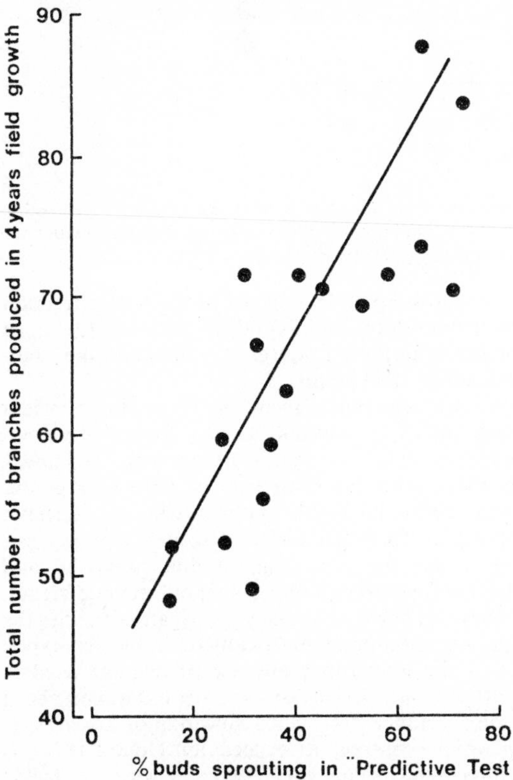


*Figure 5.* Relationship in *Triplochiton scleroxylon* between the proportion of mainstem axillary buds that actively grew 4 weeks after removing terminal buds (the Predictive Test) and the total number of branches produced during 4 years' growth in the field (Leakey and Ladipo, 1983).

With the strong relationship between form in the field and response to pruning in the nursery, we have the elements of a predictive test based on patterns of branching and enabling early selection. Total number of branches was also strongly and directly related to height in the field which in turn was positively correlated with diameter at breast height (Leakey and Ladipo, 1983). But will the relationships found after 4 years continue to be as strong? Will the harvest indices (the indicators showing the apportionment of dry matter to useful yield) of the different clones remain in the same relative positions to each other? (Sziklai, 1974).

Whatever the answers to these questions, we would argue that the predictive test, and its future variants, based on form characters, rather than volume production which is notoriously difficult to anticipate (Iwakawa *et al.,* 1967; Johnstone, 1973;), should be used to optimize the exploitation of natural variation. While mean form scores and mean stem volumes after 5 years of 14 seedlots of *T. scleroxylon,* collected in Nigeria, are relatively constant, the degree of variation found between the seven clones of each seedlot is extensive (Figure 6). A result duplicating that obtained by Kleinschmidt and Sauer (1976) who analyzed the variation in Norway spruce *Picea abies.* By restricting plantings of *T. scleroxylon* to the 33 per cent of clones with form scores and stem volumes both above average, theory suggests, if there are no interactions with silvicultural practices or severe within and between clone competition, that stem volumes would be increased by 31 per cent; the use of the best 10 per cent of clones might increase volumes by 81 per cent.

Theory is all very well but the final test is what actually happens in practice. By infusing horticultural expertise and an understanding of tree biology, we believe that many of the problems hindering the re-establishment of the resource of *T. scleroxylon* have been solved sooner than would have been the case if foresters had continued to work in isolation. Further, we strongly believe that the transfer of technology is only completed successfully if members of the team are fully integrated, in our example there

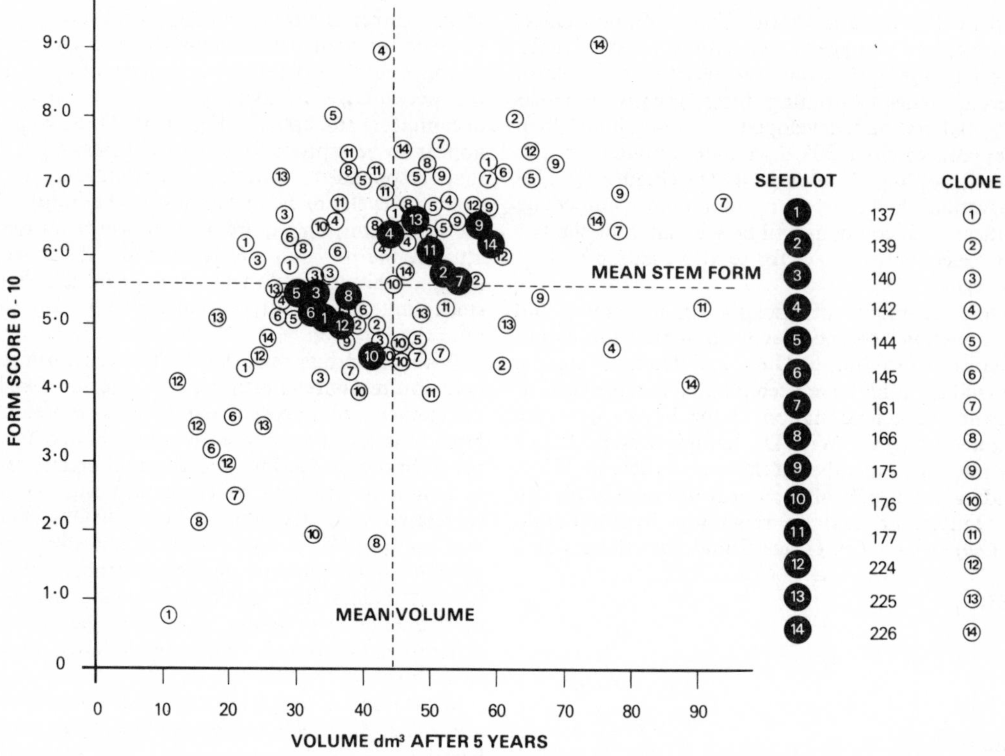


*Figure 6.* Relationship between volume of bottom log (4 m long) and score for stem form when assessed 5 years after planting rooted cuttings of *Triplochiton scleroxylon*: a comparison of variation between (i) clones (○) of the same seedlot and (ii) different seedlots (●) (137, 139, 140 . . . are seedlot accession numbers) (Leakey and Ladipo, 1983).

has been a repeated and continuing two-way exchange of staff between Nigeria and Scotland. In the type of work that we have been doing, the choice of individuals was, and will continue to be, the major consideration; the choice depending first and foremost upon temperment and then, and then only, upon scientific persuasion.

Contrary to the impression that we may have created, we have only skimmed the surface of the *Triplochiton* problem. To an extent, our task has been made easier because we have been able to devise methods, which are also being considered in the Ivory Coast, which can ensure a predictable supply of rooted cuttings compared with an erratic supply of seed; further the seed will be unselected, whereas the cuttings will be taken from selected stockplants. There still remains the problem of obtaining material from mature trees of good form which are not yielding seed. But, this problem may be more apparent than real because timber extractors concentrate their attentions on select specimens and as Howland (1975) has indicated coppice shoots from felled mature trees root relatively readily, unlike young shoots from undamaged mature trees. Thus, tree improvers would be well advised to keep an eye on the progress of extraction and the development of coppice shoots after felling a potentially important source of material for the establishment of stockplants.

We are very much aware of the need to consider wood quality in addition to stem form and vigour. Longman *et al.* (1979), working with *Terminalia superba,* found the diameters of fibre and parenchyma cells, the width of the xylem, etc., differed appreciably between different clones, and suggests that it may be rewarding in due course to add selection for wood quality to that of form and vigour.

As we all know, vegetative propagation enables the rapid exploitation of genetically desirable genotypes, but in the long run there is a predictable need to resort to controlled crosses. A start has already been made to induce precocious flowering of *T. scleroxylon* which, contrary to expectation (Jones, 1974), is outbreeding (Leakey *et al.,* 1981). However, to tackle the *Triplochiton* problem rationally, it is necessary to consider the widest possible spread of natural variation. Until now most of our work has been done with *T. scleroxylon* collections made in Nigeria but this species occurs, except for a break in eastern Ghana,

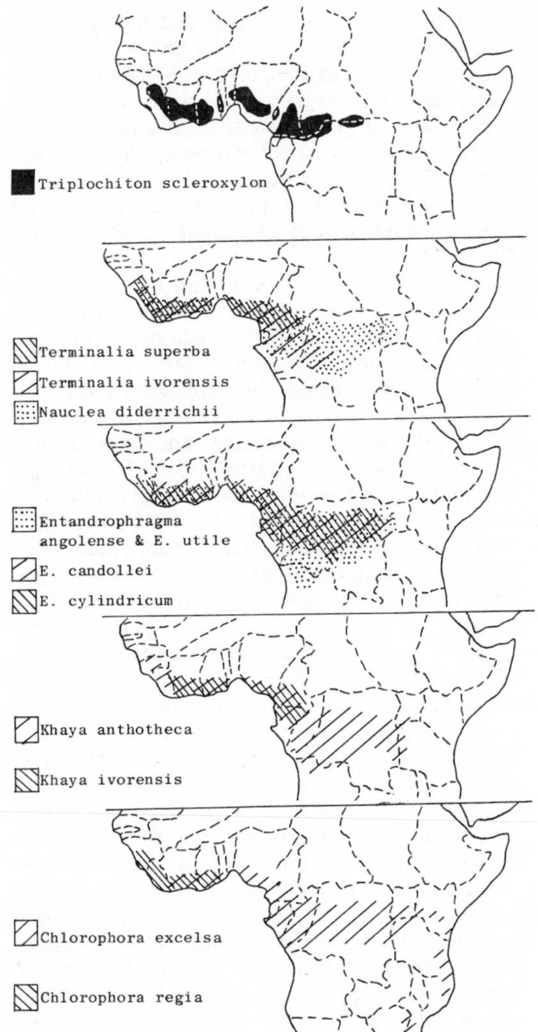


*Figure 7.* The natural distributions in Africa of 13 important broadleaved trees which are important components of the West African timber trade.

Togo and western Benin, in a coastal belt spreading from Sierra Leone in the west to Cameroon, and possibly Zaire, to the east. With knowledge of Norway spruce *Picea abies* in mind (Lines, 1974), it would be very suprising if Nigerian seed were to yield the best clones of *T. scleroxylon* for intensive management in Nigeria or, for that matter, Ivory Coast seed for the Ivory Coast. Thus afforestation in Nigeria would predictably benefit from links with Sierra Leone, Liberia, . . . and *vice versa.* But, at this stage, shouldn't we be thinking more boldly about the future? As it happens, the natural distribution of *T. scleroxylon* corresponds very closely with those of most of the important West African hardwoods, species of *Chlorophora, Entandrophragma, Khaya, Nauclea* and *Terminalia* (Figure 7).

While recognizing that there are some major pest problems to overcome and doubtless many silvicultural puzzles, should we continue to think in terms of using unselected seed for these species even if it is readily available? Our very simple predictive test with *T. scleroxylon* takes advantage of the responses of a genus whose branching pattern conforms to the Rauh architectural model (Figure 8). For the future we are confronted with the challenges of the Aubreville model, Roux and troll models as exemplified by *Terminalia* spp., *Nauclea diderrichii* and *Chlorophora excelsa,* respectively (Halle *et al.,* 1978). In doing so, however, we hope that our negotiations made with colleagues in Sierra Leone, Liberia, Ivory Coast, Ghana, Cameroon and, very importantly, the Centre Technique Forestier Tropical, Nogent-sur-Marne, France, will lead to regional collaboration in West and Central Africa, to service two priority objectives: to ensure the future availability of West African hardwoods; and to lessen the pressures on areas of tropical moist forest so as to aid their conservation.

As preliminary observations suggest that managed plantations of *T. scleroxylon* may be harvestable after 40 years, instead of the 150–200 needed in natural stands, there is some hope that our second objective will be attainable and not remain a pious hope. Both objectives are dependent upon the domestication of indigenous hardwoods (Leakey *et al.,* 1982b) and the establishment of productive plantations. In reality the transfer of technology to foresters may prove simplicity itself compared with the effort needed to persuade decision-makers of its potential worth.

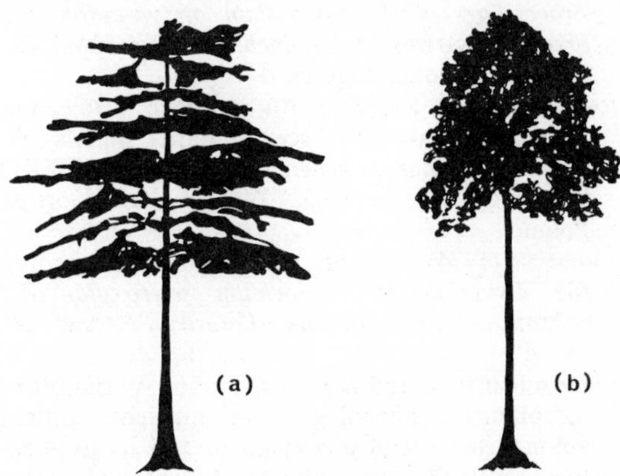


*Figure 8.* The silhouettes of (a) *Terminalia ivorensis* and (b) *Triplochiton scleroxylon,* the former conforming to the Aubreville model of branch architecture and the latter to the Rauh model.

**References**


ASHIRU, M. O. (1976). Some aspects of work on insect pests of leaves and fruits of *Triplochiton scleroxylon* K. Schum. In, *Proceedings of the symposium on variation and breeding systems of Triplochiton scleroxylon (K. Schum.).* Ibadan, Nigeria, 42–52.

BOWEN, M. R., HOWLAND, P., LAST, F.T., LEAKEY, R.R.B. and LONGMAN, K. A. (1977). *Triplochiton scleroxylon:* its conservation and future improvement. *Forest Genetic Resources Information* 6, 38–47. FAO.

BRITWUM, S. P. K. (1970). Vegetative propagation of some tropical forest trees. *Technical Newsletter,* 4, 1–15. Forest Products Research Institute, Kumasi, Ghana.

HALLE, F., OLDEMAN, R. A. A. and TOMLINSON, P. B. (1978). *Tropical forests, an architectural analysis.* Springer-Verlag, Berlin, Heidelberg and New York.

HEUSER, C. W. (1976). Juvenility and rooting cofactors. *Acta Horticulturae* **56**, 251–261.

HOWLAND, P. (1975). Variations in rooting of stem cuttings of *Triplochiton scleroxylon* K. Schum. In, *Proceedings of the symposium on variation and breeding systems of Triplochiton scleroxylon* (K. Schum.). Ibadan, Nigeria, 110–124.

HOWLAND, P. and BOWEN, M. R. (1977). *West African hardwoods improvement project research report, 1971-1977.* Federal Department of Forestry, Lagos, Nigeria.

IWAKAWA, M., WATANABE, M., MIKAMI, S., INUMA, M. and KIDA, S. (1967). Inheritance of some characters in open-pollinated progenies of *Pinus densiflora.* (In Japanese, with English summary). *Japanese Government Forest Experiment Station Bulletin* 207, 31–67.

IYAMABO, D. E. (1975). Address by the Director. In, *Proceedings of the symposium on variation and breeding systems of Triplochiton scleroxylon* (K. Schum.). Ibadan, Nigeria, 6–7.

JOHNSTONE, R. C. B. (1973). An approach to selection for second phase clonal seed orchards. In, *International symposium on genetics of Scots pine,* IUFRO Working Party 2.2.03.5., Warsaw and Kornik, Poland.

JONES, N. (1974). Records and comments regarding the flowering of *Triplochiton scleroxylon* (K. Schum.). *Commonwealth Forestry Review* **53,** 52–56.

KLEINSCHMIDT, J. and SAUER, A. (1976). Variation in morphology, phenology and nutrient content among clones and provenances, and its implications for tree improvement. In, *Tree physiology and yield improvement,* 508–517. Eds. Cannell, M.G.R. and Last, F.T. Academic Press, London.

LEAKEY, R. R. B. (1963). Stockplant factors affecting root initiation in cuttings of *Triplochiton scleroxylon* K. Schum, an indigenous hardwood of West Africa. *Journal of Horticultural Science* **58,** 277–290.

LEAKEY, R. R. B. and LADIPO, D. O. (1983). Selection for improvement in vegetatively-propagated tropical hardwoods. In, *Proceedings of 8th Long Ashton symposium "Improvement of vegetatively propagated plants".* September, 1982.

LEAKEY, R. R. B. and LAST, F. T. (1983). Past, present and future of West African hardwoods. *Timber Grower* **89,** 32–34.

LEAKEY, R. R. B., CHAPMAN, V. R. and LONGMAN, K. A. (1982a). Physiological studies for tropical tree improvement and conservation. Factors affecting root initiation in cuttings of *Triplochiton scleroxylon* (K. Schum.). *Forest Ecology and Management* **4,** 53–56.

LEAKEY, R. R. B., FERGUSON, N. R. and LONGMAN, K. A. (1981). Precocious flowering and reproductive biology of *Triplochiton scleroxylon* (K. Schum.). *Commonwealth Forestry Review* **60,** 117–126.

LEAKEY, R. R. B., LAST, F. T. and LONGMAN, K. A. (1982b). Domestication of tropical trees: an approach securing future productivity and diversity in managed ecosystems. *Commonwealth Forestry Review* **61,** 33–42.

LEOPOLD, A. C. (1964). *Plant growth and development.* McGraw Hill, New York.

LINES, R. (1974). *Summary report on the IUFRO 1938 provenance experiments with Norway spruce, Picea abies (Karsten).* Research and Development Paper 105, Forestry Commission, London.

LONGMAN, K. A., LEAKEY, R. R. B. and DENNE, M. P. (1979). Genetic and environmental effects on shoot growth and xylem formation in a tropical tree. *Annals of Botany* **44,** 377–380.

ODEYINDE, M. A. (1975). Observations on the smut infection of flowers and fruit development of *Triplochiton scleroxylon* (K. Schum.). In, *Proceedings of the symposium on variation and breeding systems of Triplochiton scleroxylon (K. Schum).* Ibadan, Nigeria, 53–56.

OKORO, O. O. (1974). *A preliminary investigation of rooting of stem cuttings of Triplochiton scleroxylon.* Research Paper (Forest Service) 28, Federal Republic of Nigeria, Ministry of Agriculture and National Resources. 5 pp.

VAN OVERBEEK, J., GORDON, S. A. and GREGORY, L. D. (1946). An analysis of the function of the leaf in the process of root formation in cuttings. *American Journal of Botany* **33,** 100–107.

SZIKLAI, O. (1974). Juvenile-mature correlation. In, *Proceedings of the IUFRO joint meeting of working parties on population and ecological genetics, breeding theory and progeny testing,* Stockholm, Sweden, 217–235.

WAREING, P. F. and PHILLIPS, I. D. J. (1970). *The control of growth and differentiation in plants.* Pergamon, Oxford.

# Application of research-based information to reforestation problems: an interdisciplinary approach

S. D. HOBBS
*School of Forestry, Oregon State University, Corvallis, Oregon, U.S.A.*

## ABSTRACT

A new program designed to intensify research and technology transfer developed as the result of severe reforestation problems in southwest Oregon. Under the leadership of the USDA Forest Service, Pacific Northwest Forest and Range Experiment Station, and the School of Forestry at Oregon State University, a two-phase program called the Southwest Oregon Forestry Intensified Research Program (FIR) was initiated in 1978. Fundamental phase scientists developed new information and technology from basic research. The adaptive phase is comprised of an interdisciplinary team of forestry specialists located in the problem area. Working closely with local forest resource managers, the adaptive phase team conducts educational and adaptive programs, and research studies designed to improve reforestation success and the utilization of existing research-based information.

### Introduction

Foresters have always recognized the need to stay informed of developing technologies and evaluate the applicability of new information to their specific management problems and forest environments. In the last decade a wealth of forestry research information has been produced, much of which is highly technical and specialized. This information often appears as mathematical models or complicated statistical procedures. Interpretation of information presented in this manner is difficult and therefore its utility is often overlooked. Furthermore, individual professionals tasked with the operational management of the forest resource are either unfamiliar with many of the technical journals or do not have easy access to them. These difficulties do not imply that forestry research scientists should simplify experimental approaches, analyses or presentations. Rather, there is a growing need for increased emphasis on research interpretation and the technology transfer process.

The lack of effective technology transfer has a particularly severe impact in locales faced with both difficult management problems and geographical dislocation from innovation centres typified by academic institutions and experiment stations. Southwest Oregon represents such an area and a new program in forestry technology transfer has been initiated to increase the level of information dissemination and innovation acceptance.

Southwest Oregon represents a five county area that extends northward from the Californian border for approximately 225 km and west from the crest of the Cascade Mountain Range to the Pacific Ocean. The total land area is 3 296 985 ha of which 2 480 327 ha represent commercial forest land (Bassett, 1979). The ecology has been described by Whittaker (1960), Gratkowski (1961), Waring (1969), and Franklin and Dyrness (1973). In general, this area is characterized topographically by narrow river valleys surrounded by deeply dissected mountains ranging up to 2890 m in elevation. Of these, the Siskiyou Mountains are the steepest and represent some of the oldest geologic formations in Oregon. The climate varies from cool and moist along a narrow coastal strip, to hot and dry in the interior valleys. A large portion of southwestern Oregon exhibits an almost Mediterranean-like climate with most of the annual precipitation occurring during the winter months. The soils are very diversified and reflect the extent of climatic and geologic variation found within the region. Many soils are well-drained and skeletal with relatively low moisture holding capacities. A mosaic of forest vegetative communities covers the landscape representing a unique flora influenced by the surrounding cover types of northern and eastern Oregon and northern California. The majority of commercial forest lands are in the Mixed-Evergreen and Mixed-Conifer Zones as described by Franklin and Dyrness (1973). Douglas fir (*Pseudotsuga menzieseii* (Mirb.) Franco) is the predominant species. Brushfields of sclerophyll species dot the landscape and reflect the historic influence of fire on the region's ecology (Gratkowski, 1961) as well as man's impact.

## THE PROBLEM

The forest industry in southwestern Oregon is not only vital to local economies but is also an important source of state and national timber supplies. During the period 1970 to 1974, approximately 33 per cent of the state's timber harvest came from southwest Oregon, as did nearly 5 per cent of the nation's lumber and 20 per cent of its veneer and plywood (Bassett, 1979). Maintenance or growth of the local timber products industry is not only dependent on national and regional economic conditions, but also on an adequate long-term timber supply. Recent large reductions in the southwestern Oregon timber harvest from public lands, as a result of actual and anticipated regeneration problems, will undoubtedly have an adverse impact on the region's future economic stability if solutions to this problem are not found. Vast areas of commercial forest land represent difficult-to-regenerate sites. The summers are long and hot with little, if any, precipitation, and many forest sites have shallow skeletal soils located in steep terrain. Surface debris and rock, known as ravel, frequently forms a constantly downward moving mantle over the underlying mineral soil, burying young seedlings in its path. Sclerophyll and deciduous brush species, as well as grasses, rapidly occupy site prepared areas, quickly utilizing limited resources. Animal and frost damage also contribute significantly to seedling mortality and growth reduction.

Prior to 1978, with the exception of Gratkowski's (1978) work on vegetation management, research efforts directed toward southwest Oregon were too few to adequately address the regeneration problem both in scope and intensity. Significant information voids specific to southwest Oregon exist in the areas of site preparation, site productivity and classification, vegetation management, site-specific reforestation prescription guidelines, and ecosystem impact of prescribed burning. While many of these problem areas represent fundamental or basic research needs where little information exists, there is a strong need to test the appropriateness of existing research-based technology. The application of research conducted in areas outside of southwest Oregon, without the benefit of well-structured local field trials, has in some cases led to reforestation failure. The need to test alternative treatments on a site-specific basis is important to the formulation of potentially successful reforestation prescription guidelines.

Technology transfer programs designed to produce change or innovation-adoption have been insufficient to meet the reforestation challenges facing foresters and other natural resources managers in southwest Oregon. This is not surprising if we consider the classical diffusion-adoption model for innovation acceptance as discussed by Muth and Hendee (1980). They identified four major factors important to innovation adoption: (1) the characteristics of the innovation; (2) the media used to communicate information about the innovation; (3) the individual and group processes required for adoption; and (4) the characteristics of the social system in which the innovation is diffused. Although existing technology transfer programs at the state and federal level met model requirements, they were not of sufficient intensity to produce rapid change. Much of this failure occurred because innovation centres dealing in forestry research and education are geographically far removed from the problem area. Consequently much effort has been directed at dissimilar forests further to the north. Geographic distance between innovation centres and clientele decrease program effectiveness by stretching lines of communication. This is not only true for information flow from the researcher to the clientele, but also the transmittal of research needs and priorities from the clientele to the researcher. Muth and Hendee (1980) recognized personal contact as a major factor influencing opinion leaders, the individuals primarily responsible for innovation diffusion through the social system. The lack of constant personal contact between the researcher and the clientele contributed significantly to the information flow problem in southwestern Oregon. Clearly, an intensification of the technology transfer effort was in order.

## INTENSIFIED PROGRAM

Recognition of the emerging reforestation problem and its potential economic impact on southwest Oregon stimulated a concerted effort by county government and local forestry leaders to seek a long-term solution. Consequently, during the 1977–78 winter, representatives of county government, the timber industry, USDI Bureau of Land Management, and USDA Forest Service, approached Oregon State University (OSU) and the USDA Forest Service Pacific Northwest Forest and Range Experiment Station (PNW) for assistance. Subsequent meetings produced the Southwest Oregon Forestry Intensified Program (FIR) under the leadership of the School of Forestry of OSU and PNW. The objective of this ambitious ten year project is to improve reforestation success in southwestern Oregon with a combination of fundamental and adaptive research, and a more aggressive technology transfer program. To accomplish this, the FIR Project was divided into two phases operating simultaneously: (1) the fundamental phase, and (2) the adaptive phase.

Under the leadership of PNW, Forest Service and OSU scientists initiated the fundamental phase in 1979. Focusing on basic biological problems confronting reforestation efforts in southwestern Oregon, researchers developed a number of diverse studies designed to produce new information and technology. Although the need for fundamental research was identified early in the development of the FIR Program, the expanded research effort would not solve two problems considered crucial to improved reforestation. These are: better utilization of existing information; and more effective technology transfer. Located 350 km north of Medford, the largest city in southwestern Oregon, Corvallis-based educators and scientists could not maintain the level of personal contact necessary to adequately address these problems. The basic problem of communication with the information user would not change in intensity with the advent of fundamental FIR. This eventuality was foreseen by the program architects and a special interdisciplinary team of OSU forestry specialists was formed to deal with the problems of adaptive research (application of existing research-based information to local conditions) and technology transfer. This OSU faculty team constitutes the adaptive phase of the FIR program.

The adaptive phase was initiated in Medford in 1978, one year before the start of the fundamental phase. Administratively, it is the responsibility of the School of Forestry at OSU. Each specialist's time is equally divided between research and extension to ensure a balanced and continuous link between research technology transfer functions. Team composition, in terms of expertise, was governed by recognition of the fact that reforestation is a complex and multi-facet process. Reforestation success can be affected at any point from choosing the harvesting system through plantation management after outplanting. Major adaptive phase problem areas were identified and specialists appointed to deal with each. These problem areas are silviculture systems, artificial regeneration technology, brushfield reclamation, soil and watershed management and forest engineering. Although primary responsibility for each problem area is assigned to an individual specialist, the majority of adaptive research studies and education programs usually involve two or more members of the team.

The identification of broad problem areas provided general program guidance, but more specific areas for effort concentration were needed. Consequently, during the first year of operation, specialists held a series of problem analysis workshops at several locations throughout southwest Oregon to seek clientele advice on adaptive research educational program direction. These meetings provided FIR specialists and clientele opinion leaders with an opportunity to interact and identify more specific problems while establishing research and education priorities. This advice has set the course in program direction for the adaptive phase. Research studies and educational programs have been initiated throughout southwestern Oregon with the assistance of local co-operators.

Adaptive research or the application of existing research-based information to local conditions, has served a valuable function in the technology transfer process. The research conducted by the adaptive FIR team is characterized by field-oriented studies utilizing uncomplicated, statistically sound, experimental designs to solve specific problems. The results of such research can usually be translated into immediate operational change. Examples of adaptive research are typified by such studies as those designed to evaluate the survival and growth of different Douglas fir stocktypes on skeletal soils or the impact of shelterwood overstory removal in established regeneration on steep terrain. The utility of such studies to technology transfer lies partly in the fact that the research sites themselves are highly visible, easily accessible, and have involved one or more opinion leaders as co-operators. The involvement of individuals in adaptive projects who can enhance innovation-adoption from within co-operating organizations, greatly improves information flow and innovation-implementation. Adaptive research conducted locally, with the co-operation of group opinion leaders, has a high degree of credibility.

The nature of adaptive research as conducted by the FIR team closely addressed the factors of the diffusion-adoption model for technology transfer discussed by Muth and Hendee (1980). The first factor concerns the characteristics of the innovation which can be divided into five components: (1) relative advantage, (2) compatibility, (3) complexity, (4) trialability, and (5) observability. Consider the adaptive research study designed to evaluate the survival and growth of different Douglas fir stocktypes on skeletal soils. If it is determined that the use of container-grown seedlings is more appropriate on sites with skeletal soils than the more widely used bare-root stock, then a relative advantage will have been gained in terms of added survival and growth.

This has particular economic ramifications because many sites with skeletal soils in steep terrain have been withdrawn from the timber harvesting base because of reforestation problems. A shift to the operational use of more container-grown Douglas fir seedlings on these sites would certainly be compatible with traditional forestry values and the economic need to maintain the commercial forest land base. Such a change would be relatively easy to put into operation and would not necessitate complex changes. Multiple, small stocktypes could be installed with little effort on a trial basis by area foresters prior to widespread use. Side-by-side stocktype comparisons are easily observed and the results frequently quite obvious. Research designed around these five innovation characteristics provides the information foundation of technology transfer.

Solving forest management problems through fundamental and adaptive research does not necessarily guarantee effective technology transfer. Adaptive phase specialists provide the media necessary to present information and stimulate the individual and group processes required for innovation-adoption. These last two represent the second and third factors in the diffusion-adoption model discussed by Muth and Hendee (1980). To accomplish this vital function, specialists co-ordinate and present information diffusion programs for southwestern Oregon clientele. A particularly useful method of mass media dissemination has been a quarterly newsletter designed for the professional forest resource manager. The status and intermediate results of fundamental and adaptive research studies are summarized, technical topics of interest discussed, abstracts of recent publications provided, and upcoming workshops, symposia and short courses listed. The clientele are exposed to a wide variety of forestry subjects and their interest repeatedly stimulated. This point cannot be over-emphasized and is one identified as significantly contributing to innovation-adoption (Muth and Hendee, 1980). In the southwest Oregon program, these contacts manifest themselves in the form of office consultations, field trips to visit and discuss specific problem sites, and advice on the design and analysis of field trials conducted by the co-operators. It is the continuous personal contact with opinion leaders that facilitates information-diffusion through organizations with established social structures. This is an important point since characteristics of the social structure have an effect on the technology transfer process (Muth and Hendee, 1980). This level of intensified effort could not have been realized had the entire FIR program been based outside of the problem area.

Moeller and Shafer (1981) studied 81 USDA Forest Service research case histories considered to be successful projects and identified 22 factors important to the innovation process. The top 13 factors they identified can be found as elements in the FIR program and have provided the framework for its formation and administration. The most important factor cited was the need for adaptation of existing technology. In particular, they described the possible requirement for SWAT (solved with adopted technology) teams to concentrate on practical problems. There is little doubt that the decision to establish a local interdisciplinary team of research and education specialists has done more to ensure effective technology transfer than any other single factor. The adaptive phase of the FIR program has provided the vital communication link between the forestry innovation centre and the forest resource managers in southwest Oregon by acting as a local centre for information-dissemination.

## CONCLUSIONS

The solution of severe forest management and silvicultural problems occurring in areas far removed from forestry innovation centres can be facilitated by the development and implementation of comprehensive programs designed to intensify research and education efforts. Such programs should employ elements of fundamental research, adaptive research and technology transfer in an integrated effort to produce innovation-adoption and the utilization of existing technology. A key factor in the organization is the permanent location of research and education specialists as an interdisciplinary team in the problem area. This greatly facilitates the flow of information to society opinion leaders and the rapid adoption of more effective technology.

### References

BASSETT, P. M. (1979). *Timber resources of southwest Oregon.* USDA Forest Service Resource Bulletin PNW–72. Pacific Northwest Forest and Range Experiment Station, Portland, Oregon. 29 pp.

FRANKLIN, J. F. and DYRNESS, C. T. (1973) *Natural vegetation of Oregon and Washington.* USDA Forest Service General Technical Report PNW–8. Pacific Northwest Forest and Range Experiment Station, Portland, Oregon. 417 pp.

GRATKOWSKI, H. (1961). *Brush problems in southwestern Oregon.* USDA Forest Service, unnumbered report. Pacific Northwest Forest and Range Experiment Station, Portland, Oregon. 48 pp.

GRATKOWSKI, H. (1978). *Herbicides for shrub and weed tree control in western Oregon.* USDA Forest

Service, General Technical Report PNW–77. Pacific Northwest Forest and Range Experiment Station, Portland, Oregon. 48 pp.

MOELLER, G. H. and SHAFER, E. L. (1981). Important factors in the forestry innovation process. *Journal of Forestry* **79**(1), 30–32.

MUTH, R. M. and HENDEE, J. C. (1980). Technology transfer and human behavior. *Journal of Forestry* **78**(3), 141–144.

WARING, R. H. (1969). Forest plants of the eastern Siskiyous: their environmental and vegetational distribution. *Northwest Science* **43**(1), 1–17.

WHITTAKER, R. H. (1960). Vegetation of the Siskiyou Mountains, Oregon and California. *Ecological Monographs* **30**, 279–338.

# A research planning strategy to assess the impacts of air pollutants on forest resources

J. E. FORCE
*Department of Forest Resources, College of Forestry, Wildlife and Range Sciences, University of Idaho, Moscow, Idaho, U.S.A.*

## ABSTRACT

A systems analysis approach is used to develop a strategy for planning a program to conduct research on the most salient relationships between forest resources and air pollutants; to determine the societal impacts of such interactions; and to consider the likelihood of implementation prior to beginning the research. A conceptual framework allows research planners and decision makers to formulate any research question as a set of basic system components and to consider such questions in the context of the entire Resource Pollutant Research System (RPRS). Given the many possible relationships in the RPRS, a normalized weighting model is proposed to assist research planners in determining the most important relationships to be examined in the research program. Additional tactical factors in research planning are also considered. This strategy can be readily adapted for planning research programs and implementing research results to other environmental stresses on resources.

### Introduction

The dependence of resource managers and decision makers on information from the research community is increasing because of expanded environmental awareness and greater demand for the goods and services provided by forests. A strategy for planning a research program that will provide results which resources decision makers can implement is presented.

The study focused on air pollution which is one of the least understood threats to the maintenance of productive forest ecosystems. Although we have been aware of air pollution effects on vegetation since the early 1900s (Swain, 1949), little research was done until the 1960s. Today there is a need for an expanded research program because air pollution is no longer restricted to easily controlled point sources; the impacts of air pollutants on forest vegetation are very complex; the National Environmental Policy Act of 1970 requires information on the environmental impacts of development on all forest resources; and we need to compare the costs and benefits of controlling air pollutants with those associated with our forest resources.

The objectives of this study were: (1) to develop a structure which allows research planners to formulate questions as a set of elements in a research system; (2) to suggest a weighting model to aid in determining the relative importance of possible research questions; and (3) to consider additional tactical factors in research planning and implementation.

## RESEARCH PLANNING

When a research program is begun, the determination of the research questions depends upon who plans the research and what process is used. There is no empirically proven best way to select the persons or the process. Within the scientific community it is often assumed that the researcher generates the next question and selects problems to study. When a formal approach is used, two models dominate the research planning literature: the convening of experts model and the problem rating model.

### Convening of experts model

The convening of experts model is widely used by the research community. (For examples see Dochinger and Seliga, 1976, and National Academy of Sciences,

1975). Although widely used, this model has several disadvantages: (1) there is often uncritical acceptance of the expertise of the speakers; (2) little time may be available for studied debate of the issues or of the contribution of any individual; (3) subjective weightings tend to be assigned to recognized authorities; (4) it is difficult to quantify the process; (5) sampling of experts may be biased; and (6) variability in the views of the scientific world may be suppressed (Holdgate and White, 1977). The last two disadvantages are sometimes considered advantages because they fulfil the traditional process of screening capability and knowledge. Care must be taken that the process does not over-emphasize already recognized problems and under-reflect more subtle but equally important ones. The research program identified using this model is often difficult to implement after the meeting ends unless one organization is responsible or compelled to proceed accordingly.

Another important limitation of this model is that it usually includes no formal attempt to determine a consensus of research priorities. Research administrators require a prioritized list of research needs and may prefer a list representing the consensus of experts. This requirement may contradict the objectives of the expert scientists who are concerned with pursuing their own research interests and may not benefit from prioritized lists reached by consensus.

**Project rating models**

The major alternative to the convening of experts model is some variation of a project rating model. This type of quantitative evaluation technique subjects the decision making process to formal analysis by making explicit the value judgements underlying decisions about research priorities. The process of formalizing and quantifying subjective judgements is often criticized because there is no empirically testable right or wrong answer (Nash *et al.,* 1975). The underlying assumptions inherent in the mathematical techniques are sometimes considered invalid or are not recognized and understood by those who are rating projects. (For examples of some rating models see Dochinger and Pell, 1976; Platt, 1969; and Sparrowe and Wight, 1975).

## THE RESOURCE POLLUTANT RESEARCH SYSTEM

In this study a systems approach is used to design a structure called the Resource Pollutant Research System (RPRS). Churchman (1968) defines a systems approach as follows:

> "Systems are made up of sets of components that work together for the overall objective of the whole. The systems approach is simply a way of thinking about these total systems and their components."

Systems can be thought of in a mathematical sense as relations defined by sets (or components) and elements of the sets which must be defined.

Relevant to this research planning situation is Ravetz's (1977) concept of 'critical science'. Critical science investigates problems whose correction will involve inconvenience and costs. Inquiry into such problems is, "largely futile unless it is followed up by exposure and campaigning; and hence critical science is inevitably and essentially political." This added dimension of the scientist assuming responsibility to transfer knowledge to the public and to decision makers and to campaign for actions to be taken is appropriate for research on air pollution, which is created by human activities. Mitric's (1977) definition of research is appropriate for a research system. He defines research as, "an information system whose goal is to facilitate a decision process." If research results are to be applied the research must produce information for making decisions.

**Components of the RPRS**

The following assumptions underlie the Resource Pollutant Research System:

1. Interactions of forest resources and air pollutants in the presence or absence of other environmental factors result in biochemical, physiological and ecological responses.
2. The observation and measurement of these responses produce data.
3. These data on responses can be processed or translated into a form that can be internalized and used by decision makers as information.
4. Changes in the socio-economic value associated with the information by society will determine the impacts of air pollutants on forest resources.
5. Various actions, which will either allow or prevent the interactions of resources and pollutants to occur, can be taken by decision makers.

These assumptions identify the following nine basic components or defining objects of the RPRS: forest resources, air pollutants, environmental factors, responses, data, information, impacts, actions and decision makers. These components are shown in Figure 1 with the arrows representing relationships between components. In the RPRS the forest resources component is composed of five major elements: timber, recreation, range, water, and wildlife and fish. Each of these elements can be further subdivided into subelements. For example, the timber element is composed of a species set and a products set. The elements of the air pollutant component are the individual substances added directly or indirectly to the atmosphere by human activities. The environmental factors component is divided into abiotic and biotic elements. The abiotic element consists of two classes: climatic factors and edaphic factors. The biotic element is composed of

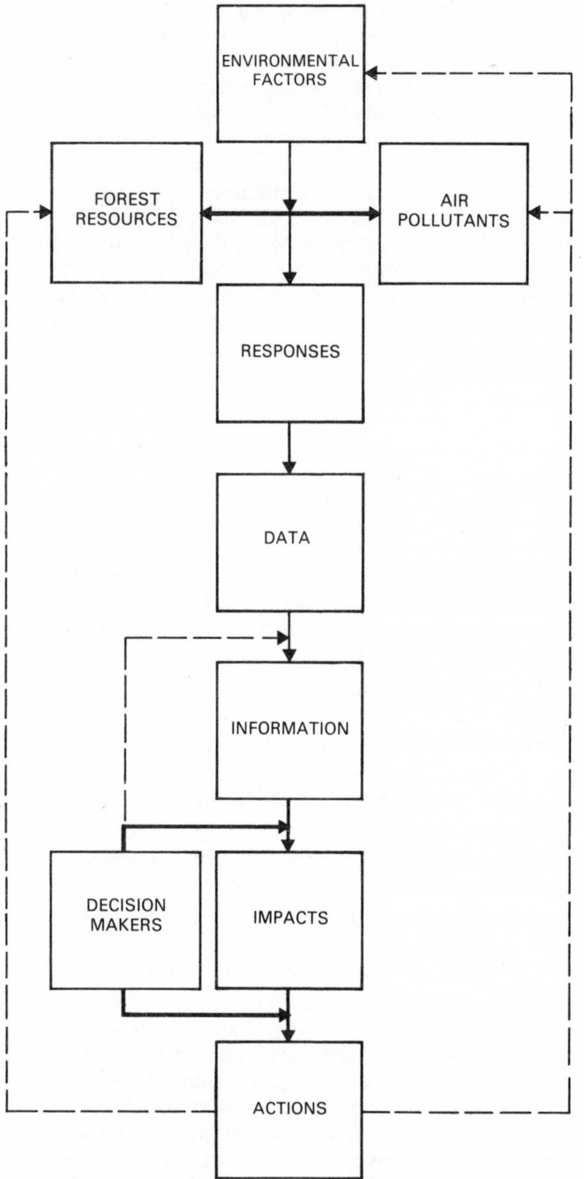


*Figure 1.* The Resource Pollutant Research System.

insects and diseases that may attack forest vegetation which is being affected by air pollutants or may change the vegetation's susceptibility to air pollutants. Responses are explicitly defined as biochemical, physiological, and ecological reactions resulting from air pollutant stimulation of elements of the biotic and abiotic forest environment.

The data component consists of observations or measurements of responses occurring when air pollutants interact with forest resources. The data component is explicit from the responses component to conceptually separate those components which represent the physical world, which the research system is concerned with, from those components representing human interpretations of that world. Data obtained about responses are not always information. For the purposes of this analysis, information is defined as data that have been processed and made available to decision makers in a form which is useful to them (Teeguarden, 1977). To some people the data set and the information set may be identical. However, this distinction is made because most of the available data have not been translated into a form that is understood by or useful to the people who have to make decisions about the impacts of air pollutants on forest resources. For example, a reduction in the rate of photosynthesis of a commercial timber species may be response data of little use to many forest managers until it is translated into estimates of reductions in annual growth. The data may require further interpretation into economic measures before it becomes information useful to some decision makers.

Impacts are defined in this system as changes in the socio-economic value of a resource as a result of forest resource-air pollutant interaction. These evaluations by decision makers are value judgements. There are not intrinsically right or wrong answers. In the above example, if we assume that a change in the monetary values is a measure of how society values forests, then there is an economic impact on the timber resource. This same response, data, and information may have no impact on the values society assigns to the forest's recreation resource, particularly if no visible symptoms are present.

These distinctions among responses, data, information and impacts are necessary if the RPRS is to be an information system. To some people there may appear to be considerable overlap between these components. The following example will make the differences clear and highlights the importance of identifying research which is an information system (Mitric, 1977) and produces results which can be applied. If we are concerned about the impact of sulfur dioxide from a coal fired power plant on commercial pine stands in the vicinity, the pathologist may observe and collect data on the percentage of dead or damaged needles. This may be information to him/her, but it may only be data on a biological response to the Power Plant Siting Commissioner who must compare it to information on sulfur dioxide emissions and the costs of preventing the emission. If the biologist can collect other data or work with a mensurationist to transform this data into measures of growth and yield and then ask an economist to assign a dollar value to this change in the pine stand, the Commissioner may consider it information. When this information is assigned a societal value or utility by the Commissioner, one type of economic impact is determined and can be compared to the impact on the society having or not having the power plant.

The actions component of the RPRS is composed of behaviours which will lessen the negative impacts and are available to decision makers. If the results of research are to be applied to improve the productivity of our forest resources, attention must be given to possible actions prior to beginning the research. If it is recognized that the cost of correcting or preventing the worst possible impacts are greater than the value of the resource, the researchers must recognize that the probability that the research information will be applied is extremely small. Also, consideration of the actions available to reduce or prevent the impact prior to conducting the research may influence the type of assessment that is performed and the information that is desired. (For a complete development of the RPRS, see Force, 1978).

The RPRS provides a structure that allows research planners and decision makers to make explicit all the various questions. Combinations of component elements generate research questions. The problem now facing research planners is one of information overload. Methods are needed to help identify those component relationships that can be most productively studied and should be included in the research program.

## IMPORTANCE WEIGHTING MODEL

The importance weighting model (IWM) provides research planners with a pragmatic approach using simple mathematics for examining and prioritizing the possible relationships between forest resources and air pollutants. The IWM is composed of four factors: (1) the physical resource base (RB); (2) the pollutant exposure (PE); (3) the sensitivity of the resources to the pollutant (S); and (4) the relative importance of the resource (RI). The following premises about research on forest resources underlie these factors:

1. The research should initially be proportional to the physical amounts of the various resources available in the study region;
2. It should reflect the proportion of resources exposed to air pollutants;
3. It should consider the variation among resources in the degree of sensitivity to air pollutants and the threat of the pollutant to the maintenance of the resource; and
4. It should recognize the difference in the values society places on various forest resources.

The importance weight (IW) for resources (r) is equal to the normalized product of the four factors:

$$IW_r = \frac{(RB_r)\,(PE_r)\,(S_r)\,(RI_r)}{\sum_{r=1}^{n} (RB_r)\,(PE_r)\,(S_r)\,(RI_r)}$$

Together the resource base and pollutant exposure factors determine the physically threatened population for the geographic region of concern. Because forest resource elements are not equally responsive to air pollutants nor equally valued by society, research planners must consult scientists to rate the sensitivity of each resource and decision makers to provide measures of the relative importance of each resource.

The final $IW_r$ in this model describes the relationship of resource r and pollutant p in comparison to the others in the study region. Because the importance weights are normalized, one possible use of the final $IW_r$ is as a guideline to describe the proportion of research efforts to direct towards a given relationship within this set.

## ADDITIONAL TACTICAL FACTORS

Several additional tactical factors in the overall strategy should be recognized before accepting the potential research program identified by the IWM. Two factors are discussed here.

### Known information

The research planners must determine what is known about each forest resource-air pollutant relationship that is identified using the IWM. Figure 2 presents a series of questions to determine which relationships in the RPRS are understood and defines specific research actions to take in the context of the RPRS.

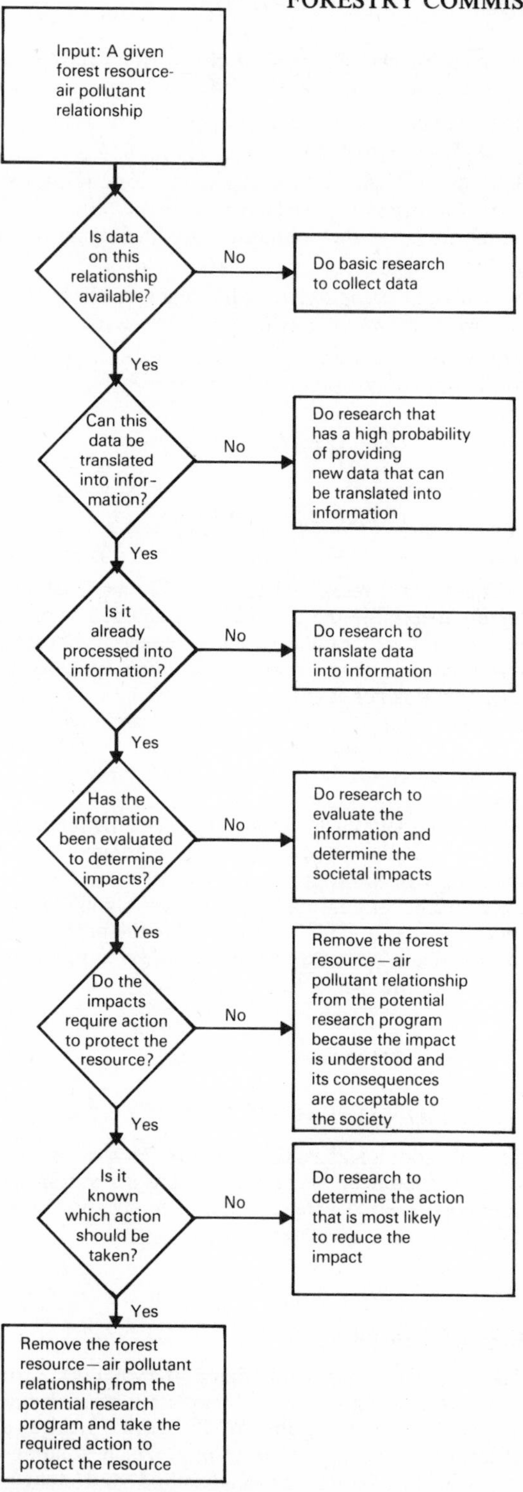


*Figure 2.* Questions to determine the known information for a given forest resource-air pollutant relationship.

## Research efforts

The probable understanding of a forest resource-air pollutant relationship is also a function of the efforts expended and the type of assessment that is undertaken. Research efforts include money expended and replications in time and space. Given a particular resource-pollutant combination, research planners and decision makers should hypothesize the relationship between research efforts and the probable understanding that can be achieved for various assessment possibilities. Figure 3 suggests example relationships for data collecting assessments of trees exposed to an air pollutant such as ozone. It illustrates that although developing an ecosystem simulation model to assess impacts may require significantly more research efforts than laboratory studies, the probable understanding is much higher.

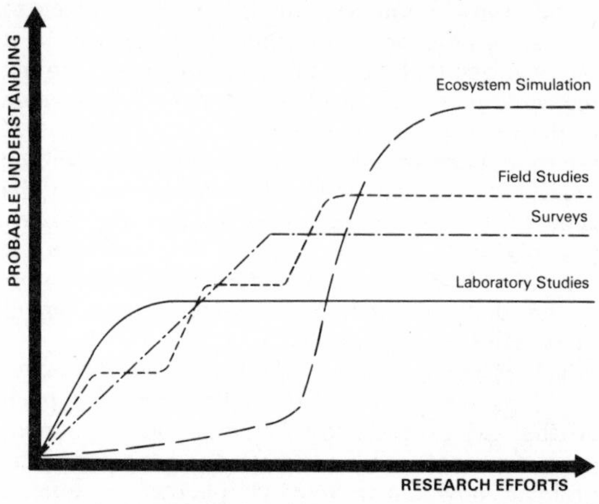


*Figure 3.* Example relationships between research efforts and probable understanding that can be achieved for data collecting assessments on trees exposed to an air pollutant such as ozone.

To estimate the relationship between efforts and probable understanding (Figure 4), research planners should locate $u_p$, (the present level of understanding); $u_{max}$, (the maximum level of understanding if unlimited research efforts were available for this type of study); and $u_{min}$, (the minimum level of understanding acceptable if any research efforts are expended) on the vertical axis.

Next, hypothesize the shape of the curve which represents the relationship of efforts to understanding between $u_p$ and $u_{max}$. Locate the minimum efforts, $e_{min}$, needed to achieve $u_{min}$ and $e_{max}$, the maximum efforts (which is the point where the curve becomes asymptotic to $u_{max}$) on the horizontal axis. (See Figure 4).

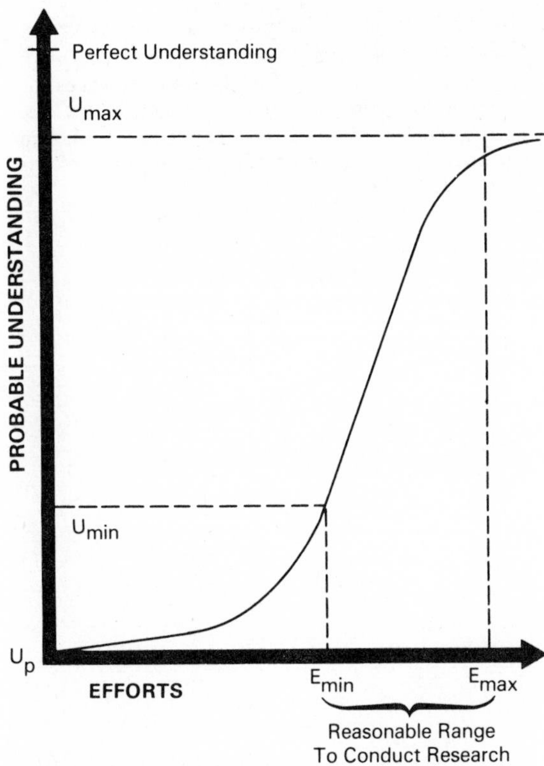


*Figure 4.* Example showing the relationship between efforts and probable understanding to define the range within which to conduct research.

The research planners now have a range of efforts, $e_{min}$ to $e_{max}$, within which it is reasonable to conduct research on this relationship using this type of assessment. For example, $u_{max}$ for a chamber study of ozone and Ponderosa pine seedlings may be quite low, particularly when compared to $u_{max}$ for an ecosystem simulation model of a forest. Continuing to direct research efforts into chamber studies beyond the point $e_{max}$ is unproductive.

Conversely, if the research planners have predetermined the amount of research effort available, then it is possible to estimate the understanding that can be gained given a particular type of assessment and effort. For example, if an ecosystem study is being considered but the research efforts available or probable are less than $e_{min}$, it is unproductive to begin the study.

## CONCLUSION

Careful planning of research endeavours is an important activity. The likelihood the research results will be applied can often be predicted prior to beginning the research if planners carefully analyze the research questions in the context of an entire research system. The strategy in this study was developed to plan a research program on forest resources and air pollutants. However, the basic RPRS structure can be used for planning other research programs to investigate stresses on forest resources. The air pollutant component can be redefined and the elements and their properties developed. The process of planning research is complex and often ambiguous. The RPRS provides a structure that enables research planners to systematically and comprehensively examine all forest resource-air pollutant relationships. This structure goes beyond traditional data concerns and explicity includes information and impact components that are critical if research results are to be applied.

### References

CHURCHMAN, C. W. (1968). *The systems approach.* Dell Publishing Co., Inc., New York. 243pp.

DOCHINGER, L. S. and PELL, E. J. (1976). *Forest and air relationships, research priorities in the Northeast.* A report prepared for the Northeastern Regional Planning Committee, Forest and Air Relationships Subcommittee. RP–2.05. 18pp.

FORCE, J. E. (1978). *Research planning in the Forest Service to assess the impacts of air pollutants on forest resources.* OSU Atmospheric Sciences Program, Ohio State University Report AS–I–105 (EES–511X–3). 258pp.

HOLDGATE, M. W. and WHITE G. F. (eds.) (1977). *Environmental issues.* SCOPE Report 10. John Wiley & Sons, London.

MITRIC, S. (1977). *The researchers and the decision-maker in urban transport: Special case of modal comparisons.* Presented at the Joint Meeting of ORSA/TIMS, San Francisco, California. May 1977.

NASH, C., PEARCE, D. and STANLEY, J. (1975). Criteria for evaluating project evaluation techniques. *AIP Journal* (March), 83–89.

NATIONAL ACADEMY OF SCIENCES (1975). *Pest control: An assessment of present and alternative technologies.* Volume IV. Forest Pest Control. Washington, D.C.

PLATT, J. (1969). What we must do. *Science* **166,** 1115–1121.

RAVETZ, J. R. (1971). *Scientific knowledge and its social problems.* Clarendon Press, Oxford.

SPARROWE, R. D. and WIGHT, H. M. (1975). Setting priorities for the endangered species program. In *Transactions fortieth North American wildlife and natural resources conference,* Pittsburgh, Pennsylvania, March 16–19, 1975. K. Sabol (ed.). Wildlife Management Institute, Washington D.C. 142–156.

SWAIN, R. (1949). Smoke and fume investigations: an historical review. *Industrial and Engineering Chemistry* **41,** 2384–2388.

TEEGUARDEN, D. E. (1977). Information resources for research in forest economics and policy. In, *Research in forest economics and forest policy.* Marion Clawson (ed.). Resources For the Future. Washington, D.C. 385–432.

# Industrial forestry research in the 1980s: the role of field stations in technology transfer

W. H. LAWRENCE and M. R. LEMBERSKY
*Weyerhaeuser Company, Tacoma, Washington, U.S.A.*

## ABSTRACT

Necessary for the success of an industrial forestry research organization is the prompt and efficient utilization of research findings by operations. Lacking an effective transfer process for placing new technology into practice, the research organization fails its mission. This rather strong statement emphasizes the importance of actively managing the technology transfer process. This paper describes Weyerhaeuser Company's evolving approach to maintaining effective technology transfer.

### Introduction

Weyerhaeuser Company is a major forest industry corporation in the United States with an annual sales volume of about $5000 million. The Company owns 2.3 million ha of forest land and has cutting rights on another 4 million ha. Raw materials flow feed some 175 manufacturing complexes of a dozen or so major product businesses. To support this activity, the Company has a Research and Development organization with an annual budget that exceeds $45 million. Product research is largely divided between solid wood and fibre projects. The management of the natural resource base is supported by a forestry and raw materials research organization with well over 100 scientists/engineers and an annual budget in excess of $10 million. We are probably the largest industrial forestry research organization anywhere.

In 1977, the senior author was invited to participate in a IUFRO Conference (Working Group 6.06) held at High Wycombe, Buckinghamshire, U.K. (Lawrence, 1977). The theme of this meeting was 'Management of forestry research for results', a subject not unlike the one before us today. In spite of the similarity of the subject matter, there was one striking difference. The metaphor, technology transfer, was not then in vogue. However, managing the process of implementing research findings remains a priority effort of research managers. This is amply demonstrated by the full attendance at this working group's conference.

A major shift in the manner that forest technology is transferred into practice has occurred within Weyerhaeuser Company since the High Wycombe meeting in 1977. The major agent in technology transfer is now becoming the scientist or engineer staffed field station. The development of a network of field stations as an adjunct to a central research organization is not a new concept. This approach is widely used to place the investigator in settings directly related to the thrust of the research program at hand. Field stations in this mode function as data collecting facilities. Weyerhaeuser is greatly expanding their traditional role to include major responsibility for implementation—the point of contact between working scientists/engineers and the operational staff. The expanded network of field stations now corresponds to all the major company operating regions (Map 1). To understand our move to field stations, it is first necessary to discuss the realities of technology transfer in the 1980s.

## TECHNOLOGY TRANSFER

Technology transfer can not be likened to osmosis, with new information flowing through an organization on a technology gradient to receptive minds scattered here and there in operations. Rather, technology transfer must be a planned process clearly supported at all levels of management—from the scientist originating the idea, through the R&D research administrator supplying resources necessary

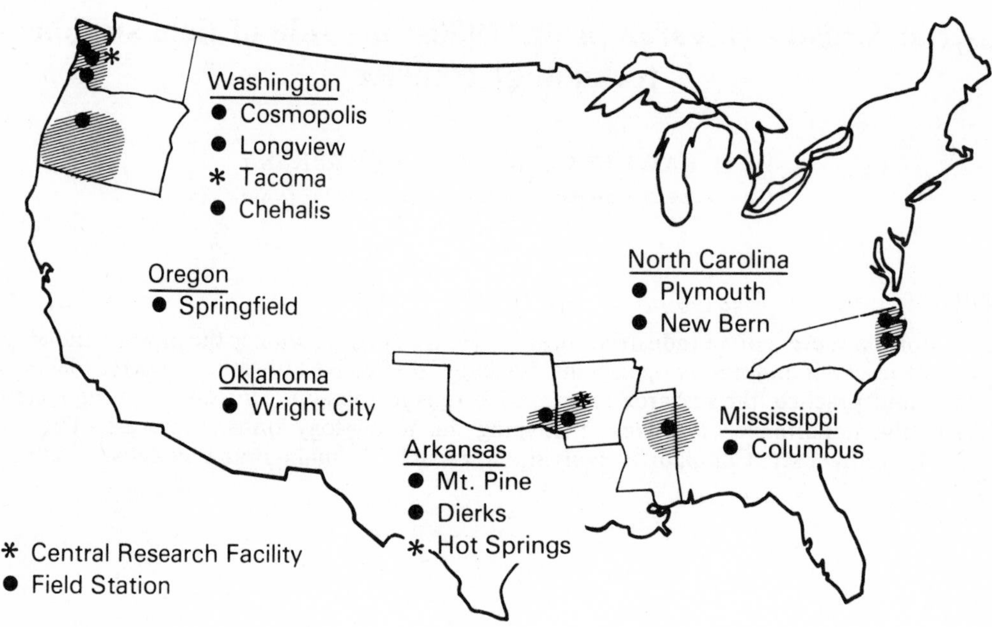


Location of central research facilities and field stations

to facilitate the transfer, to a business manager who must create a climate of receptivity that encourages the practitioner to accept new technology. This cannot be a passive process, but a process that must be aggressively pursued and supported with the appropriate people and dollar resources at each step along the way.

A carefully planned demonstration of how, when and where to apply new technology is an effective way of transferring knowledge to practice. Pilot scale field trials involving operations is an efficient way of demonstrating the benefits of new knowledge. This approach educates both researcher and practitioner in what is necessary to fine-tune the technology to better serve operational needs. At the same time, a meaningful task is accomplished for operations. Pilot scale field trials that directly involve the operational staff quickly produce a sense of ownership in the technology. This sense of ownership is a vital ingredient for *successful* implementation. This link with operations also provides the researcher with a valuable feedback mechanism that improves understanding of operational needs and realities.

Flexibility is another important ingredient of technology transfer. The operational environment is continually changing, both in personnel and objectives. A technology transfer process that worked well at one point in time may not be effective in another situation. It is essential for the R&D organization to maintain flexibility in meeting operational needs while also recognizing that operations will not itself have much flexibility to meet R&D needs in the transfer process.

The inherent resistance to change in any successful ongoing operation is a challenge that must be addressed in all technology transfer efforts. The R&D organization must make clear that the new technology will make the operation even more successful and that the increment is large. If this is not the case, the R&D organization should not be advocating the technology, no matter how elegant or outstanding it is technically. R&D should: 1) clearly identify the objective of the new technology, 2) emphasize the essential operational needs, costs and economic benefits, 3) provide a crisp statement of the non-qualitative benefits to be derived, and 4) provide a realistic accounting of the resources and time that will be necessary by both operations and R&D to implement the technology.

It is essential that the researcher be involved in all stages of the transfer process, working through the continuum from the laboratory to the field. Thus, the researcher generating the idea is also involved with the practitioner in implementing his research. This is an important relationship to foster and maintain and avoids the problems of unclear responsibilities, hand-offs and finger-pointing.

## FIELD STATIONS

A general characteristic of operations is that there is a lag (technology gap) between state-of-the-art and state-of-the-practice. By locating field stations on-site at operational headquarters, scientists and technicians are able to work directly with operational decision-makers to minimize the technology gap. Further, each of the previously mentioned characteristics of successful technology transfer are best achieved when the 'transfer agent' is in close proximity and daily interaction with operations. Field station personnel gain a unique appreciation of both the technology *and* operational realities. They are thus in an excellent position to bring forward only appropriate, useful technology. Further, the close relation with operations staff develops a credibility that is very difficult to obtain otherwise. This field station arrangement yields two major benefits: 1) the rapid transfer of new technology as appropriate to the operations at hand, and 2) emphasis on the optimum use of existing technology through applied research projects and technical service.

The role of the field stations in minimizing the technological gap between state-of-the-knowledge and operational practices is graphically portrayed in Figure 1. Keep in mind that the focus of the field station is to ensure efficient use of technology to give the solution of site-specific problems within a given operating area.

Earlier in the paper we noted that successful

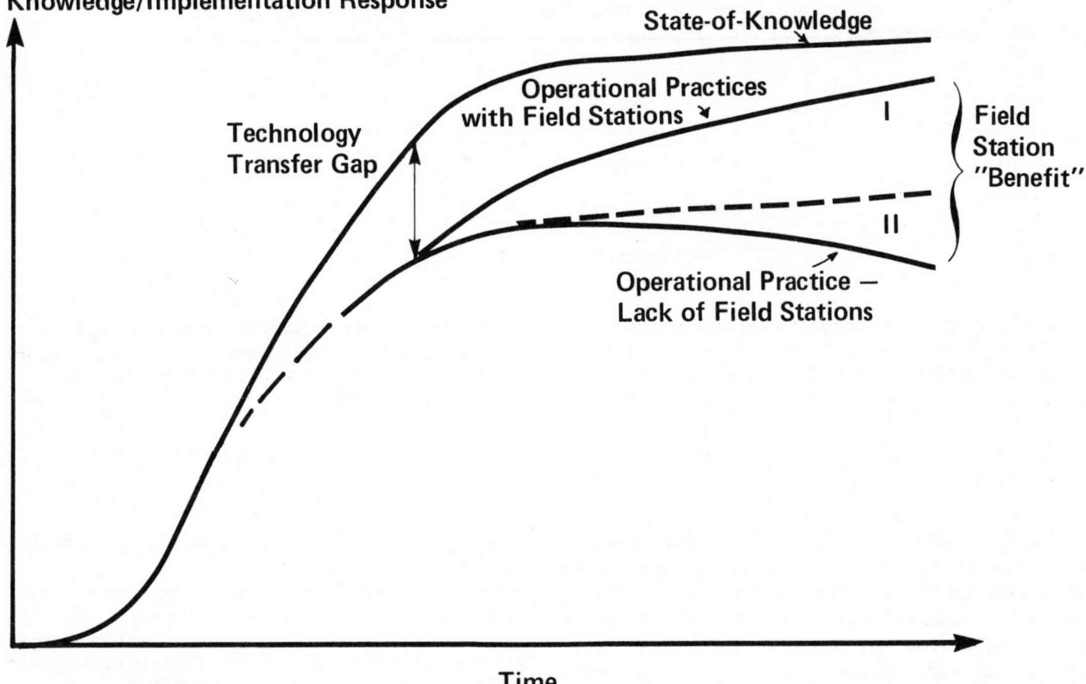


*Figure 1.* **Technology implementation.** This figure displays graphically the field station mission to assist in closing a technology gap that commonly exists between the state-of-the-knowledge and operational practices. Without an effective technology transfer process, this gap tends to widen. Over time, the field station contribution has two characteristics: 1) the transfer of new technology as it is discovered by research, and 2) maintaining an effective level of existing technology. This latter is not 'research' *per se,* but is more in the nature of applied problem solving and technical service.

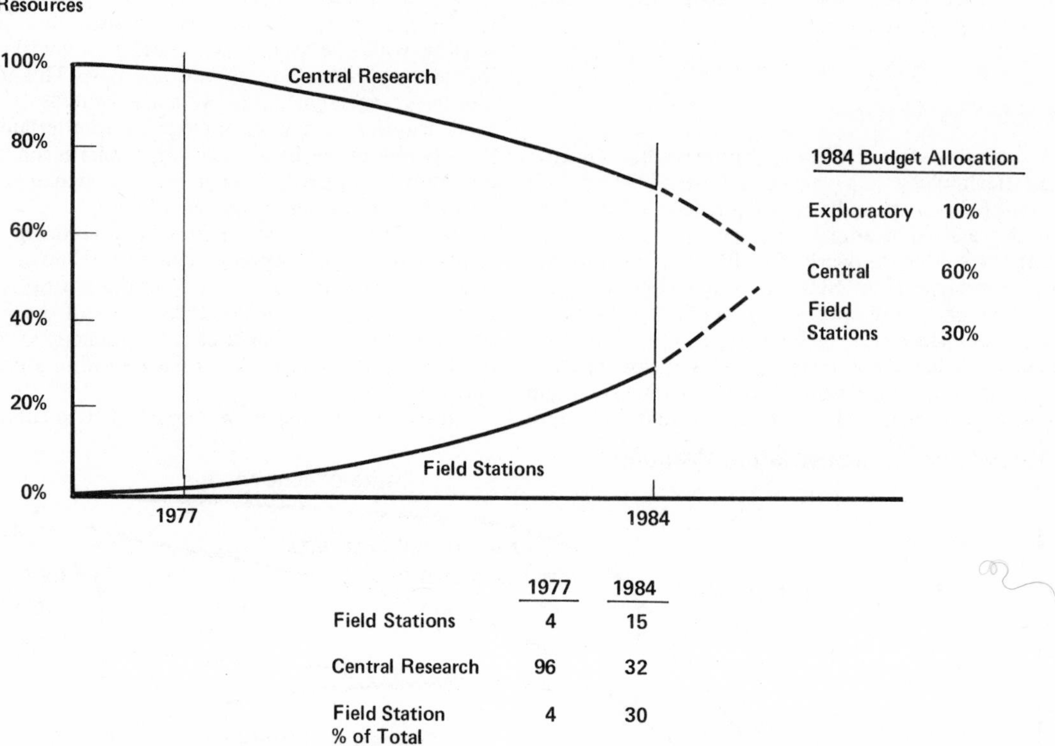


| | 1977 | 1984 |
|---|---|---|
| Field Stations | 4 | 15 |
| Central Research | 96 | 32 |
| Field Station % of Total | 4 | 30 |

*Figure 2.* **Technology implementation.** This figure displays the rise in allocation of forestry R&D resources to field stations. In 1977, field stations received about 4 per cent of the total resources. For 1984, this allocation is 30 per cent and it is anticipated that this trend will continue in the near term. A balance will be met at approximately 40–45 per cent field station resources.

technology transfer required an actively managed process with appropriate resources committed to supporting the transfer process. Since 1977, Weyerhaeuser Company has shifted the allocation of resources between centralized research facility programs and field stations consistent with this view. Figure 2 shows how Weyerhaeuser has allocated its forestry research resources. The year 1977 was the high point in the conduct of our research activities by centralized facilities. In that key year, field stations received only 4 per cent of the resources. By 1984, field stations will receive about 30 per cent of the forestry R&D budget. It is anticipated that the allocation of resources to field stations will grow in the near term to at least 40–45 per cent of the total R&D budget.

This change in forestry research organizational structure would have occurred on a natural progres-

**Table 1. Field station strategies relating to technology transfer**

| Strategy | Objective |
|---|---|
| Advocate new technology to meet region operational needs | Improve operational practices |
| Assist region operations with implementation of technologies supporting region goals | Improve operational practices |
| Conduct stand/site specific research to meet region operational needs | Maintain operational practices |
| Support high priority field research for central research programs | Support central R&D basic/applied research projects |

**Table 2. Field station technology transfer examples**

| Project | Objective | Benefits | Role |
|---|---|---|---|
| Wetlands drainage task force | Improve operational practice | ● Doubled site index rating for Loblolly pine plantation | Operations-R&D station team developed basic strategy for management plan |
| Vegetation control via new chemical | Improve operational practice | ● Increased survival 10–15%<br>● Volume gains 10–20% | Station-Operations team to facilitate technology transfer |
| Site preparation by ripping | Improve operational practice | ● Improved planting<br>● Increased soil moisture retention<br>● Site index improvement 1–1.5 m | Station-Operations team to test applicability on special sites |
| Mechanized harvest systems | Improve operational practice | | R&D-Operations team developed prototype |
| ●Whole tree logging | | ● Cost reduction; ROI more than 40% | |
| ● Wide tire logging | | ● Reduced soil compaction | |
| Provenance allocation of superior seed | Support central R&D basic research projects | ● Significant acceleration (approx. 15 years) in the realization of genetic gain in plantation management | Technology transferred to operations via field station |

sion as emphasis shifted from the discovery of new information to the application of knowledge to site-specific situations. However, two events took place shortly after the High Wycombe meeting that accelerated the development of an expanded network of field stations. These changes were: 1) the shift in the corporate structure from a centralized administration to a regionalized administration, which the centralized R&D structure of forestry research would not serve as well as the field station structure, and 2) the depressed markets for forest products that existed between 1979 and 1982, which forced company management to look at optimizing the use of forestry research results rather than continuing a high level of research effort directed primarily at developing new insights into forest technology. This is not to say the company fails to recognize the continued value of basic research; we maintain a significant amount of exploratory research devoted to examining new technologies, to uncovering new technologies with potential application to Company operations, and to maintaining a technology leading edge in selected research areas.

A set of strategies was developed coincidental with the increased importance of field stations as the agent of technology transfer. These describe both the mission of the field station and their mode of operations. The principal tasks for field stations are set forth in Table 1. Field stations are responsible for providing technical support to a region so that they can meet their operating goals. Field station scientists /engineers must be conversant with the state-of-the-art both on technical matters and operational practices.

This latter effort is directed at solving site-specific problems. The technical staff of field stations also have the mission to advocate new technology; and finally, field stations provide central research facilities with on-site help with high priority field research. There will always be additional assignments not spelled out in the strategies; usually of a technical service nature. Field station personnel are also involved in environmental issues concerning Company operations.

Five case histories of the field station approach to technology transfer are outlined in Table 2, which identifies the project, the role the field station played in implementing the technology, the benefits derived from this effort, and how the field station carried out the project mission. It is clear from this table that the

**Table 3. Benefits and constraints of regionalized forestry R&D**

| Benefits | Constraints |
|---|---|
| Fits current business structure | Disperses R&D staff |
| Direct research inputs to region strategic plans | Not all existing technical skills fit |
| Improves technology transfer | Duplication of certain technical skills unavoidable |
| Better feel for applied research opportunities | Increases R&D management problems |
| | Professional contacts reduced |
| Effective feedback to R&D management | Reduces need for technical publication |
| Builds R&D and operations teamwork to improve cost effectiveness | Increase need for exploratory research at central location |

formation of joint operational/research teams remains an important mode of operation. Today, these teams are made up of region and field station personnel, whereas prior to 1977 the teams involved corporate staff. This shift to the field level is in keeping with the corporate plan to decentralize management responsibility to the lowest effective level.

Field station staff must be selected for their ability to work with people. It is not possible to provide each field station with an array of experts to cover all aspects of intensive forest management. However, the central research facility can provide field stations with such expertise as needed. Also, there are many examples where field station personnel have assisted other nearby field stations. The central research manager still has an important co-ordinating role to play in the conduct of research and its application to operations. Field stations are not totally independent agents, but are tied to the overall picture through the central research facility.

The shift from a central research approach to field stations results in both benefits and constraints on forestry R&D. These are listed in Table 3. It is the job of the forestry R&D management team to maximize the benefits while minimizing the impact of these constraints. Management is also challenged by the dispersed technical staff. Some duplication of skills between field stations will occur because certain regional problems are very similar. For the long-term health of a forestry R&D program, it remains essential that professional contacts be maintained by the field scientists; with the dispersed staff that is a fact of the field station mode of operation, this aspect of professional development can be overlooked.

The challenge for the forestry research administrator, for the field scientists and for the operational manager is to work together as a team to maintain the quality of science while continually improving operational practices. This is the challenge of the 1980s.

## Reference

LAWRENCE, W. H. (1977). Dialogue: A flexible system for evaluating forestry. *Proceedings of the 3rd Meeting, IUFRO Subject Group S6.06,* 12– 17.

# III

# General principles of technology transfer

# The storage, classification and retrieval of research information

O. N. BLATCHFORD
*Forestry Commission, Forest Research Station, Alice Holt Lodge, Wrecclesham, Farnham, Surrey, U.K.*

## ABSTRACT

A review of the various systems and facilities available for handling scientific and technical information. Problems are highlighted and suggestions are made to help the forest researcher.

### Introduction

Researchers do two things in particular:

- they solve problems,
- they give advice.

To do these efficiently they must be concerned with scientific and technical information. Whatever project they undertake they must at the commencement consider the available literature on the particular subject to give them a basis on which to build, and to ensure that they do not repeat research which has been successfuly completed. Researchers are all, to a greater or lesser extent, experts in their particular field and frequently will be called upon to give an authoritative opinion. It is therefore essential that they keep abreast of the very latest developments so that they are always up-to-date.

Their respect for scientific and technical information is increased because the writing of scientific papers (that is the production of scientific and technical information) is an integral part of any researcher's life. Research can only become effective if it is communicated. The reputation of a researcher depends upon his scientific papers and his success is directly proportional to the length and quality of his personal bibliography. Scientific papers act as a form of currency amongst researchers who exchange their literature, thereby increasing their acquisition of information and spreading their personal prestige.

## STORAGE

This information has to be kept where the researcher can reach it with ease. Much of it, particularly that which relates to his day-to-day work, will reside in his own office or laboratory. Depending on the structure of his particular organization, he is likely to have a branch or departmental collection of information nearby, and usually in the same building. For the more general, fringe and allied subject areas most research organizations have a central library, and this library will have access to other libraries and information centres. Thus a researcher is likely to use information stored in three main libraries: personal, departmental and central. There is bound to be some overlap, but this is acceptable as the approach to classifying material will vary between each of these. For example, a forest pathologist looking at a particular disease will organize his collection according to the various strains of that disease, whilst his departmental library is likely to classify its material by host and pathogen, and central library by damage caused by the disease.

The most common form in which this information is to be found is in the printed word. This literature can be divided into primary literature and secondary literature. Primary literature, the full text of scientific papers, can be put into three broad categories: books, journals (periodicals and serials) and separates (papers, reports, pamphlets, i.e. anything not immediately recognizable as a book or journal). To assist researchers and specialists with the ever-increasing amount of literature, a whole range of abstract journals has developed covering particular scientific fields. Referred to as secondary publications, the producers have undertaken to acquire, summarize, classify and reproduce potted versions of the original (primary) publications on a regular basis.

In many scientific areas, to reduce the cost of

storage, literature has been reduced on to microfilm, either on reels or on sheets (microfiche). It can be reproduced cheaply compared with normal hard copy but requires sophisticated equipment to convert material into this form initially, and also to make use of it (i.e. to read it). The need to use a special reader has proved to be an obstacle which forest scientists in particular have been reluctant to overcome, and this medium has not been generally accepted by them.

It is now possible to ignore the scientific paper written in a scientific journal or publication and instead to put the information directly onto a computer file which can be accessed by a computer terminal. This development, referred to as electronic publishing, has already been preceded by individuals passing messages via computers and telephone lines which can be picked up from all over the world and referred to as electronic mail.

### Collections of specimens

The most obvious form of a collection in forestry is one of trees: an arboretum. Other collections are made of insects, damage (wood and plants), skulls and skins (animals), fruiting bodies, mycelia (fungi). These are built up and maintained for identification, reference and demonstration purposes.

### Photographs

Depending on the subject, these can provide: (i) visual records, sometimes the only way of describing an experiment, specimen or a feature; (ii) an aid to a lecture; (iii) an illustration for a scientific paper; (iv) material for an exhibition.

Photographic material falls into two main categories: black and white photographs, and colour slides, though you can have cine films and other forms (e.g. X-rays).

### Research registers (contacts)

Most research organizations keep a list of research projects upon which their staff are currently engaged. These registers are often available in hard copy but are increasingly becoming available as computer databases. These are particularly valuable where research work has just started and scientific papers have yet to be written, acting as signposts to researchers and organizations which can be contacted for unpublished information.

## CLASSIFICATION

Regardless of the medium used to store information, it has to be organized in some way and a record kept of that organization. The simplest way is to allocate a serial number to each item as it is received and place it on a shelf or in a filing cabinet in that order, and keep a list of numbers and items. With a very little more effort, items can be shelved or filed in alphabetical order (e.g. author), in which case it may not be necessary to have a separate list.

More often, it is considered to be helpful to have the collection arranged in some sort of subject order (i.e. classified). Classification systems can be broadly divided into two main types: those systems which use words and those which use codes (numbers and/or letters).

For collections of specimens (trees, insects, fungi, etc.) the use of biological latin names is the most obvious and most satisfactory. Photographic material however, presents a problem. Only the user of a photograph can say whether it shows exactly what he wants. His choice will depend upon a personal interpretation of the subject matter. It is essential therefore that the user is allowed to browse through the collection and select according to his own criteria. The best arrangement is to have a very few broad subjects and to concentrate on providing a facility where a large number of slides or photographs can be looked at quickly. A frame carrying 100 or more slides placed in front of a light is a good example.

For literature there have been a number of numerical and alpha-numerical systems (i.e. code systems) developed in the past but a major problem with these has been that when the system has been first created it has been difficult to anticipate exactly how many codes are going to be required eventually. A device to overcome this problem is the decimal classification whereby a subject, or indeed all knowledge is divided initially into ten areas, each of which is further divided into ten and so on until an adequate number of codes (or pigeon-holes) are designated. All the numbers are, in fact, decimal numbers with a decimal point at the extreme left of the number, though in practice this is frequently omitted, and additional full stops are used to separate the digits in the number into blocks of three for easy reading. For scientific literature in general there is an international system which is widely known as the Universal Decimal Classification, UDC. For forestry there is the Oxford System of Decimal Classification, ODC, authorized by the Rome Congress of IUFRO in September, 1953. This system is used by more than half of the forestry libraries and information centres throughout the world. Responsibility for the initial development and subsequent revision of this system rested with the joint FAO/IUFRO Committee on

Bibliography. In 1972 this Committee ceased to be responsible for the system and recommended that IUFRO should assume the work. Eventually in 1981 at the Kyoto Conference of IUFRO a Project Group, P6.01–00, was established to formally take over the responsibility for the system. The breakdown of the UDC number for forestry follows exactly that of ODC (i.e. the two systems are compatible).

Classification by words has greater attraction in that keywords can give an immediate appreciation of the subject covered. However, there are inherent problems of synonyms and in the relationships of words, not to mention the introduction of new words into a language and the change in meaning of existing words. Not only is it necessary to have a master word list, but this list may have to be structured to create a hierarchy of keywords. These word lists enjoy a variety of terms such as 'vocabulary' and 'thesaurus'.

With both code and word classifications it is essential that there is some intellectual input whereby each item of information is considered, the subject or subjects it relates to identified, and code(s) or key word(s) are allocated.

But is it necessary to think beforehand? Can you manage without a classification system at all? Modern technology suggests that you can and we shall come to that later.

## RETRIEVAL

Having collected the information and then organized it, the user must next consider how to find individual items on a later occasion. If the number of items is small and the subject area considered is narrow, then he can rely upon his own memory. If it is not he will have to make use of some aid or tool. These come in a variety of forms.

### Card catalogues

The simplest of these and possibly the most used is the 5″×3″ (12.5×7.5 mm) card catalogue or index of bibliographical citations, giving the author, date, title, publisher and bibliographical details. These can be filed by author, title and subjects, and the cards duplicated and placed in other parts of the index according to the number of routes the user may expect to follow to retrieve his information (i.e. cross-referenced).

There is a tendency in some, especially public, libraries to put these citations on to microfiche and, in fact, the card index of the Library at the Commonwealth Forestry Institute at Oxford is available on microfilm up to 1975.

A sophistication is the use of edge-punched cards where the perimeter of the card carries marked locations relating to different subjects where holes are punched and gaps can be made to enable mechanical selection of subject card with a needle.

A further advance described variously as feature cards, optical incidence cards, or peek-a-boo cards makes use of separate cards for each subject or feature. Each card is marked with a grid of squares and each square is numbered. Holes are punched on a given subject card at each location which has the number corresponding to a numbered item which covers the subject. For example, if the proceedings of this conference were allocated number 1234, the subject cards for conferences and for research would both have a hole punched in the square numbered 1234. Retrieval of all items covering the same combination of subjects can be achieved by placing the subject cards concerned on top of each other, holding them up to the light and noting the grid references (i.e. the sequential numbers) where the light shows through (i.e. where there is a coincidence of subjects).

The system has the advantage that there is no limit to the number of subjects that can be combined, but the disadvantage is that having found a number you then have to look up a list.

### Indexes

The production of abstract journals has been referred to previously. These journals are usually well indexed and save the researcher the time and trouble of classifying literature himself. These indexes are produced monthly, annually and sometimes every five years or more. This can result in certain researchers relying heavily and sometimes entirely on secondary literature rather than developing their own retrieval system.

### Computer files

Instead of putting bibliographical citations onto a card index they can be put onto a computer file. The citation can be divided into a number of fields which can be used for computer searching (e.g. authors, subjects, etc.). Not only will computers search much faster and give an exact print-out of citations, but they will search with much greater flexibility than is possible with a card index. For example, if you were to allocate four subject codes to a citation you would be unlikely to have more than four cross-referenced cards in a card index. Ideally, though, you should have 24 cards (4×3×2×1). Computers enable you make these 24 connections. Further, if you are using a numerical subject classification, you can search by a range of numbers much easier than by a card index (e.g. everything on nurseries, in ODC this would be 232.32 to 232.329.9).

**On line systems**

With the recognition that computers are able to undertake large numbers of repetitive and tedious operations quickly and accurately, the producers of abstract journals quickly discovered that it was to their advantage to feed abstracts, without any order, on to a computer which would then sort through, reorganize the layout of the master for printing, and produce a variety of indexes to authors, subjects, etc. Having once used the computer file (on magnetic tape) to set up the masters for the production of the abstract journal, the same tapes can be used to search through for references, not only according to the author or subject classification but also by looking solely for words or strings of letters (i.e. full text searching). This has great appeal as it suggests that classification and the premeditated allocation of a code to an item of literature is completely unnecessary; a massive saving in time and intellectual input, it would appear. There are, though, many pitfalls of which to beware. It is all too easy for a geneticist seeing a title *Strangulation in the orchard* to jump to the conclusion that he has found a paper on fruiting techniques. Instead he may have found a thriller about a homicidal farmer.

Language is a major problem, not only between one language and another but also between different forms of the same language, such as American English and English English (e.g. no Englishman interested in coppice would look for sprout).

However, unlike microfilm and feature cards, the use of such computer files has been widely accepted and is increasing. Magnetic tapes can now be acquired and searched through on domestic computers. A particularly successful development has been the setting up of bureaux which buy up a number of tapes and, for a fee, allow others to access and search them by telephone line. Print-outs can be obtained immediately on a terminal or (if extensive) they can be printed at the computer location and sent through the post. There is also provision to order the complete text of a paper from an appropriate library. This development is referred to as on-line retrieval, and for forestry one of the most useful is the Lockheed Dialog System in California. Not only is it very easy to use but it includes all the files most relevant to forestry (other bureaux have some but not all the files). The five most useful files are:

CAB Abstracts (Commonwealth Agricultural Bureaux)

AGRICOLA (USDA Bibliography of Agriculture)

BIOSIS PREVIEWS (Biological Abstracts)

SCISEARCH (Current Contents and Science Citation Index)

CRIS/USDA (Current Research Information System)

The last is exceptional in that it gives details of agriculture and forestry research projects sponsored or conducted by the U.S. Department of Agriculture (i.e. it is a research register).

The advantages are that access is immediate and the information is vast (e.g. CAB Abstracts allow you to scan through 1.50 million abstracts which have appeared in the 26 CAB main abstracts journals since 1972). One disadvantage is that it is not cheap (prices vary according to the files used but on average most searches will last about 10 minutes and total costs are approximately £1 per minute (i.e. £10 per search, with the cost of off-line prints sent through the post varying from 5p to 22p per citation). Another is that the information only goes back to 1972 which may be enough for many subjects but for forestry there are very many areas where the most important literature was written a long time ago.

Finally it must be emphasized that the efficient storage, classification and retrieval of the main form of information, literature, depends primarily on the researcher. He must consider carefully where his writing is to be produced (in a leaflet, in a scientific journal, in a book). This will depend on who he wants to read it (the practitioner, the researcher, the teacher) and he must use the appropriate structure and vocabulary (earthy, academic, didactic).

There is a desperate need for the researcher to appreciate the problems of accurately identifying the subject matter covered by his writing. Great thought must be given to the wording of the title and to any summary or abstract. The terms used must relate precisely to the subject(s) covered, and the researcher must resist the temptation to have an attractive sounding title at the expense of accuracy. He should be certain that if, for example, his title is *The perfumed garden* he is writing about aromatics and horticulture. Not only should he be accurate but, if possible, comprehensive. Because a paper appears in a forestry journal it is all too easy to leave out any reference to trees, forest or wood.

The addition of keywords, or ODC number, by authors is becoming more prevalent and is strongly recommended. The classifier can have great difficulty in identifying the subject, but the computer looking only at word strings is bound to be misled, overlook relevant literature and find irrelevant material. Librarians, information scientists and computers do their best, but please remember that when it comes to thinking about classification and retrieval they are only human.

# How to get the results applied

I. NORDANSJÖ
*Logging Research Foundation, Sweden*

## ABSTRACT

Every research body should attach great importance to disseminating the results of their research so that they can find practical application. Both in the research work itself and in the subsequent dissemination of the results, careful consideration must be given to the prospective recipients or users. Smoothly operating systems must exist for disseminating the results, and research bodies must possess competence and proficiency in the dissemination activity. Financial commitment is also necessary if dissemination is to be effective.

### Introduction

- Research results are of little value until they have been made known and applied.
- The more research results are used, the greater will be the benefit of the research work.

Every research worker and research administrator should reflect on these two statements. By making such claims, I have clearly underlined the view that every research body should attach great importance to disseminating the results of their research so that they can find practical application. Not least for their own benefit; not only does it help to justify their existence in the eyes of those who provide the necessary finance, but it also enhances the motivation of the individual researcher.

The relevance of what I have said and what I am going to say is not confined to applied research: it is equally important that the results of theoretical research are implemented, although in this case the target groups are small and may be reached fairly easily.

Naturally not all of the work of disseminating research results should be carried out by research bodies. On the contrary, it is vital that all conceivable resources and channels be used. Nonetheless, in my opinion, the primary responsibility rests with the research bodies.

## THE EFFECTS OF DISSEMINATING RESULTS

In theory, the relationship between the effort made to disseminate research results and the benefit to society or the field or branch concerned, from being able to share the knowledge, may be illustrated by the curve in Figure 1. The shape of the curve will vary for different types of results but, in principle, the shape of such curves should remain the same.

The interval between O and A in Figure 1 is distinguished by no efforts being made to disseminate the results. Consequently, the results are of no use. It goes without saying that it is inexcusable for a research body to find itself in this interval. Unfortunately, this does happen on occasion.

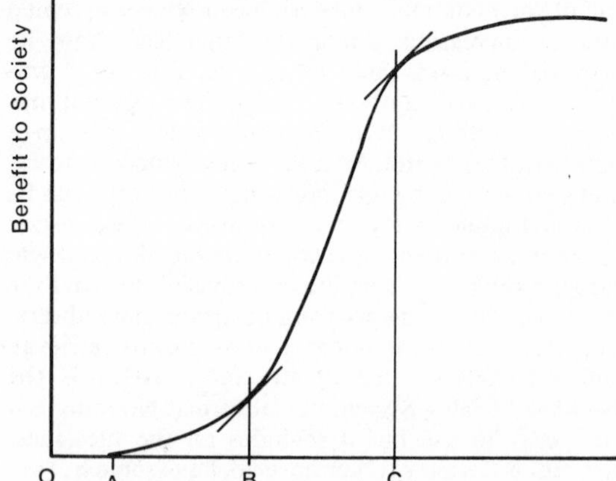


*Figure 1.* The relationship between the extent of dissemination activities and the benefit to society arising from these results.

In the interval between points A and B the results are starting to be noticed and are, therefore, of some use. However, they are still a long way from achieving maximum effect. In terms of efforts to disseminate results, the majority of research projects probably never get further than point B.

It is not until the interval between points B and C is reached that the important effects are achieved. Thus, the general goal should be to bring the work on disseminating results as close to point C as possible. Throughout this interval, up to point C, the cost of disseminating results is lower than the benefit to society derived from sharing in these results.

How then, are we to achieve effective dissemination of results? In my view, the following conditions must be fulfilled:

- Both in the research work itself and in the subsequent dissemination of the results, careful consideration must be given to the prospective recipients or users.
- Smoothly operating systems must exist for disseminating the results.
- The research bodies must possess competence and proficiency in the dissemination of results.
- Adequate economic resources must be available.

## TARGET GROUP ANALYSIS

It is natural if a researcher, after months of intensive research and with the prospect of new and interesting research work that lies ahead, takes the task of disseminating the results too lightly. In such a situation, his main concern may well be to complete his report as soon as possible and to document the work of the project in great detail. In consequence, it is quite likely that the results of the research will not become sufficiently known, nor used to the extent that is worthy of their real value.

To avoid situations of this sort, the answers to two questions should be carefully analysed by the researcher: "Who is likely to benefit from my results", and "How are they going to use them?"

Once the target groups and the objectives of the information have been ascertained, it is time to decide how the dissemination work is to be effected. Which channels should be used? What material do the respective target groups need? How should the material be packaged? And so on. Naturally it is often the case that different target groups will require the material to be processed in different ways. This means that the results must be presented in a number of different versions, for example, through various parallel publications.

Who, then are the relevant target groups for forestry research? Obviously, the list is long, but for the sake of simplicity, I have endeavoured to categorize them as shown in Figure 2.

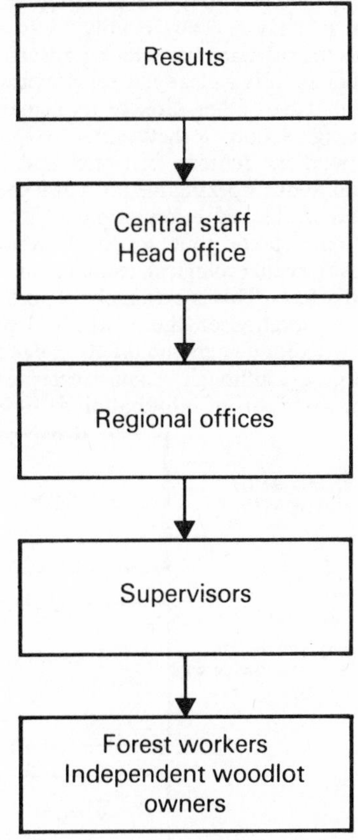


*Figure 2.* Levels and target groups within a typical forestry organization.

The first category includes the staff at the head office and other central staff. In this category may also be included other researchers, designers and the like. The persons in this group are distinguished by their good theoretical educations and the specialized nature of their work, and are therefore able to benefit from more advanced material. Moreover, in order to make their own evaluations, they also require diverse background information. Such persons are often short of time and have a wealth of information competing for their attention.

Staff with a good theoretical education are also to be found at the regional offices and, here too, work is often of a specialized nature. Also to be found in this group are the lecturers at the various institutions, the marketing and service personnel of the manufacturers, etc. This group is very similar to the previous category, but because they are closer to practical operations, their need for background information is more limited, whereas their need for results that can be directly implemented is greater.

Supervisors, advisory staff, instructors and the like have not normally had quite as comprehensive a theoretical education. They readily avoid information that is too advanced or which appears to be so. Instead, they require a clear and concise presentation of results that are either directly implementable or that encourage action on their part.

Forest workers require concrete and practical information about working methods and equipment. In the preparation of information of this nature, however, one should not forget to present and explain the relevant ecological, technical or economic causes and effects. This is extremely important to the content and quality of the work. Independently operating woodlot owners should also be included in this target group, although in some respects they also require the same sort of information as supervisors.

Often, all of the target groups should share in the results of completed research. Of course a research body may be content to pass on the information to the head office on the assumption that it will be circulated within the organization but, unfortunately, this process often takes some time, and there is also the risk of valuable information getting lost on the way. Thus, as I mentioned earlier, the research results should be presented in a form suitable for the respective target groups.

## A SYSTEM FOR DISSEMINATING RESULTS

The different target groups can be reached through a variety of channels, one of the most important of which, of course, is in the form of various types of printed matter, as is illustrated in Figure 3.

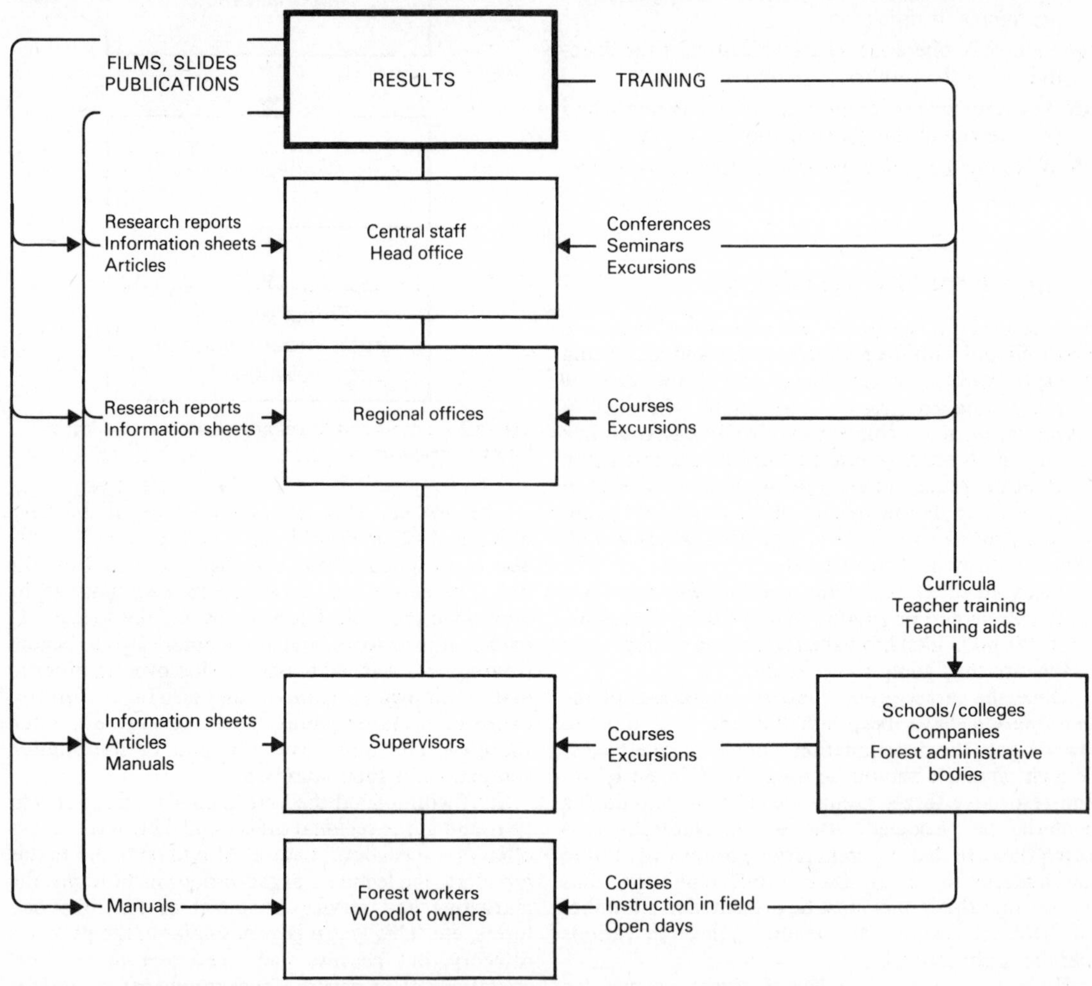


*Figure 3.* Publications, films and training are important channels for reaching the target groups.

Scientific reports providing a detailed account of the background, study methods, materials, results, etc., are suitable for those with an academic education or engaged on specialized work at the head office and/or regional offices.

To capture the interest of these busy people, the information also needs to be presented in a concise and readable form, such as articles in journals or special information sheets. Information in this form is often suitable for supervisors as well.

For the supervisors, forest workers and woodlot owners, practical directions for working methods can be presented in well illustrated manuals of a high pedagogic standard.

Instructional films and series of slides are a valuable complement to the manuals and represent an additional channel for disseminating results. Newsreels or journal-type films can also benefit all of the target groups.

Another important channel of communication is that consisting of courses and similar activities (Figure 3). Early conferences and seminars are often highly suited to reaching specialists working at central locations. For other categories more regular training in the form of courses, field days, etc., is often more suitable.

It often happens that the research institution does not have a sufficient capacity to reach the supervisors, forest workers and woodlot owners directly. Instead, the institution can initiate training to be carried out by schools, colleges, companies, forest administration bodies, etc. The research body can contribute by means of drawing up curricula, by training lecturers, providing teaching and training aids, and so on.

In this way, various channels can be opened to reach the different target groups and a complete system for disseminating the research results can be built up. After the analysis mentioned earlier has been carried out, the various channels and media, by means of which the respective target groups are to be reached, can be selected. Generally speaking, several channels and media must be used simultaneously to ensure that the information gets home.

For many years now, we at Skogsarbeten have used a system like this to disseminate our research results. According to both our own experience and that of others, the system has worked well, and we therefore intend to continue along these lines. With a staff of sixty or more engaged in research, information services and administration, each year we produce:

- Between 25 and 30 courses, with participants totalling between 800 and 1100
- About ten research reports
- About 30 information sheets
- About 30 articles for the specialized press
- One or two manuals, and
- Two or three films.

## THE RESEARCHER AS DISSEMINATOR

Are we not, then, making heavy demands on the researcher? Not only must he be able to find solutions to difficult research problems, but it seems he must also possess the combined talents of a teacher, a writer and a media expert. Yes, presumably it would be wrong to demand all this from an individual researcher. Clearly he requires the support of specialists in the fields of pedagogics and information techniques.

But the researcher himself should identify the target groups and objectives of the information work. And the earlier the better. If this is done as early as during the planning of the project, not only can this have a positive effect on the actual research work, but it also means that material, such as photos, can be collected specifically with a view to the subsequent dissemination of results.

After the target-group analysis, the various media for disseminating the results are selected. The researcher should then prepare a synopsis (for the future publication, address, film or whatever) which should include an outline of figures, tables and the like. This synopsis then serves as a suitable basis for discussion with others involved directly or indirectly in the work. If the talks are conducted at this stage, it is easier for those involved to confine themselves to the essentials in the work, rather than to become side-tracked by semantics, stylistic details, and so on. In addition, the writer will generally not have had time to become stuck with a given arrangement.

Once the synopsis has been discussed and settled, and as far as possible adapted to the needs of the target group, the researcher/author has a sound point of departure for doing the actual writing work. This manuscript may then be the subject of limited or extensive attention on the part of the editorial staff.

This entire process, then, is aimed at ensuring that, to the greatest possible extent, the content, arrangement, presentation and style of the publication are consistent with the needs and requirements of the target group. In general, for this to be successful, the researcher will require a certain amount of training and guidance, as well as the support of a number of specialists.

## THE FINANCING OF INFORMATION ACTIVITIES

But can one afford such intensive work to disseminate research results? Surely, this takes resources away from research?

Let us have another look at the graph in Figure 1 and base our reasoning on this. From the origin to point B, on the horizontal axis, it is clear that research funds must be utilized to disseminate the results. But even at point A, it is reasonable to expect part of the cost to be borne by the recipient, while from point B the dissemination activities should be financially independent.

But if the publications, courses, etc., cost money, does this not hamper the dissemination of the research results? Obviously one cannot completely rule out such an effect, but I have found that an information service that is largely self-financing has a long list of intrinsic advantages. For instance:

- The necessary resources for intensive dissemination work that are obtained without corresponding resources have to be deducted from the research funds.
- The purchaser demands high-quality information; the research organization is therefore compelled to produce products of a high standard.
- The research body has an added incentive to market its results. The greater the success in marketing, the greater the economic return.
- The market forces help to guide the activities as close as possible to point C on the graph, the optimum level.

# Technology transfer: lessons of the British experience

S. A. NEUSTEIN and D. T. SEAL
*Respectively, Head of Forest Management Division, and Chief Research Officer (North), British Forestry Commission*

## ABSTRACT

This paper focuses on aspects of the British Forestry Commission's experience with technology transfer from which useful lessons may be drawn. Object oriented research is valueless until its fruits are applied. Shortening the period of introduction confers both economic and social benefits at the commercial and national levels. A prerequisite for wide-scale technology transfer is, firstly, a firm and specific endorsement by senior level management. This must go beyond statements of broad policy. Secondly, special staff officers must be designated to major new systems or impetus.

**Introduction**

Modern British forestry can be said to have begun with the establishment of the Forestry Commission after the First World War. It was then given a clear objective to expand the productive forest estate. This objective has lasted with periodic re-emphasis and modification to incorporate financial, social and environmental values until the present. The basic resources consisted of extensive areas of bare impoverished uplands, a portfolio of exotic coniferous species the potential of which had been mainly demonstrated only on sites of above average fertility in private arboreta, and a cadre of relatively inexperienced forest officers with little forestry tradition either to guide them or to encourage innovation. Subsequent to the Second World War, when the rate of afforestation accelerated, rapid development and application of mechanization fuelled the afforestation drive to an extent that yielded prodigious results but also promoted a degree of over-confidence in the forester's ability to overcome all limiting factors.

The overall achievements during the post war period are described elsewhere in these proceedings (see paper by Holmes). There is no doubt that these accomplishments were remarkable. However, this paper focuses on aspects of the British case history from which useful lessons may be drawn. Mistakes are as instructive as successes, both are used to illustrate principles and promote discussion without apologies for hindsight or claims that the authors could have done better.

## RESEARCH STRATEGIES

The Forestry Commission at its inception in 1919 concentrated on the applied empirical approach in research. Existing methods were applied to new conditions and where found inadequate subsequent inputs were modified to overcome the assumed limiting factors. The obvious benefit of this tactic was rapid and maximal extension of existing technology, as exemplified by a major programme of trial plantations, opened up large new tracts of afforestable land. But there have been significant penalties. Investigation of site constraints was undervalued and the contribution that soil scientists, climatologists and physiologists might have made were delayed, while silviculturists proceeded with reiterative and sometimes costly field experimentation. For decades experimental treatments were unduly constrained by practical cost factors, whereas, even accepting the validity of the philosophy, more progress might have been made by the exploration of extreme inputs followed by their simplification. Some investigative specialists were used, often university researchers on contract but, particularly where their recommendations did not support current practice (e.g. W. R. Day's warnings about the implication of gleyed soils), little credibility was given to their contribution, and their influence on management was small. The weaknesses of over-emphasis on the practical approach was not institutionally recognized until the 1970s when a separate agency was established to fill this gap, an organizational dichotomy which should have been avoided.

## RESEARCH PROGRAMMES— INVESTMENT PORTFOLIOS

Technology transfer starts here. As forestry is an applied science of lesser national importance than its sister disciplines of agriculture and horticulture, botanical and biochemical advance will generally be derivative. Nevertheless, the selection and periodic re-appraisal of the best portfolio is a key challenge at national, regional and organizational levels. Proposals are infinite but resources are finite. An analogy has been drawn between the ration of basic/applied research and the exploration of a mineral and the mining and utilization of the metal. There is no easy guide to the total justifiable research budget of an industry nor to the above division, as it depends on the scale of the enterprise, current and forseeable technologies, prospects for improvement, as well as estimates of probability of disasters. Suffice to say that in Britain the cost of R&D on forestry subjects has been estimated at 4.5 per cent of total expenditure and this level is unlikely to be significantly increased.

Until 1982 there was no national strategic coordination. The Forestry Commission's project register was strongly influenced by managerial requirements. Managers identified current problems and researchers, with close organizational links with field practice, plus a deeper view, more often saw longer term projects for improvement. Research in universities was less tightly harnessed to perceived needs and prospects, although a degree of navigation was achieved via funding of contract research and the university researcher's natural desire to make relevant contributions. Research by other agencies, and to some extent that of the Forestry Commission's R&D Division itself, was steered by a network of advisory committees which, having some members in common, produced a loose national co-ordination. However in 1982 it was recognized that better coordination was required and the Forest Research Coordination Committee, previously described by Mr. Holmes, was established. It has already shown signs of improving the national portfolio of forestry research.

The Forestry Commission portfolio (direct and contracted) is reviewed annually in consultation with the Forest Management Division both to ensure that justifiable new topics are considered, promising projects reinforced and, equally important, that obsolete subjects are abandoned. The private sector also has opportunity to influence the research programme.

The balance of forces in the class struggle between the fundamentalists who claim intellectual superiority, and the applied researchers who place high value on relevance, deserves continual re-assessment. The Forestry Commission's mix within one organization confers notable advantages.

## FINANCIAL APPRAISAL

A research director must not only adjudicate among the perceived needs of managers, economists, and environmentalists, but must also, in seeking to meet these needs, take into account the potential of the researcher, his technological competence and his ability to evaluate objectively his own contribution.

Environmental aspects are often particularly difficult to quantify and hence they have tended to receive less attention than more readily measurable factors. In the 1960s the Forestry Commission attempted to compare all current and proposed projects by means of simultaneous financial appraisal. Cost/benefit ratios of projects were brought to a common scale by taking into account the area of applicability. More speculative projects were modified by a numerical co-efficient of their probability of success. Much effort and time was devoted to these calculations by project leaders, for proponents of the approach argued that its value depended on its precision. However it proved no panacea, there being no belief in results based on estimates multiplied by guesses, especially when the track records of the originators and the quality of their presentations could not be brought to a common standard. Another systematic failing, especially when one species is dominant, is that, if slavishly applied, any project promising even minimal improvement in the predominant species will oust work in other areas. Financial appraisals of course have an important place but they must be used with discretion, especially as to timing.

Short term projects susceptible to a Work Study approach are commissioned directly by management. In this area delusions of scale or over-ambition of engineers and 'meccano minded' staff can promote a 'Concorde syndrome' namely, lengthy resource-consuming development of machinery whose market has not been adequately appraised. It is very unlikely that a small British forest industry with commensurate R&D input will be able to compete with countries having similar problems on a much larger scale. Thus Britain, having a unique need for forest ploughs, achieved pre-eminence in this relatively simple field, but wasted significant effort in attempting to develop harvesting machinery. Even where a promising concept was identified, as in the hydrostatic skidding tractor, limited development resources so delayed success that the need disappeared with the arrival of a new generation of forwarders from abroad. Other analogous projects, including the capstan and the self-powered skyline carriage, have now been aborted for these reasons and the Work Study Branch now rightly concentrates on evaluation and modest modification rather than development.

## INERTIA, MOMENTUM AND CHANGE

Research is basically a creative process. It is dependent on a sympathetic climate and the enthusiasm of individuals. On the other hand research managers are most aware of the need for economy, co-ordination and discipline and have a natural tendency to impose centralized control systems to ensure that effort remains within approved avenues. This conflict of emphasis is unavoidable. To a large degree the Commission's organization and staff deployment policy has encouraged project leaders to strive for the esteem of managers rather than to compete with their research peers by giving priority to esoteric publications.

The history of British forest research shows how the pendulum has swung between periods of more or less centralized control. For example, Neustein (1977) described major advances in post war plough development made by a succession of local, strongly motivated three-man teams (comprising a forester, an engineer and a co-operative manufacturer) in contrast to an official centralized machinery development team which contributed little. Likewise, windthrow research was originally conceived by researchers, and their advocacy of its importance and implication was sceptically received. However the 'Concorde syndrome' needs strong centralized control.

Inertia arises when too many people have to be convinced of a need. Its consequence is frustration and discouragement of the researcher. The crucial role of exotic species and the need for provenance investigation was recognized by Steven in 1924. But North American species were not systematically examined until 1965, perhaps because the value of narrow-object-oriented foreign travel was not favoured and the limited funds were absorbed by attendance at conferences and symposia. By their nature the latter attract well established work which could be equally well disseminated by publication and also promotes a momentum more of mass than velocity. The scale of past British research into poplars could exemplify this tendency. It is also apparent in the work of some research institutes. Currently there is some danger that mycorrhizal research is developing a momentum without supporting practical indication of its value. Whereas there is justification for parallel studies of subjects where regional variation is to be explored (i.e. the IUFRO provenance experiments), there is perhaps scope to impose more specific direction of fundamental research on an international basis.

## IMPEDIMENTS TO TRANSFER

The very existence of this conference demonstrates that technology transfer is a scientific art in its own right. Object oriented research is valueless until its fruits are applied. Shortening the period of introduction confers economic advantage at both the commercial and national economic level. It has long been alleged that it is a British national weakness to fail to exploit research even in the private manufacturing sector where self-interest motivates. In the public sector there can be an analogous unwillingness to innovate borne of a desire to avoid the risks and hassle of untested procedures, even though shortage of capital and personal consequences of mistakes play a lesser role.

The British mix of communication between researchers by publications in learned journals, and between researchers and managers by articles in professional and trade journals is well known. In the past year the Commission's technical publications have been divided into two broad categories, differentiating the prescriptive from the explanatory and justificatory in order to focus most sharply on the needs of different types of readers. It is still not clear whether it is more useful for the manager to obtain entry via regional or operationally based publications or how best to combine these approaches. Certainly few managers have time or inclination to undertake much time consuming indexing and cross-referencing of a plethora of over-lapping publications.

The broadly directed blunderbuss technique of offering knowledge to the whole population both by technical publications and staff training, in the hope that staff will extract what is relevant to their conditions and sphere of influence, has become seriously inappropriate. In the Commission the functional Assistant Conservator has long had the responsibility of acting as a middle man and booster station for the two-way flow between users and suppliers. This function, though enshrined in formal job descriptions, was by no means universally fulfilled and it has been suggested that the gap between existing knowledge and its extensive application is now greater than it was in the 1930s.

Obviously one cause is the larger variation of crop and site conditions now recognized and another is the greater sophistication of treatment and equipment and the wider spectrum of specialist advice being offered at the same time as the managerial pace is accelerating. Hence the manager tends to give priority to those facets in which he has personal expertise or enthusiasm, and progress over the enterprise as a whole is uneven and slower than justified. The results are regions of excellence in particular subjects which have incidental and unintended virtues as extension trials.

Equalization has been customarily promoted by staff succession, a procedure which can be unduly personality dependent and slow. Examples include the introduction of chemical weeding, fertiliser usage, introduction of forwarders and the all-encompassing lack of cutting edge in the professionalism of technical audit achieved by generalist managers.

## USE OF SPECIALISTS

In countries where scale justifies an adequate extension service between research and practitioner these failings can be minimized. Another solution is to establish sufficiently large demonstration units to illustrate the integration of novel treatments into managerial systems which could serve as regional models. The diversity and smallness of the British forest industry has favoured neither of these approaches.

In some instances the Education and Training Branch or the Work Study Branch have been charged to identify deficiencies but their position outside the direct management line has militated against their routine use in this capacity, especially as both Branches fear, probably correctly, that their necessary relationship with management and staff could be jeopardized.

A prerequisite for wide-scale technology transfer is firstly firm and specific endorsement by senior level management. This must go beyond statements of broad policy with attention being drawn to sources of available information and options. Secondly, because of the complexity of demands upon middle management which in the Commission cover both Enterprise and Forest Authority functions, special staff officers must be designated to introduce major new systems or impetus. This has been effectively demonstrated in many fields including acquisitions, harvesting, recreation planning and seed collection.

## SUMMARY OF BRITISH EXPERIENCE

1. Applied research must have an appropriate backing of more basic targeted investigations.

2. Financial appraisal of research projects must be used, but with discretion.

3. Senior management endorsement is essential. (Natural disasters, leading to unequivocal priorities, elicit exceptional progress).

4. Communication of results and prescriptions is akin to salesmanship. Personal communication is more powerful than publication. Exchange of specialist staff is very helpful.

5. In the absence of an extension service, applied researchers should have to act as advisers and be judged on their effectiveness in this regard. If the topic demands it, designate special officers to be responsible rather than merely increase the volume of exhortation.

6. A climate of innovation should be encouraged organizationally by allowing and if necessary by assisting local short term trials, and permitting local commissioning of specialist investigations. The risk of wasted effort might be less than over centralized control killing local initiative and delaying innovation.

7. Concentrate attention on identified priority subjects rather than attempt to influence the full spectrum.

8. In publication, identify readership and treat the subject accordingly in terms of content and style.

9. Distinguish between confirmed research results and best current estimates by researchers. Do not let preoccupation with the former discourage the latter.

10. Ensure that all levels of staff are motivated and trained in appropriate phase.

11. Avoid half-hearted or premature introduction of new technology. It can queer the pitch.

### Reference

NEUSTEIN, S. A. (1976, 1977). A history of plough development in British forestry. *Scottish Forestry* **30,** 2–15; 89–111; 253–274 and **31,** 2–12.

# Fostering and managing innovation

R. SEGMAN
*USDA Forest Service, Pinchot Institute, Milford, Pennsylvania, U.S.A.*

## ABSTRACT

Foresters and their organizations need to be innovative to survive vigorously and productively in today's uncertain world of rapid, almost continual change. With this paper we examine innovation and propose ways of making the process work better for us. In forestry, innovation has countless variations in dimensions, complexity, source, and pathways of development and spread. Fostering and managing innovation requires commitment; recognition that most people, given encouragement, will be innovators; a management style that features flexibility and some looseness; and several common techniques or methodologies. The challenge is to make these elements work together naturally, easily and effectively.

### Introduction

There is more innovativeness available in most organizations than is mobilized.

Innovativeness is a talent we all have to some degree. It can be made to flow like water from a spigot. The managerial trick is to keep the pipes clear, the valves open, and the flow under control. If you're not getting enough innovation in your organization, don't blame the reservoir—it is always full.

Some observers feel that management often stifles innovation. Up to a point, perhaps, but it is also true that uncontrolled innovation tends to be inefficient and disruptive.

Within the past few years in the USDA Forest Service the demands for change have become incessant and themselves have kept changing. The public requires new ways of assessing social impacts. The Congress wants longer-term planning than ever before. The Forest Service is being computerized down to its roots. It needs to deal with dwindling natural resources and increasing forest-product competition from other nations. Budgets are cut, personnel ceilings lowered.

This is our world, full of change and uncertainty. Not much traditionalism or stability left. If we resist change we wither. The way to respond and survive —survive productively and in good mental health—is to innovate, to steer the changes in the most propitious directions for ourselves, our clients, and the public.

Since the Forest Service obviously has accepted innovations as a way of life, it is useful to begin an examination of the processes of innovation and to search for better ways of making it work for the organization. This paper discusses innovation and recommends ways in which a large, dispersed organization can foster and manage the process. It brings together ideas about innovation and management that until now have been dealt with separately. The integrated approach offered here is intended to help managers foster and control innovation more knowledgeably and sensitively, therefore more effectively.

Sponsored by the U.S. Forest Service's Pinchot Institute, the report is based on an analysis of field observation, a literature survey, and discussions with nearly 200 Forest Service people and some outside management professionals. It is organized into three sections: innovation, managing innovation, and fostering innovation.

## INNOVATION

Innovation is a beneficial response to a changing situation. Pressure to change may come from The President, The Chief of the Forest Service, a forest technician, public sentiment, an insect infestation, an altered climate, a desire to make things better, or combinations of these and many other factors.

While there is no firm blueprint for an innovation process, it may be described for the sake of discussion as a sequence of stages: definition of need or opportunity; search for solution; research, if required; development, if required; field testing and debugging; implementation by early adopters; and diffusion to the mass of potential users. The sequence is influenced by people, organizational characteristics, management styles, and characteristics of individual innovations.

Innovations may be big or little, complex or simple, technical or non-technical. Of the productivity and other economic benefits accruing from innovation, more than half come from the minor innovative improvements that generally follow major changes.

People are the sources of innovation. Virtually everyone is blessed with innovativeness, not just a few creatives. Sources of innovation are found in all branches and at all locations of the Forest Service, and outside as well. One of the more prolific sources of new ideas and improvements, major as well as minor, is the often-ignored hands-on user, who best understands his own needs and opportunities.

It doesn't matter whether an innovation is truly novel or has been developed or used elsewhere. What is important is that the technology method, improvement, or system be useful to the Forest Service, whatever its pedigree or age.

The shifting sequences, the great range in dimension and complexity, and the manifold sources of innovation suggest that we should not rely on research as the prime source, on major new technologies as the prime innovations, and on media specialists as the prime diffusers. To do so is to neglect the totality of innovation and the interactions between sources and users that are essential if our innovations are to be appropriate and widely diffused.

## MANAGING INNOVATION

The challenge to Forest Service leadership is to understand the intricacies of innovation, to create conditions that stimulate the flow of innovative ideas, and to sensitively and flexibly guide each innovation through the most rational sequence.

The effective innovation manager knows his organization, knows himself, has goals, knows and respects his people, values their ideas, and depends on them for performance. He accepts the need for innovation, makes it clear to his people that he is personally committed to the idea of it, and provides staff and other resources to back-up his commitment. He champions innovative ventures and accepts responsibility for the risks associated with them. And, particularly important, he has the courage to suspend ongoing work if a proposed innovation is not living up to its promise.

The degree of a manager's involvement in innovation is not pre-set. Generally, the higher his level, the more time he devotes to it. Specifically, his involvement is determined by the innovation's characteristics; his managerial style; the functional and social structures of his organizational unit; his place in the hierarchy; innovativeness of his staff; resources he controls; and his organization's need for what the innovation promises.

He is most heavily engaged early in the sequence when the incipient innovation is more susceptible to his influence. He sees to it that the sources or developers of an innovation and its most likely early users work together from the start. Continual interaction between developer and user, an almost universal recommendation in the literature, produces more suitable innovation and faster diffusion.

Simple recognition for good work is often neglected and undervalued by supervisors. The informal, intangible word or note or gesture of approval from the boss is a potent innovation motivator. So is pride in workmanship, which the manager may give to his people as opportunities to use their skills and talents, as intellectual challenges, and as freedom to pursue their ideas.

Reward, the formal, tangible acknowledgement of long-term accomplishment or estimable performance, is most effective as a validation of ongoing recognition. The manager should be careful that the promotion, bonus, or medal does not come unexpectedly; it could be misinterpreted by the recipient and backfire.

Innovation performance standards are tricky but worth considering because they have the potential for enhancing a whole organization's innovativeness. They should concentrate on improving personal interaction, should be appraised qualitatively, and should not under any circumstances result in accusations of failure.

## FOSTERING INNOVATION

In this paper, 'fostering' means encouraging and cultivating the innovativeness that is in us all. Some of the suggestions for managing innovation may also be regarded as fostering methods. The separation is arbitrary. What's important is that the manager understands that his people are innovative, talented, loyal, and eager. This may sound like a cliché, but it is nothing to be cynical about. The manager who takes advantage of these personal characteristics can develop a spirited, productive organization.

The goal in this section is to allow innovation to be an easy, natural process.

The key to achieving unselfconscious innovation is informal interaction. The management and innovation literature is nearly unanimous on the subject of word-of-mouth. It is regarded as the most efficient way of spreading ideas and information that will be used.

Word-of-mouth can be used as a management tool, first by striving to remove such communications barriers as interbranch rivalry, interdisciplinary moats, hierarchical walls, and physical remoteness. Then the manager can encourage broad, informal interaction; provide means to communicate; minimize restrictions; and leave people to their own social devices. Under the right conditions, the managers can even join some informal huddles in the halls or at coffee break. In order to be kept up-to-date on the ferment, he should maintain respectful and trusting relationships with his people and should tolerate some looseness in his organization.

He should not try to control his staff's interactions. The delicate mechanisms of informal relations and innovativeness will crush under a heavy hand.

Another consensus technique from the literature is linking in the form of a change agent or facilitator. While their number is small and there are no formal personnel slots for them, the Forest Service has spawned some unauthorized linkers who spread information as credible sources and bring people together in ways that enhance the development and use of innovations.

Whatever their assigned jobs, linkers tend to be irrepressible. They manoeuvre around, over, and through communications barriers both inside and outside their organizations. Their success as facilitators has something to do with a combination of personality, prestige, broad range of interests and knowledge, contacts, competence and motivation. They are the informal authorities people seek out when they have problems or ideas to discuss, unofficially.

There is no preferred way for a linker to operate. The role is a personal one.

The relationship between a manager and linker is delicate. The manager, first of all, needs to know who his main linker is, which he may find out very discreetly by asking his staff. The next step is to talk with the linker about helping him improve his effectiveness. Linker willing, preferably enthusiastic, they should decide on one of at least three possible basic relationships: (1) the linker performs autonomously, bringing information to the manager at his own discretion; (2) the manager prudently encourages and supports the linker; or (3) the linker is given the assignment full time and is supported fully and formally. The latter relationship is particularly tricky, for the staff might stop responding if they see him as the boss's man. Yet, if he is the right-boss's man, the linker might find himself in a more potent position.

Innovation can also be fostered by networking. Perhaps the best way to do it is through computer conferencing, which simulates proximity for far-flung collaborators. It is an easy, efficient, cheap way for people at several locations to have ongoing discussion at their individual conveniences. Anybody can start a conference in minutes. In many cases involving innovation, it would be ideal for a linker or any involved person to originate and moderate region-wide conferences.

Basically, the conferencing system accepts, stores, catalogues and reads-out messages. Any time a participant enters a conference (at his convenience) the system tells him what messages he has not yet seen. On his command any or all of the messages are printed out. He may respond to a message immediately, hold it for later response, or ignore it. He may enter a message himself and check back the next day or a week later for responses. Messages may be broadcast to the membership or addressed to an individual. Two or more persons may have a running debate in full view of the membership, any of whom might join in. At any time the elected or self-appointed moderator might ask for a consensus. There are no winners or losers, as long as the moderator keeps the conference under control. On a regional or forest level, such computer-conference networking can enhance all stages of the innovation process.

Another way of fostering innovation would be through a national innovation newsletter, published by the Office of Information. It could provide insights into the diversity of innovation and its sources, recognize individuals and organizations, carry case-histories of significant or unusual innovations, describe benefits from specific innovations, run briefs on implemented but not widely-diffused innovations, offer rewards, and carry stories on relevant outside innovations.

## AFTERWORD

It would cost very little to gain the benefits inherent in the recommendations proposed in this paper. What gives the recommendations validity is the fact that they are based on widespread talents, existing skills, and common techniques and methods. Mainly they require the innovativeness we all possess, normal social behaviour, a well-used computer-conferencing system, and a flexibility of management. Even the makings of the suggested newsletter already exist in the form of several specialized publications. The challenge is to make these elements work together naturally, easily and effectively.

Indeed, where the Forest Service will be in 5 years will depend largely on the innovative responses of our managers under continual, shifting pressures of change.

# IV

# Conference recommendations

## Recommendations

The final session of the conference was used to assemble and record recommendations for improving technology transfer in forestry. Recommendations for forest managers, that is for the *users* of research results, were distinguished from those intended for the researchers themselves. Both kinds of recommendations are set out below. There was, of course, some difference in opinion between conference members as to the relative importance of these recommendations, and it was acknowledged that circumstances must change the order of value. Nevertheless the degree of agreement was remarkable considering the range of countries and experience encompassed by the conference participants, and it is clear that all the points covered below deserve the most careful attention.

**What can users of research and their organizations do to improve technology transfer?**

Users must be actively involved in the early stages of research planning:

- Identify and prioritize their research needs
- Make sure researchers understand these needs

Users must create an organizational environment that encourages innovation:

- Establish a user liaison person to research
- Involve researchers in management teams
- Encourage interaction and co-operation between researchers and managers
- Provide managers with technology transfer training
- Allocate staff time to attend meetings, demonstrations, workshops, etc.
- Set up an administrative structure to ensure technology transfer
- Monitor technology in primary and related fields
- Be open to new ideas
- Reward people who innovate
- Establish a technology transfer advisor in a senior staff position
- Interchange staff with research whenever possible
- Form user co-operatives to encourage innovation

User must be involved in research application and evaluation activities:

- Help fund application efforts

Test and demonstrate innovations and inform research about results

- Make a solid commitment to trying new technology
- Conduct benefit/cost and cost effectiveness studies

**What can researchers and their organizations do to improve technology transfer?**

Research must involve users in early stages of research planning:

- To help identify problems and set priorities
- To establish reasonable expectations and commitments
- To understand the user market

Research must create an organizational environment that encourages innovation:

- Encourage direct contacts between researchers and users
- Keep users appraised/involved throughout the research process
- Attend management meetings
- Encourage staff exchanges between research and management
- Train researchers in technology transfer and communication techniques
- Commit adequate resources to technology transfer
- Recognize and reward scientists for application work
- Establish an organizational focal point for technology transfer
- Take initiative to motivate managers
- Recognize technology transfer as a continuing commitment

Research must be involved in application and evaluation activities:

- Whenever possible, quantify benefits of research
- Concentrate efforts on most beneficial results
- Involve users in application efforts
- Understand users capability to implement results
- Provide state-of-the-art summaries
- Use most appropriate means of transferring results—demonstration and personal contacts whenever possible
- Ask for and use evaluation feedback from users.

# Appendix

APPENDIX

# National situation reports

*Commonwealth Forestry Research Course Student Reports*

# Forest research in Honduras

S. ALI
*Corporacion Hondurena de Desarrollo Forestal, Tegucigalpa, Honduras*

## Forest resource

The Republic of Honduras, a tropical country of Central America, lies between 12°58′ and 19° north latitude, and between 79°30′ and 89°17′ west longitude. It covers an area of 112 090 km$^2$ and has a population of approximately 4.0 million inhabitants, the country is almost half the size of Great Britain.

The forest resource is natural and has been estimated to be 7.4 million hectares of which, 3.0 million are covered by pine forests, the remaining 4.4 million correspond to broadleaved forests. In reality, less than 50 per cent of the forest cover remains productive, the rest has been degraded and destroyed by early uncontrolled cutting, shifting agriculture, grazing, fire and erosion.

## History of forestry-relevant aspects

The year 1974 marked an important date in the history of forestry in the country. The Honduran Forest Development Corporation (COHDEFOR) was created, charged absolutely with managing, harvesting and the commercialization of the forests. This included responsibility for organization, enforcement, research, investment and forestry education.

Prior to 1974, forest management and exploitation were functions of the Ministry of Natural Resources, but very little control and care was taken. Revenue from forests ended in the hands of private enterprise, and outside the country. The forest resource was rapidly dwindling.

After 1974, the Forest Corporation has placed emphasis on the management of pines only. The country has been divided into Forest Districts and Management Units. The management and harvesting control has improved considerably. Revenue from its forest is handed into the Central Government, mainly to finance development programs.

## Research

Despite the bulky multipurpose research undergone in the nation since the 1940s, there has not even existed a research policy, nor have priorities been drawn. Research has always been a function of individual likes and project needs. This has led to unco-ordination, duplication, resources spent in low need projects, lack of publication of results in the official language, unfinished work, and no research training. In the last 10 years, worst of all, there has been a complete lack of communication between management and research, therefore, the budget for research is at its minimum. Application of results is non-existent, perhaps because of lack of knowledge for implementation or because of fear to apply results from research that has not been seriously evaluated or conducted.

The Forestry Corporation, through the National School of Forest Sciences at Siguatepeque, has in the last couple of years attained important progress towards improving and organizing the present research situation, but much more needs to be done.

## Work plan

The Forestry School has begun working on the following goals:

1. To define policy and priorities.
2. To develop a research plan.
3. To obtain financing of the research plan.
4. To offer research training.
5. To continue publishing and transferring of results.
6. To find measures to incorporate results into management practices.

This effort cannot ever succeed without involvement, true commitment, understanding, and agreement from the Government, International Aid, and forestry technicians, on the need for a research plan by priorities.

# Forest research, organization and technology transfer in Kenya

B. N. KIGOMO and G. M. KINYANJUI
*Forest Research Department, Kenya Agricultural Research Institute, Nairobi, Kenya*

Forest research in Kenya is aimed at supporting the forestry department in its policy of 'Forest for development'. This involves managing the forest estates on an increasing sustainable forest production in perpetuity. Various constraints however present difficulties in pursuing these goals.

Suitable land for agriculture and forestry covers only one third of the total land mass. This area supports 75 per cent of the human population and forestry is, therefore, in competition with mainly agricultural land which utilizes 25 and 50 per cent of the total human and livestock population, respectively. The latter land comprises the arid and semi-arid areas of low unreliable rainfall. Establishment, survival and adaptation of tree crops in these lands is difficult to achieve and priority in forestry research has been given to them in the current five year development plan. Indigenous forests have suffered irreplaceable losses due to past unrestricted exploitation and replacement by industrial plantations of softwoods. Present intention is to manage the remaining indigenous forests as a renewable crop, thus adopting a less conventional option to meet the rapidly increasing consumption of wood. Some tree species despite their productivity have to be dropped from industrial plantations due to various disease attacks. These include *Pinus radiata* and *Cupressus macrocarpa* due to *Dothistroma* and canker attack respectively. This calls for protective research measures.

It is in the light of the above problems, and other minor ones, that the Forestry Research Department is currently required to transfer technology to forest managers and farmers in areas relating to expansion of forestry into drier areas, devising techniques for integrated agricultural and forestry disciplines, agroforestry, and improvement of yield per unit area of unexpanding existing forests which are found mainly in the highlands. This is being undertaken by five divisions with substations spread over different ecozones. Agricultural and forestry research are now combined in one research institute (KARI) leading to closer co-operation in research on agroforestry and community forestry systems.

The Department's research findings are disseminated to professionals through technical notes, newsletters, quarterly and annual reports and the East African Forestry and Agricultural Journal. Research findings get to farmers through the latter's participation in experimentation, the local forester's demonstrations during the annual tree planting day, Agricultural Society of Kenya (one week), field days and advisory services given to individual farmers with forestry and related problems. Transfer of technology to farmers in arid and semi-arid areas is difficult. Afforestation of these areas started recently and not enough data is authenticated. Regional transfer of such knowledge is not up to date and needs to be enhanced. Communication, water availability for nursery work and financial limitations retard work and transfer of knowledge in these areas. Farmers with small holdings cannot adopt agroforestry disciplines easily due to patience and risk elements and, since this category of farmers constitutes the biggest number within the farming community, it is most likely that transfer of technology down to this group may remain a problem for some time. Our aim here is to encourage planting of trees along boundaries of smallholdings. There is also a need to revise and devise a more accessible method of transfer of results among the professionals and especially down to field forest and agroforestry managers who may not have easy access to publications. This will help this group acquire a positive realization of possible future changes in management and therefore foster a willingness to carry out authenticated management changes.

# Co-ordinating research activities in Nepal

B. P. LAMICHHANEY and M. JOSHI
*Forest Research Information Centre (FRIC), Nepal/UK Silviculture Research Project*

Prior to 1976, the results of the forest research studies have been scattered, wasted and in some cases even involved unnecessary duplication resulting in wastage of money, time and efforts due to the absence of a responsible organization. However, in 1976, the Research Division (now called Forest Research and Information Centre) was created to co-ordinate and control such studies, by whatever agency, and also to ensure that the results are stored for retrieval and implementation elsewhere. Furthermore: to ensure (1) adequate co-ordination of all research activities on a national scale, including non-Departmental organization; (2) the correct priorities of individual programmes; and (3) the necessary staff and financial support for agreed programmes.

# Forest research in Zambia

C. MEKI
*Chief Research Officer, Forestry Department, Kitwe, Zambia*

Silvicultural research in Zambia started in the early 1930s and took the form of species trials using species and establishment methods that had been tried elsewhere in Africa, particularly South Africa and East Africa. This early work resulted in the identification of species best suited to Zambian conditions. Among these were a number of tropical pines like *Pinus kesiya, P. oocarpa* and Eucalypts mainly *Eucalyptus grandis* and *E. cloeziana.*

Land preparation and establishment methods had to be worked out following the selection of species together with other cultural methods that would ensure proper establishment of the young plants. This included working out fertiliser levels and protection measures against termites in the field in the case of Eucalypts. Weeding regimes had to be worked out too.

The present research programme is concentrated on some projects which were started when commercial plantations were introduced but which are still continuing. These include work on provenance trials, tree improvement, post establishment cultural operations such as pruning and thinning, growth and yield studies, and work on insect pests and diseases.

All research projects are approved by the Chief Conservator of Forests who also issues directives to plantation managers on implementation of certain research recommendations. Most of the research work is carried out within the Forest Department but a few projects have been carried out in conjunction with international agencies. Research results are disseminated by means of reports, Research Notes and publications in journals. The extension branch of the Department writes simplified publications to assist farmers in establishing their own wood lots.

The major problem in research has been that of staffing in that there has usually been no continuity. Staff get transferred to other sections of the Department quite frequently, mainly because there are fewer promotion prospects in research. There is a need to have more senior posts in research to reduce the inevitable transfers to senior post in other sections of the Department. Small budget allocations make it difficult to carry out meaningful research and result in frustration among research workers as it becomes difficult for them to operate. Wood users who have been used to imported timber are sceptical about using locally grown timber, considering it to be of inferior quality.

## Forest research in Sierra Leone

H. R. S. MOHAMMED
*Ministry of Agriculture and Forestry, Sierra Leone*

The main lines of forestry research, organization of the Forest Research establishment in Sierra Leone and the successes and problems of technology transfer are discussed.

Finance is a severe restraint to forest research activity and achievement. This is reflected in the standard of buildings, nature of services, the strength and quality of staff in relation to promotion prospects, allocation of priorities, availability of transport and equipment, the recruitment and holding of personnel, the movement of personnel around the country on duty trek and the purchasing of essential materials.

Forest research projects in Sierra Leone, in contrast with other agricultural and land use projects in a great many developing countries where partial or entire financial sponsorship is by International Aid Agencies, such as IDA, ADB, etc., have tried without success to attract foreign aid and are therefore exclusively dependent on government funding. The establishment cannot, on this count alone, be expected to conduct its business adequately, implement government forest policy successfully and achieve its objectives.

Sierra Leone is thus a good case in point where local budget limitations and lack of foreign financial sponsorship are major deterrents to progressive forest research and consequently to technology transfer in the field of forestry.

## Forest research in Uganda

J. R. OCHAKI
*Nakawa Forest Research Centre, Kampala, Uganda*

Eight per cent of the area of Uganda is reserved for forestry under management by the Department of Forestry within the Ministry of Agriculture and Forestry. The Department carries out research through the Research Division. The purpose of research is to probe into the problems encountered during management and utilization of the forest resource.

The Division is made up of three major sections: Silviculture, Protection and Utilisation. Under Silviculture is included work on seed, nursery, plantation establishment and tropical high forest research. The Protection section is only involved in entomology work. The Utilisation section deals in logging, sawmilling, preservation, seasoning, strength properties of wood and wood products, wood wool and charcoal research. The objectives of the Division include isolation of problem areas, priority assignment to the problems, full definition of the problems, provision of periodic review, assessment of the work and publishing results in an appropriate manner.

There are, however, several problems. These range from lack of funds (both local and foreign exchange) and hence lack of equipment, vehicles, etc., to failure to spot priority areas and hence the poor distribution and allocation of the scarce resources, poor organization, lack of good technical staff, or even a training programme, and lack of a co-ordinating system. It is, therefore, necessary not only to provide funds but to re-organize the whole set-up in view of the pressing needs of the country's population.

# Research needs of forestry in India

S. C. SHARMA
*Deputy Conservator of Forests, Uttar Pradesh, India*

Much of the existing forest area of India is dedicated to production of industrial raw material or protection of sensitive areas. The out-turn of fuel wood is just incidental. It cannot be used in the industries economically.

Fuel wood is the main source of energy in India and its demand cannot be met with this incidental output of fuel wood. However, it is also not possible to divert any sizeable portion of existing forest exclusively for production of firewood because of economic and conservation considerations.

With this in view, the government of India has launched a massive tree plantation drive in areas outside reserve forests under the Social Forestry Programme with the help of World Bank, USAID and SIDA. During the VI Five Year Plan we propose to raise over 1.26 million hectares of community land plantation. It is also proposed to plant about 3500 million seedlings during the plan period on private lands and along roads, railway lines and irrigation channels. These plantations will enable us to meet the requirement of the rural community for fuel wood, leaf fodder, fruit and small timber.

Such a massive programme cannot be implemented successfully without proper research. The Forest Research Institute, Dehra Dun, which is the principal research centre for forestry, is at present engaged in working out silviculture and management principles of the species that are being planted under this programme. The research priorities are:

1. Identification of suitable species (indigenous or exotic) for fuel wood, fodder and other needs of the rural community.
2. To evolve suitable nursery and plantation techniques for these species.
3. To work out silvipastoral and silviagricultural combinations to ensure maximum utilization of land.
4. To standardize seed collection and seed storage techniques, including tree improvement.
5. To determine proper harvesting age and techniques.
6. To improve the utilization of forest produce.
7. To develop rural cottage industries.
8. To quantify indirect benefits of forests and their dissemination to rural community.
9. To evolve suitable extension methodology.

Suitable extension methodology for the transfer of technology to the rural population through demonstration plots and nurseries at community level is being developed. The integration of the social needs of people with forest management is essential. No significant work has been done in this direction. We look to this conference to provide support and guidance to us in evolving technology on various aspects and to transfer it to the users' level efficiently.

Printed in the UK for HMSO
Dd 737614 C40 9/84 4235 Job No. 841159C